TWISTS AND TURNS

Episodes in the Life of Ambassador

Eric M. Javits

To my boyhood pal and lifetime friend,
Ed Downe,
with gratitude for his valuable
help and support the role he has always
played in my life — as my closest
friend.

Eric M. Javits

Oct. 28, 2013

DEDICATION

I dedicate this memoir to my parents who gave me my education, values, work ethic, and desire to give back to others; to my children and grand-children that they may know my life and understand their heritage; and lastly and above all, to my wife, Margaretha, who made my life complete with joy, love, and loyalty for which one can only wish.

TABLE OF CONTENTS

CHAPTER I

I watched the camouflaged military jeep drive up with a soldier at the wheel and two more in the back seat. The front passenger seat was empty. The driver asked if I was Señor Javits. When I said that I was, he motioned for me to get in.

The moment we drove away from the Panama Hilton the soldier sitting behind me slipped a blindfold over my eyes. I remember how uneasy I felt, although I realized it was probably done to intimidate me. I asked a few questions that went unanswered, but I felt sure there was no intention to harm me.

Perhaps I was being taken to a place that Omar Torrijos, the dictator of Panama, did not want known in case an assassination attempt against him was being planned. I tried to remember each stop and turn, and the approximate times between each, but I soon lost track as there were so many. It became muggy and hot in the jeep. My confidence that I was not in danger was melting away. I felt like an actor in a movie who had not read the script. My armpits felt sweaty, and the jeep's exhaust fumes were making me nauseous. The blindfold was not a small one. Breathing grew extremely difficult as the morning heat in Panama City had already become oppressive, and the humidity made it worse.

After about half an hour and many turns over rutted roads, the jeep came to a stop. I expected we had arrived at some military headquarters or government building, but when my blindfold was removed I discovered we were in a jungle clearing. The driver pointed toward a group of three Quonset huts that looked like they were made of aluminum. He pointed for me to go to the middle one. The soldiers remained in the jeep as I

1

walked slowly toward it. I remember wondering why, in the cinema-like scene that was being staged, they didn't frisk me before sending me in, but I entered as they instructed.

Before me was a dimly-lit hut about 100 feet wide and perhaps 30 feet deep. After having been blindfolded, my eyes were unaccustomed to the strong sunlight in the clearing, and going through the doorway into the unlit structure was such a quick change that I could not discern much. I was aware of a hard-packed dirt floor under my feet and a rich aroma of damp earth, gun oil, leather, sweat and perhaps a touch of cordite. I hesitated just inside the entrance to allow my vision to improve a bit. Soon I was able to make out a row of at least thirty heavily-armed men in jungle camouflage seated on low wooden benches all along the back wall. The rag-tag bunch all wore menacing glares and large caliber cartridge-stuffed ammunition belts crisscrossed over their shoulders. In front of them, behind a small wooden table, sat Panama's dictator and strongman, General Omar Torrijos. The only thing on the table was a large Colt .45.

My mind raced. I began to think of how I had gotten myself into this pickle and how, or if, I might get out of it . . . .

It all had started in 1975 with a call from my uncle, Senator Jacob Javits, who was then in his fourth six-year term as the most senior Republican on the Senate Foreign Relations Committee. I knew he had not called just to chat. Normally he would call to let me know when he would be coming up to New York and to make a dinner date. This time it was to tell me about his close friends, Dame Margot Fonteyn, England's world-renowned prima ballerina who had been awarded the equivalency of knighthood in 1954, and her husband, Dr. Roberto Arias.

2

Jack spoke fondly of Dr. Arias whom he referred to as "Tito", explaining he was a prominent international lawyer whose father, Panamanian President Arnulfo Arias, had been deposed in a coup led by the family's arch enemy, Lt. Colonel Omar Torrijos, who at the time headed the Panamanian National Guard.

Tito, Jack explained, had served briefly as Panama's ambassador to London in the '50s but later got involved in attempting a failed coup against the Panamanian government in power at the time. In 1964 Tito was elected to the National Assembly and was preparing to seek the presidency of his country when he was gunned down in a failed attempted assassination that left him a quadriplegic unable to move from the neck down.

Torrijos eventually exercised total power. He exiled Tito, stripped him of most of his assets, and sought to deprive him of his one remaining piece of Panamanian real estate—a tract of land consisting of hundreds of hectares called "La Pulida" that bordered on the main road leading to the Panama City airport.

My uncle explained that Tito and Margot had approached him to get America's help in dealing with Panama's dictator, General Omar Torrijos, but that he had been obliged to tell them there was nothing the U.S. could do to be of assistance. If the American government could not even protect and defend national interests as vital as the freedom to control the only canal linking the Atlantic and Pacific oceans, obviously he and the Administration were in no position to assist on a much less vital private matter involving a Panamanian national and his wife.

When his friends asked who might be able to assist them, Jack hesitated, then acknowledged mentioning me and pointing out that my specialty in the law was "difficult international negotiations". He told them that I had earned a reputation for negotiating skills that succeeded where others had failed, and that I only charged a fee if I was successful.

I was quite unprepared to hear Jack tell me he had recommended me to his friends! I never expected him to diverge from our strict family practice. He had never recommended me to handle a legal matter, and I had never referred legal work to his law firm that did mainly real estate law and no federal work. He and I had always been close, but after the death of my father, we had grown even closer. However, the Javits' antipathy to nepotism was sacrosanct, and so was trading on the family name, or doing anything that might appear to be taking advantage of one's public role. That was why we each headed separate law firms with no common partners, and I would not represent clients who sought to use me, or my uncle through me, for federal favors or government dispensations.

I had never met Dr. Arias, but I presumed after Jack's suggestion that Dr. Arias would check my reputation with his brother, Gilberto Arias, who was the senior partner of Arias & Arias, the prominent Panamanian law firm to which my law firm often referred matters. I already knew Gil and his wife, Toni, quite well. Gil was an internationally respected maritime lawyer—a useful legal specialty when so much of the world's shipping flew Panama's flag for tax purposes. Gil represented, among other shipping magnates, Aristotle Onassis. Ari, Gil and I sometimes met at New York's signature night club—El Morocco—where we would sit together with its owner, John Perona, at his corner table, along with other of Perona's friends who happened to drop in without spouses or dates.

A few days after the call from my uncle I heard Dame Margot's sweet voice with a faint British accent come across the telephone line saying that she and her husband, "Tito," were in New York and would like to come to my office.

I still can run the mental movie in my mind's eye of that couple as they came into our law firm's suite—Tito in a wheel chair pushed by his faithful Panamanian male nurse, together with one of the world's greatest prima ballerinas, to tell me they would lose everything if I could not help them.

I had never met Margot, the first to walk through my office door. Her elegance, her grace, her dignity, her wispy figure and wafting step, her chiseled features and those piercing eyes that missed nothing, were stunning. When all were in the room, Tito politely asked to be taken from his wheelchair and seated in front of my desk. The tender grasp and incredible strength of his male attendant amazed me. He lifted Tito's inert body with its flopping limbs as if it were weightless. Then he set Tito down gently without the slightest impact before retiring to our waiting room.

Meeting Tito Arias for the first time, my impression was of a strikingly handsome, amazingly warm, gentle yet very manly character, unable to use his arms or legs but not seeming at all handicapped—so strong was his intellect and ability to articulate his thoughts. His countenance was that of a highly dignified intellectual. Despite his infirmity he had the aristocratic bearing of a former athlete, and his olive complexion was flawless without lines or blemishes. His slightly-graying full head of hair was brushed back in classic Latin fashion.

We three spoke for almost an hour. Tito had difficulty breathing, so he spoke in almost a whisper. Margot said that when they had met, Tito was strikingly handsome and quite a playboy, so theirs was a stormy and troubled romance at first. She said with Tito's infirmity, and as years passed, they found harmony and joy together despite his condition, and although her career meant they spent considerable time away from each other.

She did not dwell on the tragic events that befell her husband, but she explained their financial predicament. She was thinking about retiring, Tito could no longer earn a living, and they would be confronting increasing medical costs and living expenses.

Margot asked if I would go with her to Panama to negotiate with Torrijos since Tito, as an exile, could not return to his country. Margot explained that Torrijos, in order to deprive her husband of La Pulida, had placed hundreds of squatters on Tito's property who were soon to gain ownership by right of adverse possession, meaning that if they had stayed on the land for the requisite number of years, and the owner had taken no action to remove or evict them, it would legally become theirs.

I remember how comfortable we all felt with each other. When Margot had finally finished recounting their story, I wanted to know if they were willing to give me complete latitude in the terms that I could negotiate on their behalf, and whether they would be satisfied with whatever I could salvage for them. Tito said since they were on the verge of losing the property by adverse possession anyway, I could have total discretion in any negotiation, and could agree on their behalf to terms by which they would be bound. They both acknowledged the chance of any recovery was remote.

As they were such close friends of my uncle's, I said would take their almost impossible case—not on the usual contingency arrangement whereby I would receive a share of whatever I could recover for them—but only my travel expenses were I unsuccessful, and if successful, only a per diem while on the trip.

As they left my office I wondered if anything could be done to snatch even one hectare away from peasants who, for almost two decades, had eked out their meager living on Arias' land.

A couple of weeks later Dame Margot Fonteyn flew in from London to meet me at the Panama Hilton where she had made room reservations for us, and after checking into our respective rooms we dined together in the hotel's modest restaurant and retired early after our long day of traveling.

The next morning I rose with the sun at 6:00, pulled on a sweat suit and jogged along the curved concrete rim that circumscribed the Bay of Panama. I needed to get in motion physically after my flight down there, and jogging helped me think. I urgently needed to devise a strategy for the upcoming negotiation. Unfortunately, in those days there was no worldwide web on which I might have researched the background, personality or character of Panama's dictator. I only knew he had snatched the Panama Canal away from the United States and of his reputation for ruthlessness. I would have liked greater insight into my imminent adversary. The sun was already burning hot. There was not the slightest breeze, and with every breath and step I took, the stench of sewage in the Bay—much of it still on the surface—filled my nostrils. The stench propelled me to jog faster, but I could not think of any way to get Panama's strongman to clear off the squatters from La Pulida.

By 7:00 am I had showered, dressed and was headed to the lobby. Margot was nowhere to be seen. I knew that somehow I had to get to see Gen. Torrijos. I had forgotten to set a time with Margot to meet for breakfast, so while waiting for her to come down to the lobby I decided to take a chance and approach the Concierge at the front desk. Everyone on the hotel staff knew Dame Margot who was very popular in Panama. Since she had made my hotel reservation, and we had checked in at the same time, it was no secret that I was accompanying her. I presumed that we were being watched, so I felt I did not have to do much explaining. I simply told the concierge that I was Dame Margot's attorney and would like to meet General Omar Torrijos. I felt reasonably confident that my request would get to the right place. The Concierge on the desk said he would contact me if an appointment could be arranged. Later that day there was a message on my phone. It said to be at the front door of the hotel on Monday morning at 9:00.

On Sunday morning, I rose again at 6 to run around the Bay before the temperature climbed to broiling. Once more the stench was awful, but the exercise was what I needed, so I just went into a yoga-like trance and ignored the sewage and the floating dead animals. As I jogged, I turned over in my mind imaginary scenarios of my upcoming meeting. By the time I returned to the hotel and hit the showers, I thought I might finally have a plan that would work . . . . . .

The General sat patiently waiting behind the small wooden table on which his Colt .45 rested. I walked over, smiled warmly, and before sitting down on the folding chair opposite him, introduced myself in the faulty Spanish that I had picked up in New York City and my many trips to Spain.

I was somewhat surprised and relieved that I did not feel intimidated. Perhaps it was because I had already had so much experience in my lifetime with powerful people and difficult clients that I figured this was just another instance where bluff, showmanship and bravado were the order of the day. So I wasted not another second eyeing his horde of gorillas. I focused on the general instead, trying in a few seconds to appraise my adversary and decide on my opening move.

I confess I liked his good looks, his self-assurance and his ready-for-business demeanor. His rugged face was clean-shaven, exposing a leathered complexion. His dark eyes drew me to him, but gave no indication of what he was thinking. He, like the others, wore a jungle-camouflaged outfit without epaulets or insignia of rank.

I don't know where I got the inspiration, but I opened our conversation by exclaiming emphatically, "General, you have given me the greatest compliment I have ever received!" He looked at me quizzically. "What do you mean?" he asked. I pointed at his Colt .45. "If you think you need *that* for me, that is the greatest compliment I have ever received."

The stern look immediately left his face. With a slightly embarrassed sheepish grin, he put the gun away. That lucky one-liner changed the whole tenor of our meeting.

I explained that I had come with an offer that I hoped he would find acceptable—an offer of tribute from a former adversary—one to honor him and to begin a new chapter in the Torrijos-Arias saga. I explained that Tito and Margot both wanted to honor him by creating a foundation called the Omar Torrijos Foundation to which Arias would deed all of La Pulida except a strip of land fronting along the airport road through which rights of way would provide access to the deeded land behind it that would represent most of the property. I further explained that the sole trustee of the Foundation would be Gen. Torrijos himself, thus giving him complete and unquestionable right to the deeded property. He could have his Foundation deed over to each of the squatters the precisely described parcels to be owned by them, thus avoiding myriad future boundary disputes between squatters. I pointed out that our suggested method would perfect title to each of the peasants in an incontestable way that otherwise might have been left in doubt. Furthermore, I argued, each squatter would know the land came as a gift directly from General Torrijos—a better alternative for political purposes than having squatters believing they earned it themselves by right of adverse possession.

Torrijos probably thought he was going to be threatened by the New York lawyer with the powerful uncle in the United States Senate, and he had set the scene to ensure it would be me who would be intimidated. I waited expectantly to see if my ju jitsu-like tactic would work.

The general's facial expression softened, and he seemed to hesitate. What had just transpired must have come as a total surprise. No more than a few seconds passed before Torrijos stood and said that he would accept our offer, and that the necessary legalities could proceed without delay. He came toward me and shook my hand with a look of utter satisfaction. I could feel it was a genuine gesture, as he obviously relished accepting that tribute from a vanquished political enemy. As I rose to leave I glanced again at his crew of desperados spread out along the back wall. This time my eyes had adjusted fully to the lack of light. Their hostile and threatening glares had not changed one bit.

My flight back to New York via Miami lifted sluggishly from a dank and soggy Panama and struggled into clouds that hung low over Panama City and the isthmus. Margot had business to finish and friends to see, so she stayed behind at the Panama Hilton. I settled into my airline seat to savor what had been accomplished.

First and foremost, retaining the valuable strip of road frontage close to the Panama City airport meant that when warehouses would be built on that land, Tito and Margot would realize some monetary benefit from their only remaining Panamanian asset.[1]

Besides Tito and Margaret's profuse gratitude, my greatest gratification came as I mentally anticipated telling my uncle how I had dealt with General Omar Torrijos.

CHAPTER II — MY FORBEARS

My father was curious about the origin of our family so he eventually decided to have our family tree researched by scholars at the Jewish Theological Seminary. They told him that the Javits family name had originated during biblical times in Israel where our ancestors were scribes—those few who could read and write the written word recording laws, deeds, contracts and other important records. The ancient Hebrew word for God was Yawa, so our family name may have been a derivation, i.e. Yawitz, meaning people of God. I have a small library of books in Hebrew that my father was given by the Jewish Theological Seminary documenting their research on our family.

In the seventeenth century we had an ancestor in Germany, Jacob Ben Tzvi (Emden), 1697-1776. Yavetz (an acronym for Jacob ben Tzvi) did not serve as a practicing rabbi. A prominent Jewish theologian, rabbi and philosopher, Yavetz Emden studied under his father who was also a noted halachic authority. Yavetz disseminated his views through the press. He is famous for his acrimonious dispute with Rabbi Jonathan Elbeschuetz, whom he suspected of following a false Messiah.

My father told me that we had a cousin who had been a cardinal in the Catholic church in Eastern Europe, but I never got his name or what country he was from. But I did meet our cousin, Nahum Levison in the 1960s who was close to retirement after a long and distinguished career as a minister of the Church of Scotland! Nahum's older brother, Leon Levison (1881 -1030) had been one of the most eminent leaders of the

Church of Scotland while their brother, Morris Levison, was a Jewish lawyer practicing in Tel Aviv, Israel!

The Levison family lived in the town of Safad in Israel during the 19th century, where the family patriarch, was the town's Rabbi. The family owned vineyards and pastureland on which they grazed their flocks of sheep and goats. When the heads of the Church of Scotland made a visit to the Holy Land, they went to Safad, one of the holiest places in the country that held Israel's oldest synagogue. There the church fathers met Leon and his younger brother, Nahum as boys. I was told that little Nahum so impressed the Church leaders with his brilliance and charm that they asked the family if they could take him back to Scotland and educate him. The family agreed and Nahum was raised in the Church. Leon made his decision to accept Christ as the messiah at a later age, and now there are congregtions all over Scotland with male and female Levison family members as their ministers. When I met Nahum and his wife, Margaret, in the '60s, I was with my parents in London. We took them to the Savoy Hotel for lunch. They were a delightful couple, and I found Nahum to be a compassionate and engaging man.

We had other notable cousins amongst them Fanny and Oscar Schachter (1915-2003). Oscar had graduated first in his class from Columbia Law School in 1939. He served as counsel to the United Nations Relief and Rehabilitation Administration (UNRRA) in 1944 and 1945. He served for many years as Counsel to the United Nations right from its inception in 1945. Later he distinguished himself in international law, lectured at Yale Law School, and from 1980 until his death taught as a Professor on the faculty of Columbia University School of Law.

Another cousin, Naum Rekhtman, a businesman who lives in Minsk had been the manager of the Belarus Tractor Works under the Soviet Union; his mother, Rosa Javits, lives in Odessa, Russia; and Jaime Javits, in Montevideo is a leading figure as head of their performing arts center in the cultural firmament of Uruguay.

I never met either of my grandfathers. They both had passed before I came into the world. I have almost no knowledge of my maternal grandfather and very little about my paternal grandfather. As a child, I came to know only my two grandmothers.

My maternal grandmother, Ella Birnbaum, stood only five feet tall, was frail of figure, testy of temper, and mean of spirit. She must have been beautiful in her youth, but I never saw her smile or felt her embrace. When I was only three or four years old, my sister and I were left in her care while our parents were off traveling somewhere. One winter morning she dressed me for kindergarten by simply pulling a snowsuit over my pajamas. When I got into the car to be driven to school, the chauffeur had no way of telling I was not properly dressed, so he dropped me off at the school. When I went in, all the children were gathered in the main entry hall. All them had taken off their galoshes and snowsuits. It was there, in front of all the children, the teacher asked me to take off my snowsuit. I refused. She offered to help me, but I still refused. She then began to remove it, but I got visibly upset and embarrassed, as I did not want the children to see me in my pajamas. Once she realized the problem she sent me upstairs to wait in privacy while she phoned home to have someone come to pick me up. The chauffeur came back where he found me still in my snowsuit. From that day on I intensely disliked my maternal grandmother.

The five immediate forbears that I will describe in detail—Grandmother Ida Javits; Grand Uncle Martin Birnbaum; Mother Lily, Father Ben, and Uncle Jack Javits—were all formidable personalities. Each had a lasting impact in shaping my life.

IDA LITTMAN JAVITS

In contrast to how I felt about "Grandma Ella", I adored my paternal grandmother, Ida Littman Javits. Grandma Ida resembled Mrs. Khrushchev, built like a truck, with facial features of typical peasant stock. She had been born in Palestine, but went in search of other relatives in Odessa, walking all the way to the Ukraine behind a camel caravan because she could not stand her mother. She was fluent in Yiddish and Russian. Her English was spoken with a heavy Jewish accent. She had a heart of gold, and nothing was too difficult for her. When she kissed or hugged you, it was from the heart, not a social ritual. She could hardly see for the cataracts covering her eyes, and the lenses in her glasses were the thickest I had ever seen. To support her family, Grandma Ida had labored as the janitress of three slum buildings on the lower East Side of New York, while her husband, Morris, whom she always called "Mr. Javits" spent most of his time in the shul (synagogue) with his buddies.

Grandma Ida used to bake strudels for my sister and me in her apartment in Brooklyn and then smuggle them into our house in Westport when she would come to visit on the train from New York, despite the ban our mother had on her bringing us pastry or sweets. The smell of camphor permeated her strudel and rugelach. She must have kept it for days in Brooklyn in a drawer along with woolen items in preparation for her trip to Westport.

Ida was devoutly patriotic. So much so that in World War II as a volunteer worker for the American Red Cross she rolled the most bandages of any volunteer in Brooklyn! She was enormously proud of her two sons, Benjamin and Jacob—or "Jakela" and "Bennela" as she called them; but she was especially proud that Jack had enlisted in the army and had achieved the rank of Lt. Colonel during the war, and that thereafter he had been elected to the Congress of the United States! The singular idealism, determination, and strengths of will of both her sons were, in my judgment, a testament to her and her alone.

Ida was a stoic who accepted without fear or complaint what each day brought. In her mind the whole world was Jewish. When she was invited to accompany her son—then Congressman Jacob Javits—to meet Cardinal Spellman of New York, upon being introduced to His Eminence, she exclaimed "I am so happy to meet you, Cardinal Spelnik".

Ida was incapable of guise, deceit, or mouthing niceties. Her demonstrations of feeling were unmistakably forthright and adoring. From her I learned the value of honesty in bestowing one's affections.

MARTIN BIRNBAUM – 1878-1970

My mother's uncle, Martin Birnbaum, was born in Miskolc, Hungary in 1878—the same year that calamitous flooding took an enormous toll of life in that country. Martin's mother had to climb atop a porcelain chimney ledge directly under the highest point in their attic ceiling and remain there for days with her infant children to escape being drowned by the floodwaters that rose inside their house. When the family immigrated to the United States through Ellis Island following the flood incident, the immigration officer, on learning the family name was Kertezy, urged his mother to dispense with that Hungarian name meaning pear tree and take instead

Birnbaum, the German word for pear tree which was easier to say and spell.

Martin grew to be a tall, handsome, mustachioed man of athletic build. He was an accomplished violinist and noted explorer who travelled with the Natural History Magazine's first photographic exploratory expedition to Africa in the early 1930s. He gave me photos he took of a horned cobra, and another of him standing erect and wearing a pith helmet with a Watussi chieftan horizontal in the air, clearing his head by at least two feet. He told me that many members of that tall tribe were able to jump over his head, each higher than the Olympic world record at that time.

A man of letters and a giant in the world of art (over 1600 of his letters and correspondence can be found in the Smithsonian Institution's Archives of American Art and at Harvard University), Martin became one of the world's most eminent art experts—a distinction he shared in his day with Bernard Berenson and Lord Duveen. His record of having given his expert opinion or testimony on many of the world's great paintings without ever making a mistake was unmatched in his era.

Martin was a child prodigy who graduated with Phi Beta Kappa honors from City College of New York that he entered at the tender age of only fourteen! A graduate of law school, he spoke perfect English, Italian, Hungarian, French and German. He was in charge of the Berlin Photographic Company branch in New York from 1910 to 1916 and then became an art dealer and partner in the then preeminent New York art gallery, Scott & Fowles, which he managed. He built one of the most important private art collections in the history of the United States for his friend, Grenville Lindall Winthrop, whose amazing collection is now housed at Harvard University's Fogg Museum in Boston.

Martin wrote books on Ingres, William Blake, Oscar Wilde, Watts, Edmund Dulac, Alexandre Jacovleff, John Singer Sargent, the sculptor Paul Manship, and other artists. His first book was published in 1919. Entitled "Introductions", it was dedicated to his close friend, Annie Bertram Webb, and it "introduced" Aubrey Beardsley, Charles Conder, Charles Ricketts, Charles Shannon, Leon Backst, Maurice Sterne, Paul Manship, and Edmund Dulac, among others. A magnificent graphite portrait of Martin by John Singer Sargent hangs in our apartment in Palm Beach. Manship, who is best known for his magnificent statues at Rockefeller Center of Prometheus Bound and Atlas holding up the world, was instrumental in the art deco movement. Manship also was quite adept at low relief. He produced a large number of coins and medals, including JFK's inaugural medal. A beautiful sculptured head of Martin on a large bronze medallion sculpted by Manship hangs in my study. Other works by artists who were the subjects of his books decorate our apartment's walls. Martin wrote each of his manuscripts intended for publication fastidiously in his own hand. He showed me some of his handwritten edited manuscript before submitting them to his publishers. I marveled at his penmanship that rivaled that of a calligrapher. His explorations and travels were documented in his books "Angkor and the Mandarin Road" in which he recounts his travels through Indo China; and in "Vanishing Eden— Wandering in the Tropics" in which he narrated his explorations and travels in the South Seas, Africa, Asia and Central America.

Martin's final work, "The Last Romantic" published in 1960 for which Upton Sinclair wrote the introduction, told his life's story. In it he recounted his career at Scott and Fowles and how he built the Winthrop collection. Upton Sinclair's words are illuminating and worth quoting in part:

"Martin Birnbaum is my oldest living friend. We were together at the age of twelve, in the old Public School Number Forty, on the East Side of New York. At thirteen we entered City College of New York, and were in the same class for five years, and you can learn to know each other very well in that time. When I came out of college I became a writer of 'half dime novels' and Martin became my violin teacher for a matter of three years. Since that time we have met when fate made it possible, and have corresponded frequently.

Martin became an art expert—one of the best known in that profession; and the stories he told me impressed me so that when I started the Lanny Budd series of novels, I decided to have Lanny follow in Martin's footstepts. His views of art are sound, and his knowledge of artists and their work is infinite.

So now here is the book—the life story of one of the kindest, gentlest and wisest men I have met during my life's pilgrimage. You may not know many of the artists or art works that he tells about; I certainly know very few of them. But you will learn what love of art means, and what it can do to make inspiring pleasure and to preserve the past alive in the present and immortal in the future."

Martin was a truly colorful figure on the international stage. His circle of intimates encompassed not only the artists about whom he wrote, but many of the world's wealthy art collectors. Martin resided for many years in an art-filled apartment at 14 East 60th Street in Manhattan. As a child I hated to visit him there because of the unusually wide space between the elevator cab and the building's floors. I felt like I would fall down the shaft when I left or entered the elevator. Later, Martin moved to a splendid town house in Manhattan's East '70s with his valet, and his pet boxer—an affectionate watchdog he named

Prince Ruppert of Westport. He also kept a Myna bird that could whistle all the bars of Yankee Doodle Dandy in perfect pitch and cadence. The bird's speaking ability was also amazing. It would imitate Martin's voice so exactly one could not tell who was speaking if both Martin and the bird were in another room. Every time the phone rang the bird could be heard reciting "Hello! This is Martin Birnbaum. How are you? I am fine!"

In his early youth Martin had fallen deeply in love. His many love letters had gone unanswered. Not until many years later did Martin learn that any replies had been intercepted by his mother. Martin never married. I suspect as an adult he was homosexual, but he gave no hint of it by carriage or demeanor. He was masculine, handsome, aristocratic, and international in manner and outlook. He owned a palazzo on the Giudecca canal in Venice where he always spent the summers. He organized and served as the Commissioner of Fine Arts of the International Biennale Art Exhibits held in Venice in 1934 and 1936 for which he was decorated by King Victor Emmanuel of Italy.

Martin had a playful sense of humor. He would tease my sister and me as we approached a doorway together, saying "you go first and I'll precede you"; or he would recite this self-effacing limerick for our amusement: "Artin, bumbartin, tiddieartin go-fartin, tee-legged toe-legged bow-legged Martin." I recall one whimsical poem he would recite that had a message:

> A wise old owl sat in an oak
> The more he saw the less he spoke
> The less he spoke the more he heard
> Why can't we be more like that old bird?

Because Uncle Martin had no children of his own, he would accompany my sister and me from a very young age to the

Metropolitan Museum of Art at least once, and often several times a year. He would dedicate each of those visits to different wings of the museum. Being a young boy, I loved the medieval wing best where I could gape at swords, maces, crossbows and suits of armor. Each time we visited the museum our uncle always explained that he was teaching us "to see."

At his death in 1970, Martin left his net estate to my sister and me, yet his most meaningful and lasting gift was not pecuniary. It was appreciation of art, esthetics and creativity; and his precise and demanding instruction in English composition during my summer vacations—far more valuable to me throughout my life than his testamentary bequest.

LILY BIRNBAUM JAVITS

1894-1986

My mother, Lily, a woman of innate effortless style, was born in New York City and educated by nuns in the catholic elementary school in the Yorkville district of Manhattan where she was raised by her parents, Max and Ella Birnbaum, who had immigrated to the U.S. from Vienna, Austria. Lily had a petite sylph-like figure, a thick helmet of jet-black hair, perfect facial features; and—though dresses were then worn long—a pair of shapely ankles that drew stares like two magnets. Lily's sturdy character and personality sparkled. She was self-sufficient, inwardly happy, and radiated warmth and charm. She enjoyed the company of others, loved to share her many stories and experiences, and was deeply caring of those she loved.

Lily's parents were without higher education, property, privilege or wealth; but she was incredibly bright and beautiful, with a quick wit and an endearing and spontaneous laugh—so much so that she became known in the early 20th century as the Belle of Yorkville. She could speak German, Yiddish, and a little Hungarian; and in her youth she danced with the celebrated Isadora Duncan Dance troupe and had many wealthy and prominent suitors. Firmly decisive in her tastes and judgment, highly intuitive and psychically gifted, she declined many offers of marriage, and instead chose to manage for her aunt what was then New York's most fashionable and exclusive millinery shop located on the Upper East Side. After years of working for only a pittance on the expectation that her aunt would leave the store to her, she was crushed to discover the store was being left to her aunt's son.

Lily wasted no time in leaving her aunt's employ. She began scanning the help wanted pages where she noticed an opening being advertised for Manager of the Mode Costume Company that produced all of the costuming for Shubert's theatrical productions. By 1920, the Shubert family had built the largest theatre empire in America and established the Broadway theatre district as its hub. With virtually no experience in the theatre, Lily somehow inveigled her way in for an interview. It went fairly well until she was asked if she was familiar with all the exotic fabrics, furs and feathers that were used in costuming the splendid Shubert showgirls. When she replied "of course" she was asked if she knew how to work with egret and lamé. Lily had no idea what lamé or egret were, but she replied "Bring me samples, and I will show you how I would work with them." When she was handed a bolt of the slippery metallic gold fabric and the egret feathers she instantly knew how to drape the fabric on the bias so it would appear as if it had been poured like liquid over the torso and hips, and how to accent it majestically with egret feathers. Her alacrity and artistic skill pulled her through that interview, and in the following years as Manager of Mode Costume Company, she got to know intimately many showgirls, stage door Johns, leading theatrical figures, and the two Shubert brothers. In the course of holding that key role, she became privy to their lives, sexual affairs, drug habits, abortions, and more. She kept their confidences, and proved a trusted loyal and faithful friend.

By 1920 Lily was earning $300 a week—a salary unheard of for a woman at that time! It was then she met my father at a dance. Dressed like a chauffeur and almost penniless, it was his intellect, idealism and ambition that intrigued her. A long and stormy courtship followed, but eventually they married in 1926.

Once my sister and I were born, our mother focused on us almost to the exclusion of everything else. Although she had help from governesses, she was compelled to be a hands-on caregiver, as I was born a colicky RH baby with lactose intolerance and yellow jaundice. For my first two years I could drink only soymilk. I was constantly sick as a child. At the age of three Lily was told I had to undergo immediate surgery for a double mastoid infection. Knowing the operation would disfigure me for life, against the doctor's advice she insisted on waiting overnight to see if the mastoids would abate. Somehow, miraculously, they were almost gone the next morning!

With each fall season thereafter, I invariably contracted a streptococcus infection in one or both ears. My fever would reach 104 or higher. Lily would summon the local pediatrician and he would prescribe sulfa drugs that made me delirious. I can still remember watching the ceiling spin while hearing excruciating noises in my head. Other antibiotic drugs had not yet been developed. With each illness an ether-soaked gauze pad had to be placed over my face and my ear abscesses lanced. Year after year, Lily nursed me around the clock, giving me sponge baths to bring down the fever and special foods to nourish me. It was not until I was a teenager that I no longer fell victim to infections with the arrival of the fall and colder weather.

When I was only six years old Lily took me to the funeral of Lillian Wald—the woman who had started New York's Henry Street Settlement. Her funeral was held at her Westport home—the "House on the Pond"—at which a large crowd was gathered to hear classical music played by a string quartet in which my violin teacher, Paul Bernard, played first violin. Lily, always the realist, was making sure I became acquainted early with mortality.

Lily was never idle nor would she tolerate idleness around her, so she programmed us to do something useful every day. She made sure we had a schedule tacked up in our room that told what we should be doing for every half hour of every summer day. It included minor chores like making our bed, brushing our teeth, cleaning our room, putting our things away, etc., and she insisted we adhere to it.

One summer she took me to the local liquor store in Westport where many model airplanes, some with gasoline engines, hung from the ceiling! She wanted to interest me in taking up the hobby, and explained that the owner of the store would come to our house and teach me how to build a model airplane. I loved the idea, and on our next trip to NYC she took me to Polk's Model Shop where we bought a kit to build a model airplane of balsa wood covered by silk span paper. Its propeller was powered by rubber bands. She had a wooden workbench set up in my bedroom, and she bought X-Acto knives, single edge razor blades, airplane glue, dope and the paint that would be needed. Building model planes was one of the things that I learned to love as a boy.

Lily loved nature, wilderness, and wild animals. Her flower gardens usually won best of show at the Westport Garden

Society, but she also took great care of her bushes and trees of which she had some magnificent specimens. It was not surprising, therefore, that she hired a naturalist to come to our house one summer to teach my sister and me how to collect butterflies. The woman showed up with two butterfly nets, a bottle of chloroform, some cotton, a few cigar boxes, and a package of long pins with round heads for mounting our collections. She taught us the names of the different butterflies and in those early days in Westport, there was a plethora of Monarch and other beautiful large moths. We assembled a creditable collection in just a few visits from our naturalist mentor. I hated the smell of the chloroform and felt sorry for the beautiful butterflies that fell victim to our collector's urge.

Lily was afraid of fire, as she had been a witness in 1911 to the Triangle Shirtwaist Company disaster in New York City—one of the worst fires in its history in which over a hundred women and children, working in the top three floors of a loft factory, died in the first fifteen minutes because the Triangle factory owners had locked the exits to keep the women at their sewing machines. That tragedy gave rise to the International Garment Workers Union and New York's child labor law.

So once my sister and I were old enough to each have our own bedroom, mother insisted that we each had a rope ladder lying next to the windows of our second floor bedrooms in Westport; and she made us practice descending the ladder. The trouble was that the wooden dowels that served as footholds would unexpectedly rotate under one's weight, and one could slip if one's grip on the ladder was not tight enough. Also the ladder was attached to the windowsill by just a single U-shaped metal hook. That made it difficult to get one's feet on the first rung outside the window without tipping the ladder one way or another. Either you had to plant your foot exactly in the middle of the dowel, or you had to hold your weight by gripping both rope sides of the ladder. I was afraid of heights and practicing on the ladder was torture for me. My fear resulted from of a visit to the Empire State Building with my father when I was very young. My father had held me over the edge of the observation floor parapet to look down at the view, and I thought his grip would loosen and that I would fall.

Once my sister and I were both away at college and prep school, Lily no longer concentrated on her children. She continued spending winters at our home in Palm Beach, became more social, and helped to found the Palm Beach Festival that showcased aspiring musicians competing for acclaim and public attention. She had always enjoyed sponsoring the talents of others. She would often befriend someone in the process and then encourage them to fulfill themselves through various forms of self-expression.

One noteworthy example of this was when Lily became acquainted with Russell Kuhner who had become a mundane bank teller at the Westport Bank and Trust Company because he had no other means of support. Russ and his wife Elizabeth were a charming couple that loved photography, so Lily convinced Russ to quit his job at the bank and open a photographic studio. She referred clients to help him become successful. His wife joined him in the enterprise, and eventually Betty eclipsed Russ to become one of America's foremost family photographers. She was chosen to photograph family photo albums for many of America and Palm Beach's leading families, including the Kennedys. Betty Kuhner's "scrapbook" style, using natural light and unpretentious natural background settings, led the way for other famous photographers such as Bruce Webber. Lily's own artistic and intuitive gifts guided her selection and endorsement of many talented people.

Another person Lily discovered and mentored to fame was young, handsome David Webb. David designed jewelry, but he had no retail outlet, no backing and no clients. At the time, his only assets were his amazing talent and burning ambition to become eminently successful. Lily invited David one weekend to come to Westport, during which he drew some jewelry designs with her guidance. She commissioned him to make those pieces for her and showed them to her admiring friends. She relayed their positive feedback to David, and encouraged him to prepare a collection of his work. Once it was ready, she had him return to our home in Westport where she had invited many of her well-to-do, fashionable friends. Lily did this for David on a number of occasions. Each time David was able to sell out his entire collection. Eventually the name David Webb found its place among the pre-eminent names of fine jewelry, and women representing the pinnacle of style and elegance such as the Duchess of Windsor and Princess Grace became devout Webb customers.

In 1956, my parents sold their Westport home and moved to an apartment in New York City. Lily then turned her attention to the Professional Children's School. Its mission was to enable young students who were pursuing professional careers as actors, dancers, singers, and musicians to also, at the same time, be able to get their high school educations. The school was located in Lincoln Center, and it had a dedicated staff and a star-studded student body, but its building was run down and its coffers were empty. Lily decided she would save it from bankruptcy and help build its endowment. The school that was affectionately called "PCS" was a cornucopia of talent. Lily would celebrate her birthday each October by having PCS students put on a recital in her apartment to which she would invite wealthy friends. These became known as the Lily Javits Musicales, and they were the main source of donations for PCS for many years. Lily also provided scholarships for the most needy and talented students. She mentored Emmanuel Ax with the approval and appreciation of his newly immigrated parents, paying for much of his PCS education. She also helped Midori, YoYo Ma, Pinchas Zuckerman, along with many others who appeared in her Musicales.

Then, at the age of 65, her fine facial features still beautiful and framed by her helmet of now silver hair, Lily turned to oil painting as a way of expressing her artistic talent. She had never touched a brush or held a palette, but inspired by the magic of richly saturated colors, she attacked her easel with a vengeance. By the time she died at the age of 91 she had turned out 400 paintings of which the family still have 300. Lily set up a studio in the poolside cabana in Palm Beach where she painted landscapes, flowers and bridges in a style derived mostly from fauvism and impressionism, but which she clearly made her own. She continued painting with looser, broader brush strokes until she became almost blind from macular degeneration. These last canvasses, some of which were not even signed, were among her strongest artistic achievements. She had only four gallery exhibitions during her lifetime, two in New York and two in Palm Beach, some of which were reviewed by the New York Times and art magazines. At each she displayed only 25 of her works, and each sold out. I loved her paintings so I used to go into her studio as she was finishing a canvas to cajole her, tell her how beautiful it was, and that I would take it to Heydenryk's in New York (framers of choice for Picassos, Monets and Bonnards that hang in the Metropolitan Museum of Art) to be expertly framed if only she would give it to me—which she often did.

At her death the obituary in New York Times with her photo was as long and prominent as her husband's who died thirteen years earlier. Lily was no shrinking violet. She was a creative force in her own right, a philanthropist as well as an advocate for nurturing talent in others. She is still present in her beautiful paintings that surround us.

BENJAMIN ABRAHAM JAVITS

1894-1973

My father, Ben, was born with the help of a midwife in the family's basement apartment on the lower East Side of Manhattan. In 1894 the Lower East Side was the ghetto slum district receiving most of the Jewish immigrants to America from which thousands of achievers eventually emerged to make their way to prominence, fame and fortune. My father wanted me to personally see the poverty in which he had spent his youth, perhaps so that I would appreciate my privileged life and the opportunity for upward mobility afforded by the American Dream.

So one fine summer day when I was ten he took me on the train from Westport into Manhattan and then down to the Lower East Side. We walked around in the midst of teeming humanity and abject poverty on Stanton and Orchard Streets where his mother had been a janitress in charge of two slum buildings. He told me how his baby sister had fallen off the kitchen table and been killed when she hit the floor; and how, as a child, he had contracted thoracic empyema, a painful infection of the chest wall and ribs. The surgery to remove one of his ribs was performed as he lay on the kitchen table. For the rest of his life he had a deep and disfiguring gash in his back. He told me the illness made him so weak that he had to be pushed in a baby carriage for years until he was strong enough to walk.

He took me into one of the walkup slum tenements in the neighborhood. It was hot outside and suffocating inside. The stench of urine and garbage was almost unbearable, and I became nauseous as we climbed the stairs. He explained the apartments in that building were called "railroad flats" because they were long and narrow like the inside of a rail car, without light or windows except at each end, and lacking any toilet facilities. There was only one shared bathroom on each floor, so tenants would urinate on the stairs or in the hall if it were occupied; and they would throw their garbage out the rear windows of the building, rather than carry it down the stairs to the basement of the building. I was almost to the point of throwing up by the time we left.

We then walked down one of the avenues on which an elevated train was running with pushcart vendors on both sides of the street hawking their wares. My father bought me a couple of shirts at $2 each that had long sleeves, cuffs that buttoned and wing collars. They were rough to the touch. He said he wanted me to feel the inferior quality of goods that were on offer.

We walked a bit further until we came upon an orthodox synagogue in a dilapidated dump of a building with a forbidding entrance and almost no lighting once we stepped inside. It took a couple of minutes for our eyes to adjust. Eventually we could make out some shabbily dressed men grouped together hoping to make a *minyan* (the quorum necessary to start a prayer service), but when they saw the intruders were a well-dressed stranger with his young son, they glared at us with such anger and ferocity for invading their precious sanctuary that we backed out lest they became physically violent. I had never experienced and could not understand that kind of hatred, although my father certainly could. He had rebelled at his own father's overzealous and fanatically strict Jewish orthodoxy. Neither my father nor my mother was deeply religious, and although they were longtime members of the reform Temple Emanu-El in New York City, their attendance was limited to high holy days once or twice a year. My grandfather, Morris Javits, on the other hand, preferred to delegate to his wife, Ida, the support of the family while he spent most days with his buddies in *shul*.

Later, when we got home to Westport, my father made me try on one of the shirts he had bought me. The fabric was so coarse and abrasive that it caused unbearable itching. I couldn't wait to take it off, and I never wore it again.

That single day on the lower East Side imprinted for me the gulf between the haves and the have-nots. I was stunned and depressed by the poverty and filth I had seen. I began to comprehend how it might motivate those with ability and ambition to strive to escape the slum life and conditions of poverty. I felt sad for those unable to make it. For the first time then, and thereafter, I have been deeply grateful for the privileges I enjoyed.

Before he contracted pleurisy, my father had attended enough elementary school to learn to read and write. He even took violin lessens at 25 cents a lesson from an impoverished musician that lived in a slum building nearby. Ben's younger brother, Jacob, was born when Ben was ten. It must have been hard at first for a sick and frail elder brother to relate to a newly born baby brother, and perhaps that is why my father in later life felt somewhat parental towards my uncle. However, once my father reached his teen years he began a reading program of self-education and a daily regimen of deep breathing and exercise that restored his physical fitness and strength. He stood only 5'4", but his muscular physique at maturity was that of a bantamweight pugilist. It spoke loudly of the dedication he must have devoted to rebuilding his wasted body.

One could not call Ben's stature imposing or his facial features handsome. However, he had such intensity and force of personality that when he entered a room all eyes turned his way, and the sound level muted. His piercing grey eyes, ready wit and singular intelligence combined to project charisma and personal magnetism. Above all, he was a futuristic thinker and an idealist. He believed one could make things happen by sheer strength of will. If he had a motto it would have been "Think Big!"

Due to his illness he had missed much formal schooling, but once he regained his health he put himself through night high school, and then attended City College from 1909 to 1911 while at the same time working to help support the family. To get his first job he took the elevator to the top of the Flatiron Building—a skyscraper at 23rd Street and Fifth Avenue—called that because it was wedge shaped and resembled one of the old cast-iron clothes irons. Ben proceeded to walk down from floor to floor. He knocked at every office until finally he got a non-salaried job collecting delinquent debts on commission. From 1911 to 1922, in addition to attending Fordham University night law school, he continued collecting bad debts and working in various positions in sales, management, industrial organization and business counseling.

Ben finally earned his law degree from Fordham University, an institution run by Jesuits; and in 1922 at the age of 26 he was admitted to practice by the New York bar. His younger brother was then only 16 and about to graduate high school. Four years later, having put his younger brother through college and law school, Ben made Jacob—then only twenty years old—an equal partner when, in 1926, the firm of Javits & Javits was formed.

Ben collected a seven-figure receivable for a client that year. That launched the firm on its path to international recognition in the fields of bankruptcy, reorganization, trade regulation and corporate finance. It also provided the means for him to buy the Westport acreage and to build the family's Connecticut homestead.

In his ensuing lifetime of legal practice with famous law clients like B.C. Forbes and Charles E. Wilson of GE, my father's cases included many celebrated proxy contests for corporate control including American Can, Niles Bement Pond, Pratt & Whitney, MGM and Twentieth Century Fox. He also represented Eddie Gilbert in his attempt to take over E.L. Bruce, the hardwood flooring company, that created a rare "corner" on the American Exchange in the market of Bruce shares by an enormous "short" position that could not be covered.

Ben's full head of black hair—like his youthful predisposition in favor of socialistic principles—started to thin when he reached the age of 32. Making his first big fee changed his simplistic view that capitalism was unfairly stacked in favor of the wealthy and big business. His focus now was on his belief that the anti-trust laws forbidding price fixing, monopolies and conspiracies in restraint of trade—instead of ensuring fair competition—were causing cutthroat competition and were not in the public interest. So that year, 1926, Ben sponsored a movement to amend the anti-trust laws. The American economy and stock market were booming, but then along came the Stock Market Crash of 1928.

In 1929, Ben organized a national conference in Washington, D.C. in support of national economic planning. His hopeful optimism for reforming capitalism and free enterprise was blueprinted that year in his book *Make Everybody Rich, Industry's New Goal,* (Forbes Publishing Company), but the stock market's crash that October shook America's confidence and rocked it to its very foundations. It was as though a kaleidoscope had been shaken. The national picture had drastically changed, and everything had to be reassessed.

Ben's proposals were spelled out in his next book—*Business and the Public Interest; Trade Associations, the Anti Trust*

Laws and Industrial Planning, published in 1932 (Macmillan). With the election of Franklin Delano Roosevelt later that year, Ben's thesis of amending the anti-trust laws to be in "the public interest" really took root. Millions were jobless. The Great Depression was threatening to end "The American Dream."

Following Roosevelt's inauguration, Ben immediately went to Washington to assist in the drafting of the National Recovery Act. Under that Act, FDR established the principal New Deal agency in 1933. Its goal was to eliminate the "cut throat competition" that many now thought was fostered by too strict anti-trust law, and to create codes of "fair practices" to set minimum wages and prices with the goal of making competition less ruthless and destructive.

In 1933, Ben also assisted in the drafting of the National Industrial Recovery Act, another major effort by FDR's New Deal to regulate industry by permitting cartels and monopolies in an effort to stimulate economic recovery. By 1935, both of these regulatory efforts proved to be failures and were declared unconstitutional by the Supreme Court.

Though Ben started life in his teens as a socialist, he went through a metamorphosis following his experience with the New Deal and its failures. By the time he reached his thirties he recognized the pitfalls of central planning and the virtues of free enterprise and free markets. In 1936, recognizing the failures of government control of industry, his book *The Commonwealth of Industry, the Separation of Industry and the State* (Harper Brothers) was published.

Ben ultimately was convinced the means to democratize capitalism was by vastly expanding public share ownership of corporations and business enterprises. Recognized as one of the pioneers of the shareholders movement in the United

States, Ben founded United Shareowners of America in 1950, a membership organization to fight for more equitable treatment of, and accountability to, shareowners by corporate managements.

The Second World War had been over for five years, and the Marshall Plan had proved a success in rebuilding Europe, but foreign aid came entirely from our government. By this time Ben sought answers not from government but from the private sector. He postulated that vastly expanded investment by US companies abroad was a more sensible form of aid to help rejuvenate Europe's business sector and economy.

He began to befriend and correspond with Jean Monnet in France and Herman Abs in Germany, and helped to encourage the formation of the European Coal, Iron and Steel Communities, the forerunners of the European Union. His book *Peace by Investment* (Funk & Wagnall 1950) outlined a transformative plan for America's companies to become multinationals by vastly expanded US corporate investment overseas.

On November 8, 1962, the Benjamin A. Javits Halls of Law at Fordham University were dedicated at a memorable ceremony attended by Father Lawrence McGinley, President of Fordham University, by the Dean of the Fordham School of Law, and by members of our family including Senator Jacob Javits. It gratified my father to be able to give back to the Jesuit educational institution that had welcomed him as a young man eager to learn and succeed.

Ben's forward thinking and revolutionary concepts were visionary. They inspired my and his brother's thinking, and that of many other prominent leaders of government and business in America and abroad. His political and economic philosophy was succinctly expressed in 1962 in an historic document entitled,

"The Manifesto of Freedom for Mankind," that was subscribed by many members of the United States Senate at the time.

Ben was fearless and tough. He could be passionate with a quick temper or even shed tears when emotional. He was strict as a father, and somewhat ascetic in that he did not smoke or drink hard liquor, detested lipstick and heavy makeup, and considered cocktail parties a waste of time. But his ardent love of family and infective smile were radiant, and his humor contagious. He appreciated good food and wine, traveling, the arts, making new friends and discovering the world. He was my tennis partner, my law partner and my closest friend.

JACOB K. JAVITS

1904 - 1986

Senator Jacob K. Javits was more than a famous family member to me. Because my uncle was so much younger than my forceful father (who was paternal to us both) Jack and I shared a certain quasi-brotherly relationship. Jack became my pal—the brother I never had.

His career and accomplishments are legion. He served eight years in the House of Representatives, then two years as Attorney General of NY State, and finally twenty-four years in the United States Senate. Among his signature legislation was the 1973 War Powers Act that limited to sixty days a president's ability to send American armed forces into combat without congressional approval, and ERISA that regulated and helped to protect the solvency and portability of the private sector's corporate pension funds. I will not go deeply into his political record or accomplishments. They have been chronicled and assessed by him and many others. Suffice it to say that while he took a hard line on fiscal, defense, and financial policy, he was much softer on social issues. He was proud to be considered a liberal Republican like Nelson Rockefeller, Mayors Fiorello LaGuardia and John Lindsay, Senator John Sherman Cooper and others—promoting strongly civil rights and a safety net for those in need. Consequently, I will write of the private man and some of my own experiences with Jack during our lifetimes.

Jack stood 5'10" tall. He had a muscular build and was a great endurance swimmer. When I was a child, we would go together to Westport's Compo Beach, where he would swim a slow and steady tireless crawl far offshore in Long Island Sound for at least forty minutes before coming back to the beach.

He was equally good on horseback and at tennis as he was in the water. He was something of a bon vivant who had had travelled and tasted the good life in many of the world's capitol cities. From London came his love for a glass of sherry. From France came his love for fine food and wines. He ate like a European, not an American—spearing food with the fork in the left hand and cutting with the knife in the right—rarely putting either down to take the fork in his right hand. He loved to dance, and he excelled at "tripping the light fantastic". He could do them all—Samba, Mambo, Meringue and Cha Cha Cha.

Jack's pate began to bald quite early. He had a roundish head and face that conveyed intellect, a serious mien, his lips were full, his nose was slightly spread but straight, and his perfect teeth gleamed like ivory when he smiled. He had a great capacity for friendship. With his engaging manner and charm, he found it easy to make new friends and retain strong friendships with close friends as diverse as Max Fisher and Douglas Fairbanks, Jr.. Above all he loved life, ardently aspired to improve the lives of others, and yearned to be all that he could be. He was tenacious and disciplined in striving for his goals. He possessed inordinate patience and persistence, whether in arguing his point, courting a beautiful woman, seeking a trial verdict, passing legislation or gaining higher office. Perhaps he had developed those traits as a long distance swimmer. His ego was robust and he took no pains to hide it. When Jack was a youngster attending George Washington High School in New York, after hours he would practice orating to an imaginary audience in its vacant auditorium. At times he could be haughty and vain to a fault and at other times likeably modest.

During the early years of the Javits & Javits law firm, although Jack possessed impressive speaking ability, he did little trial or appellate work. He basically just carried my father's briefcase and apprenticed. That must have bridled him. But as the years passed he was delegated increasing responsibility. Jack acquired a consummate set of legal skills to become a tenacious litigator and superb tactician. Those skills served him well even after he left the practice of law.

Jack withdrew from the family law firm early in 1942 to enlist as a major in the Chemical Warfare Division of the Army. He attended the Army's War College at Fort Leavenworth, Kansas and soon rose to the rank of Lt. Colonel. During WW II Jack was second in command of the Army's Chemical Warfare Division. He returned briefly to the family firm in 1945 before running for Congress in 1946 in the upper West Side of Manhattan known as "Washington Heights".

I was just a toddler when Uncle Jack started courting Marjorie Ringling. She was a statuesque blond, strikingly beautiful to behold. I clearly remember the complete awe she inspired in me. My sister and I were introduced to her one weekend when she came to Westport with our uncle, but soon thereafter our mother took us into New York City to the Ringling Brothers

Barnum and Bailey circus at Madison Square Garden. There, sitting atop the head of the massive lead elephant in the parade that entered the Big Top to open the show, sat Marjorie Ringling, her spangled sheer skin-tight outfit displaying her every curve to its optimum advantage. She was radiant and unforgettable. Uncle Jack and Aunt Marjorie were married at our home in Westport; but after only a couple of years, Marjorie's promiscuity ended their marriage.

Losing stunning Aunt Marjorie was, for me, a devastating blow; but according to my mother just before she died, not a blow to my uncle. She said that on their wedding day she went upstairs to the bedroom that Marjorie was using to help her get into her wedding gown, only to find her in bed with one of the male members of the wedding party. Lily Javits had seen sordid betrayals many times in her theatre career. She discreetly backed out, quietly closed the door, and decided not to disrupt her brother-in-law's choice to marry that day. Nor did she ever tell Jack about it.

After WW II, not only was Jack still single, he was a bit of a rake. He used to drive to Westport to spend his weekend with us in the countryside. In 1946, Buick introduced a dashing convertible with a stunning grill reminiscent of a shark's smile. When we knew he was coming on Saturday mornings, my sister and I would wait expectantly to see him sweep into our driveway in his shiny new Buick convertible with the top down and each time with a different beautiful lady in the front seat beside him.

My mother eventually convinced Jack to buy a ramshackle house on Cross Highway in Westport as an investment. It had lopsided floors and needed painting desperately, so after a couple of years when property values went up, he sold it; but meanwhile it brought Jack even more often to Westport with good friends like the renowned Broadway choreographer, Agnes DeMille, and others from the theatre or the arts.

Jack was elected for the first time to Congress in 1946 and took his office in January 1947. New York's 21st congressional district covered much of the upper West side of Manhattan known as Washington Heights. Later that year, Jack married Marian Boris who had worked in his campaign. Their wedding took place in a synagogue on Washington Heights, and it was more of a political event than a personal one. They moved into a large apartment on Riverside Drive just below the Columbia University campus and proceeded to have three children—their son, Joshua, and daughters Joy and Carla. I used to visit Jack's family when I was attending Columbia. Often Jack would be in Washington, so I would spend time with Marian and the children.

Sometimes we would go into Riverside Park across the street where we would talk about our lives and family. It disturbed me that Marian was critical of my father for being a dominant influence in my life. She was constantly trying to convince me to split from my parents and sought to undermine my family's closeness. She was probably projecting her own insecurity at the close emotional bond Jack shared with his older brother, and the immense influence Ben had in Jack's life. Instead of seeing it as something positive, she felt threatened by it. In later years I realized that Marian, for whatever reason, chose not to edit her opinions that could be deliberately hurtful and create lasting rifts. She sought to control by attacking and to destroy relationships and her target's self esteem. Despite her perverse and complicated nature, I tried to maintain a cordial relationship with her after Jack's death, but I finally had to completely sever it some years ago.

In 1954 I was still studying at Columbia Law School when the Republican nomination for State Attorney General opened up.

That gave Jack the chance finally to leave the Congress and to run for higher office against FDR Jr., a former member of Congress and the bearer of a formidable political name. Frank Roosevelt was the name partner in a prominent New York law firm, and no one thought he could be defeated for office. He was a clone of his father's patrician good lucks, resonant oratory and irresistible charm.

But beneath that seeming invincibility was an Achilles heel of having traded on his father's name and not having "made it on his own". Jack Javits, on the other hand, was a popular liberal legislator, a fighter for the common man whose appeal reached across party lines. Jack was statesmanlike in his thinking and public commentary. If Jack could defeat Roosevelt, he would become a political giant killer that could go on to even higher office.

Jack did receive the Republican nomination and the Liberal nomination as well, thanks to my father's friendship with David Dubinsky and Isador Dubin, the leaders of the Liberal Party that had backed Jack for Congress six years earlier when he had defeated Paul O'Dwyer, the Mayor's younger brother in Washington Heights area of NYC where registration of voters was three to one Democrat over Republican.

Thus, in early September, 1954 at the age of twenty-three, I was put in charge of setting up the Citizens for Javits campaign headquarters. We knew that a third "Citizens" movement would be indispensable to defeating FDR, Jr. because it would invite and attract independents and persons of all political parties—outside of the Republican party's efforts—and would reach across party lines. "Citizens" could vote for Jack either on the Republican, Liberal or the newly formed Independent line. We had to get enough signatures of registered independents to establish another line on the voting machines, and we did.

I recruited at least one hundred volunteers from Columbia College and the Columbia Law School who worked with me day and night for two months to help stuff, address, seal and stamp a few million letters to independents. We solicited votes in Jewish neighborhoods with flyers that purposely misspelled Jack's last name with a z. We even had some of our literature done in comic book form which we mailed to immigrant slum neighborhoods, to tell of Jack's journey as a child of immigrant parents rising from the slums of the lower east side to the halls of Congress.

When the votes were tallied on election night, ticket splitting was rife. Instead of voting the straight Democratic ticket all the way down the line, many Democrats had voted for their party's nominees but then "split" their ticket by crossing over to the Liberal line to vote for Attorney General. The voters put in office a Democratic Governor, Lt. Governor and State Controller. Jack was the only Republican to win statewide office that year to become Attorney General with the largest vote in NY history.

That election was my chance to learn the nuts and bolts of electoral techniques, and to cut my teeth on a campaign fought block by block, building by building and suburb by suburb throughout the state.

Two years later in 1956, Nelson Rockefeller was nominated by the Republican State convention to run for governor and Jack received the nomination to run for the United States Senate. The only problem was that once again Jack had to face another "giant" in Robert F. Wagner, Jr., the well-liked former mayor of NYC. Wagner's father had been a highly respected and very popular Democratic U. S. Senator from NY whose name was synonymous with the Wagner Act—a cornerstone of federal labor law.

I was no longer in law school during this election. I could not call on classmates and students to turn out as volunteers. But I had a network nevertheless, and again Jack called on me to set up the Citizens for Javits headquarters in vacant office space in a building owned by Samuel Rudin, a warm and wonderful friend of our family who was also one of the leading developers of Manhattan real estate. The only problem was that Jack gave me less than a week to get the headquarters open and staffed, with phones, furniture, office equipment, mailing machines, signage, stationary and literature printed etc. Still it opened on schedule.

Many wonderful people came to help at Citizens for Javits headquarters, including many prominent Democrats. Ann Rubensohn and Mrs. John L. Loeb (who went by the nickname Peter) led the army of female volunteers. My father set up office there and kept busy non-stop raising the money. I was spending eighteen-hour days recruiting and managing the rest of the campaign volunteers. Suddenly one morning, right in the midst of the campaign, I awoke with such excruciating abdominal pain I could barely move or even speak.

Despite pain so acute I could hardly breathe or walk erect, I managed to get a cab to Lenox Hill Hospital where I had immediate surgery for acute appendicitis. Following the surgery, I was seized by extreme nausea and repulsive delusions in violent reaction to the morphine.

Despite a brutal campaign schedule that would have taken him that day to far reaches of New York State, Jack took time off from campaigning to call on me in my hospital room. My only concern was not for me, it was whether my absence would hurt or compromise the campaign effort. When Jack walked in I guess I must have looked a mess. I never thought he would take time away from his campaign schedule to make a hospital call. When Jack saw me with IVs and drainage tubes, tears came to his eyes. That touched me deeply.

Though I could not get back to work in the Citizens headquarters for the rest of the campaign, I was able, by election night, to join the small group that sat in a private room at the Republican Campaign headquarters watching the election returns.

The evening began by Jack lagging behind in early returns from heavily Democratic neighborhoods in New York City. Voting returns came in earlier than those from the remote areas of upstate that were heavily Republican. But when those upstate voters began to slowly make up the deficit, and then when Nassau and Suffolk counties came in, Jack was again declared the winner with a record count.

No sooner was he elected than a dark cloud loomed over him in the person of Senator Joe McCarthy and the Senate Internal Security Subcommittee that was investigating communists in government and Hollywood. Enemies of liberalism like Roy Cohen, and ultra conservatives like J. Edgar Hoover, were not happy to see a liberal from New York in the U. S. Senate, and they hoped that somehow they could prevent his being seated.

A senate subpoena was served on Jack to appear to answer questions about his early associations, and the trip he took to San Francisco in 1946 to be at the creation of the United Nations. My father and I flew down to Washington to be present at Jack's Senate hearing, but since it was held in secret session, we had to just wait outside the Senate hearing room.

When Jack emerged, he told us the committee had been given his answers to all their questions and that the committee had indicated they were satisfied with his replies. By coincidence, it was that very hearing that marked the beginning of the end of the McCarthy reign of terror.

When Jack had been elected the Attorney General of New York State, he separated entirely from the Javits & Javits law firm because of the obvious conflict of interest, as well as the New York legal prohibition against the State Attorney General practicing law privately. But two years later when Jack was elected to the United States Senate, he had the option of going back into the practice of law so long as he or his firm did not handle any matter that involved the federal government or that could raise an apparent or potential conflict of interest.

Jack's wife, Marian, did not want her husband to re-affiliate with his brother in the family law firm. Marian was always trying to disrupt the relationship between her husband and his older brother, as she saw Jack's closeness to his older brother as somehow diminishing her husband's stature and diluting her control of him.

Probably due to Marian's influence, Jack eventually did decide to establish his own firm. He chose Jim Moore, a prominent litigator in Buffalo, NY, and John Trubin, his former First Deputy Attorney General, to be his partners. Later, Jim Moore withdrew from the firm to be replaced by other lawyers, including Albert Edelman, the latter a well-known NYC real estate lawyer. This was logical since almost all of the firm's business would come from real estate closings and mortgage loans done for Citibank where Jack's close friend, Bill Spencer, was the President and CEO.

Jack tried to woo me away from Javits & Javits to join his new firm. I was unwilling to join him, not only out of admiration for and loyalty to my father. I did not want to benefit from the patronage of my politically powerful uncle. I am proud to be able to say I practiced law without ever trading on my uncle's political position—I did no lobbying, no use of his name, received no business because of my familial relationship with him, and no legal business was referred either from him or his firm to our firm, or visa versa (other than the Arias negotiation I have described earlier).

After Jack lost his last race for the United States Senate in 1980 his doctors identified the weakness he was experiencing in his limbs as amyotrophic lateral sclerosis, otherwise known as Lou Gehrig's disease or ALS. The family knew then that his life expectancy was short. Jack was a stoic. He never complained about his illness. The most he ever indicated was in response to a remark I made to him in St. Mary's Hospital in West Palm Beach where I had gone to visit him after he underwent surgery for an oxygen tube to be inserted in his throat so he could be assisted by a breathing machine. Now our roles were reversed. He was the one looking like a sick chicken in the hospital bed, and I was the visitor with tears in my eyes. The noise of the machine was rhythmical as he took each breath. I exclaimed "Oh Jack, I am so sad to see you like this." He did not reply. He just looked skyward and rolled his eyes as though he wanted sympathy from God, not from me.

Jack's mettle was sorely tested, but he used his mind and what little physical capacity he still had in his wheel chair and breathing apparatus to instill hope and renewed determination in those who also suffered with terminal illness. His lectures to hospital staffs began with the statement, "I have a terminal illness, and so I am what you call a terminal case. But all of you are terminal cases. It is only a matter of when and how you are going to die."

In Jack's mind there was no point in dwelling on death or brooding. He just felt one should use whatever time one had to be all one could be.

Jack's nurse, a beautiful and adept professional, was Jack's angel of mercy who tirelessly endured through his slow deterioration with grace and forbearance. The support and affection she gave Jack, and that he so needed, was a gift of pure love.

When he died in Florida, his body had to be transported up to New York for his funeral. Jack's intimate friend and confidant, Max Fisher, offered to have his private jet transport the coffin, but it was too bulky to get into the passenger cabin, so the Air Force sent one of its cargo planes to carry him back for his funeral. I rode with his casket on that flight. We landed in New York, and along with Jack's coffin were escorted by a cavalcade of motorcycle police into Manhattan—sirens blaring and red lights blinking.

Jack's funeral was held at the Central Synagogue on Lexington Avenue. The service and the funeral orations were poignant and wonderful, but most touching was when the procession of limousines following the hearse pulled away from the curb, people lining both sides of the Avenue for blocks stood with their hats removed, tears in their eyes, and their hands on their hearts mouthing "goodbye" to the Senator of "All the People of New York".

Lily and Ben Javits on the boardwalk in Atlantic City
circa 1934

Jacob Javits with Martin Birnbaum,
photo taken in November, 1962

Ida Javits with her sons Jacob and
Benjamin circa 1920

The Javits brothers at Fordham Law School dedication
Nov. 1962

ADDENDUM (2)

e, the Free Peoples of the World, endowed with love of liberty, respect for the inalienable rights of man, and devotion to the Divine Spirit, requiring a new Manifesto of Freedom for Mankind, believe: The threat of human extinction by war can only be overcome by all uniting to achieve the Purposes of Peace. The Purposes of Peace are to release all mankind from ignorance, poverty, disease and insecurity, so that life, liberty, the protection of personal property, and the pursuit of happiness shall be mankind's heritage. The Purposes of Peace, thus clarified, can now for the first time, because of man's moral, material and scientific advancements, be realized by universal consecration to these twin commandments: No longer shall man or the State exploit man. All men together shall exploit the machine only. The State shall be man's, not man the State's. All men shall be owners, not owned. To these economic, political, and social commandments, we dedicate all of our moral, material, human and scientific resources, both public and private. We shall do this together with peoples everywhere. We shall do this with our enemies as quickly as they accept these commandments. We are not the enemy of any peoples, nor do we believe any peoples are our enemies. Despotic state leaders may tell them so, but just as we do not believe their leaders, so they may not. We seek all peoples economic liberation from whence shall come their political freedom. We condemn those and their remedy who impose political bondage in order to cure economic and social ills. We shall everywhere reduce the walls between the governing and the governed by bringing to all a true share in the processes of government. We shall everywhere reduce the walls between the owner of property and the toiler in plant and field by bringing to all a fair share in the creation and enjoyment of its profits. We shall translate the potentials of mass production into the blessing of mass consumption. We shall expand wealth vastly through peoples capitalism until consumer capitalism is achieved. We shall expand personal profits into social profits. All may not be equally rich, but none shall be poor. We seek that those at the top shall lift upward those at the bottom rather than that those at the bottom pull downward those at the top. We seek to uproot all political, religious, social and traditional barriers yet remaining, born of fear, prejudice or ignorance, halting man's political and economic emancipation. With a common cause, a common purpose, we seek togetherness for peace. This is our Testament as Free Peoples. This is our Decalogue as Leaders. This is our Gospel as Nations. To these, the Purposes of Peace, we pledge our lives, our fortunes, and our sacred honor, lest mankind perish from this earth.

Manifesto of Freedom for Mankind written
by Benjamin A. Javits

We endorse this Manifesto and commend it to the American people

[Signatures]

Affirming Signatures of Members of the United States Senate

CHAPTER III —
WESTPORT

I had taken nothing to read when flying home from the adventure in Panama to New York, so my thoughts for some reason eventually wandered back to my childhood years in Connecticut. Westport in the 1930s was a quaint and picturesque artist's colony of about 2,500 year-round residents where household names like Steven Dohanos and Harold Von Schmidt turned out illustrations for weekly magazines like Colliers and the Saturday Evening Post. Most of the houses were white wood Colonial-style structures on more than a few acres, accented by black or green shutters, with brick chimneys and asphalt tile roofs.

Our house was a two-story four-bedroom white colonial with black shutters, nestled back along a curve on Greens Farms Road with well paved tree-lined country lanes. In the spring the blossoming dogwood was breathtaking to behold; and in the summers the well-tended velvety lawns, flower gardens and shrubbery were lush and colorful. A youngster could easily find an opportunity to earn "two bits" in the summer, cutting grass and weeding vegetable gardens, or raking leaves in the fall.

Land was plentiful, and nothing but dairy farms surrounded the 30-acre tract of farmland that my parents bought in 1927 as a place to build their home and raise their children. Prior thereto, they had rented in Forest Hills, NY, but when my father earned his first major fee they decided to move out of the city and invest in a permanent home. Their tract of land was composed of meadows, rocky knolls, wooded areas demarcated by long neglected stone walls that must have dated back to colonial times.

Westport had an elementary phone system in the 1930s, mostly composed of "party" lines. You might pick up the receiver and if not polite, listen in on a neighbor's conversation. There were only four digits to our phone number—4900. One had to lift the receiver and click for the operator to place even local calls, no less one to a neighboring town or to New York City.

Our kitchen had only an insulated icebox in which to keep perishables. The iceman would come every few days to deliver a large block of ice held with calipers slung over his shoulder. The white milk truck came every few days with early morning deliveries of milk, butter and eggs. The milkman, dressed in a white uniform, delivered the milk in glass bottles sealed with paper caps. The empties had to be returned in wooden cases to get the next delivery.

There were Methodists, Episcopalians and Catholics living in Westport, but no Jews. My mother, Lily, had attended parochial school in the Yorkville section of Manhattan where she received her education from Catholic nuns. My father, Ben, had earned his law degree at night from Fordham, an institution run by Jesuits. Neither of my parents were orthodox, conservative or deeply religious, so being one of the first Jewish families to settle in Westport was not unfamiliar to them.

The construction of their country house was still not completed when my parents moved there in 1928 right after the arrival of their firstborn, my older sister, Joan. The challenge that confronted my mother—my father being too busy as an attorney to pay much attention—was to turn a virgin farmland tract into a country estate. Fortunately, she had the pioneering spirit, determination, esthetic taste and green thumb that was needed.

However, to do the job, she needed help. She turned to two Italian immigrants—Sebastian Pengallo and his wife, Tessie. The Pengallos lived close to the Westport railroad station in an Italian immigrant enclave called Saugatuck. Sebastian was an expert mason, carpenter and farmer who became our gardener and caretaker. Tessie would come over occasionally to clean or do other chores.

Lily designed the landscaping, terraces and rock gardens. She chose the flowers, the shrubs and their placement. Sebastian laid the stonewalls and terraces. He built the grape arbor, tennis court and tended the flower and vegetable gardens.

With 1941 came the onset of World War II. I was just ten years old. Sebastian convinced my father to buy a Ford Ferguson tractor so he could fully farm our fields of hay, corn and vegetables. Sebastian built a chicken shed and a large barn to house the new tractor and its equipment, along with bales of hay, various tools and supplies. Close to it stood a smaller barn that housed a couple of sheep, two cows and a goat.

Sebastian would usually let me milk one cow for a while in the morning or evening, and then he would take over until she was milked dry. The cat that lived in the barn used to mew until I would divert a few squirts in her direction. I did not have to feed the cows or shovel out their waste, but I did have to feed two hundred chickens, clean out their coop and collect their eggs. The hens were obstinately proprietary, but I soon learned how to slip my hand beneath them to deftly remove eggs without getting pecked. The chickens ranged in a grassed area into which I would dump old vegetables and other edible farm waste.

Once a week Sebastian would weed the flower and vegetable gardens, and then ride a gas-powered Locke lawn mower around the extensive lawns surrounding our house that took all day to cut. I used to beg him to let me run the mower, but he would only let me stand behind him on the sulky as he drove. He finally taught me to drive the tractor,and eventually trusted me to plow some furrows. He had a grasp of English, but when he spoke he was difficult to understand. Whenever it would start to rain I can still hear him saying, "Jeezama Chriis, she's a rain!"

Sebastian had served as an infantryman in one of Italy's wars, and he taught me how to handle the family's 12-gauge shotgun. One lovely day we were out behind the barn trying to knock down some crows that were in the young cornfields making an annoying ruckus with their cawing. I can still feel the kick of the stock against my shoulder and hear the shotgun's deafening reports. We went through a box of shells without success, so we gave up in disgust and sat down in the barn.

Perhaps because I had been targeting much less predatory birds than crows with my BB gun that Sebastian decided to relate to me an incident from his wartime experiences. In his broken English, he described in detail the no-man's land of trench warfare, the relentless shelling by enemy artillery, the terror of dying slowly in pain and the senselessness of the slaughter. He went on to tell me how one pitch-black night the battlefield had suddenly gone quiet. Overcome by exhaustion, he dared to crawl into a trench to sleep because he thought he was alone; but when dawn broke he opened his eyes to find an enemy soldier in the very same trench with him. They stared into each other's eyes, leveled their weapons at each other, but then both realized the senselessness of killing and neither fired. But for those two combatants spontaneously valuing life over death, I would never have met Sebastian or heard his story. That vignette made a deep impression on me. Killing songbirds or wildlife other than vermin became unthinkable after that.

A person's sense of right and wrong can often be traced back to childhood incidents. One summer day when I was only four or five my mother took me into Westport to look for some items she needed. After she made those purchases, we went into Breslow's stationary store. I saw a cap pistol that I really wanted, and when my mother started to walk out of the store, I ran back into one of the aisles, took the gun and as I walked out with it in hand I said to the proprietor who was standing at the cash register "charge it" which I had heard my mother say earlier when she made a purchase. He did not object or try to stop me, so I ran up the street to join my mother, gun in hand. When she saw me she asked where I had gotten the cap pistol. I told her that I had bought it, and she asked me how I had paid for it. I explained that I said "charge it". She explained that money was required to buy things, and if I could not pay for what I had charged, or had not asked permission to buy it, then I was stealing it. She marched me back and had me apologize to Mr. Breslow for taking it without asking her if I could have it. I can still feel the humiliation I felt that afternoon.

The Kindergarten I attended in 1935 or 1936 was Miss Paul's in Westport. Among the students were Mark Rudkin, whose mother started Pepperidge Farm bakeries by preparing whole wheat bread for Mark who had TB or asthma and could not eat white bread. Mrs. Rudkin would take her loaves into the only grocery store in Westport, Sam Friedson's Economy Grocery. She would personally solicit and sell her whole wheat bread to the townspeople who shopped there; and in those days, since only Silvercup white bread was commercially available, Mrs. Rudkin's loaves sold like hotcakes.

Another student in my class at Miss Paul's kindergarten was Justin Dart who later became an important industrialist, entrepreneur and figure in American public life. He was instrumental in influencing Congress to pass legislation to make life easier for Americans with physical disabilities. He and I used to climb up on the big wooden railroad engine that was erected in the kindergarten yard and pretend we were the engineer and the fireman.

As each summer drew to an end Westport's public schools opened; and once I became six I started in the first grade. Each day, I was driven to school in our four-door forest-green Lincoln sedan by Huevelt, the family's handsome black chauffeur. The Greens Farms Elementary School was housed in a red brick building that sat atop a grassy knoll with a winding driveway leading up to its front entrance. My mother would always dress me for school either in a little sailor suit or in short pants and a shirt that had a Lord Fauntleroy collar.

Each morning five or six of the tough Italian kids from immigrant families in Saugatuck would loiter outside the school's entrance until the starting bell rang that marked the beginning of the school day. The moment I would step out of our car, and before I could even get inside the school, they would surround me. They would knock me down and mess me up as much as possible until the bell rang. Whether it was envy at my being chauffeur-driven, or contempt for what appeared to be a rich sissy, it was torture for me. Each afternoon when I got back from school my clothes were grass stained and muddy. My mother's only response was, "Don't fight, don't take dares, and stay out of trouble".

After repeatedly seeing me humiliated, Huevelt decided he had to intervene, despite my mother's admonitions. He had been a professional bantamweight prizefighter before turning to chauffeuring, and unbeknownst to my mother he bought a punching bag and boxing gloves and proceeded to coach me in our basement. After some weeks of training in how to make a fist correctly, jab accurately, throw right crosses and left hooks, I was told, "You is now ready."

Then he gave me my instructions. "When it's one up against a gang, surprise is de bes' defense, so when they comes at you look scared and point to the groun' jus' a little to the side of the firs' bully. When he turns his head to look where you're a-pointin', hit him in the jaw with all you got." I carried out his instructions exactly, and the boy went down like a ton of bricks. All the others backed off as I walked proudly into the school. I was never picked on after that.

Huevelt used to sit me in the driver's seat on his lap and let me steer the car. I soon had the feel of the big Lincoln and felt ready to drive it, but my feet could not reach the pedals. So I nagged Sebastian to allow me to learn to drive the old Ford truck and the Ford Ferguson tractor. He gave me instruction, and by the age of 8 I was able to drive both around our property.

Another memory I have of Huevelt was the warm summer day when my father insisted that Huevelt accompany our family to Compo Beach for a picnic, and that he bring a bathing suit with him. Huevelt said he did not own a bathing suit, so my father said he would lend him one. Huevelt's eyes grew as big as saucers and he said, "No siree, Massah Ben. I ain't agoin' to that white man's beach. I be killed if I swim there." My father promised to protect him, and explained that Connecticut was not the South where Huevelt had grown up. People might not expect to see a Negro swimming at Westport's Compo beach, but there was no discrimination in Westport's public places, and there was no reason to be afraid.

Huevelt, who as far as I knew feared nothing, reluctantly did go to the beach with us. He changed out of his chauffeur's attire in the small changing locker that we rented from the town every summer. Huevelt looked like a happy six year-old as he capered about in Long Island Sound, splashing water in every direction. It was, I believe, the first taste of real freedom from discrimination that Huevelt had ever experienced. That day I came to understand what a prison without bars discrimination could be for human beings. Huevelt taught me not only how to defend myself but to judge people by their character and not by their skin color.

In the summer of 1938, Eric "Hartzy" Boehm was my German Jewish tutor and companion during his summer vacation. I was seven that year. I had gone away to camp Wigwam in Maine the preceding summer, and my parents wanted me home for a summer before sending me away to another camp the following year. We called Eric Boehm "Hartzy" because he was from the Hartz Mountain area of Germany. He would take me fishing, sailing, on hikes and camping trips to keep me busy. He turned 18 at the end of that summer, and so was of draft age when he was scheduled to go back to Germany in September. My father pleaded with him not to go back because of the way Jews were being treated in Germany and to seek asylum in the U.S. instead.

Hartzy insisted that he was a loyal German ready to serve in the German army and would not suffer the fate of Jews generally. He said if he did not go back he would be a deserter and would never be able to go home to Germany. Some years later, around 1943, a stranger came to my father's office in New York to deliver a letter and diary that had been smuggled out of the concentration camp where Hartzy had been imprisoned. Hartzy wrote that he was surviving by being a trustee guard with a German shepherd that he would have to kill after a year. He wrote that he did not expect to survive much longer because of the conditions in the camp, so he wanted the world to know what was happening there. He described the extermination of the prisoners by starvation, exposure to freezing, being worked to death, summary execution, or gassing and cremation, and his cover note asked my father to give his diary to the American government.

My father took the letter and diary to Washington as requested. Nothing happened. I have often wondered why America never took action to try to rescue or give sanctuary to German Jews, never bombed the rail lines to the concentration camps, and why Roosevelt enjoyed such lasting adoration by American Jews despite the paucity of American policy in that regard. But once I read "The Secret War Against the Jews" I came to understand that there were those high in Roosevelt's Administration who shaped those policy decisions, not the President himself.

In 1939 our mother took us to the World's Fair at Flushing Meadows in NYC. The Fair's color theme was blue and orange, and its symbols were the Pylon and Hemisphere. Small trolley-like vehicles filled with visitors crawled around the Fair grounds. The most fascinating exhibits were Billie Rose's Aquacade Show that starred Eleanor Holm, a champion swimmer and diver that he later married. Also, General Motors' Futurama Pavilion showed what the future would be like. The first cup of coffee I ever tasted was one offered without charge to those who visited the Brazilian pavilion.

Around that year, our family received a gift of one of the first television sets from David Sarnoff, one of my father's close friends who headed Radio Corporation of America. It was almost beyond human imagination then to think that pictures, not just sound, could be sent over the airwaves. The small box that housed the television set was prominently placed in the living room of our Westport home. It had a tiny screen, and for the first year showed only a broadcast test pattern. I could barely conceive of it actually displaying a picture! Eventually, it did display a tiny black and white picture, but we soon got a larger set.

In the thirties I remember watching the Graf Zeppelin, one of Germanys' dirigibles, fly over Westport on the way toward New York. The dirigibles that attracted most attention were Germany's giant gas-filled, propeller-powered, steerable passenger airships that made hundreds of transoceanic trips during the twenties and thirties. In 1937 I saw the Hindenburg flying past our house in Westport after crossing the Atlantic, on the way to its doomed landing in New Jersey.

On my sixth or seventh birthday, my father's client and close friend, Bert C. Forbes, the founder of Forbes Magazine, who was known to close friends as "B.C." came to our house in Westport to attend a party my parents were hosting. I called B.C. "Uncle Bert" because he was very much a godfather figure for me. On that occasion he was wearing his kilt because he was enormously proud of his Scotch upbringing and heritage. I had never seen a man wearing a skirt, so I asked Uncle Bert why he was wearing one. He explained that a kilt was a male's formal regalia, even a fighting man's garb, and the design of one's plaid signified one's clan in ancient Scotland. Next he asked me if I knew the meaning of the word "thrift"—a word he explained that was very close to every Scotsman's heart. I said I did not, to which he replied with a heavy brogue, "Thrift is when you squeeze a penny so hard that it screams!" I never forgot the true meaning of thrift after that. Years later, for my thirteenth birthday, Uncle Bert presented me with a leather-bound Webster's Collegiate dictionary that he had inscribed "to Eric with love from Uncle Bert".

The year 1940 was a presidential election year. President Roosevelt was running for a third term and my father was no longer enamored of the President's policies. So when his friend Samuel Pryor, then Vice President of Pan American Airways, called and asked if he could bring Wendell Willkie, a Republican, to our home in Westport to garner Ben Javits' support for his presidential campaign, my father was eager to comply.

It was on a beautiful sunny day early that year that Sam Pryor turned into our driveway on a magnificent red motorcycle with sidecar. It had twin red lights and a siren, and Sam explained that he had bought it from the Greenwich Fire Department to squire Wendell Willkie around Connecticut without having to worry about speed limits or getting through heavy traffic.

The visitors promptly repaired to my father's study where they conferred for about an hour. At the conclusion of their meeting my father agreed to back Mr. Willkie. As they emerged and were about to leave, Mr. Prior asked if I would like to go for a ride with him. Of course I beamed eagerly with enthusiasm, so he instructed me to get into the low sidecar and hold on tight. When I got in, I found myself almost flat on my back with my head sticking up over the coping. Once we were out of our driveway and on the Shore Road he opened it up and tore away with siren screaming and red lights blazing. The feeling was one of flying barely two feet off the pavement. I could hardly breathe, so strong was the wind in my face. We only sped for a few minutes before he turned around and headed back, but the thrill of that ride still leaves me joyous and smiling, even after almost seventy years!

As I was approaching my thirteenth birthday, mother arranged for me to go to the neighboring town of Norwalk, Connecticut, to study Hebrew so that I could be Bar Mitzvah'd. My father had explained that in the Jewish faith when a boy reached the age of thirteen he would become a man—in a rite of passage celebrated by family and friends in synagogue where the boy would be allowed for the first time to read from the Torah.

Even by 1944 there were hardly any Jews in Westport, so naturally there was no temple there. I went to the synagogue in

Norwalk a couple of times and learned almost nothing from the Rabbi there. Discouraged with my disinterest and lack of progress, and with almost no time remaining before my birthday, the Rabbi showed me a phonetic text in English that I could read and sound like I was reading the Hebrew. My father said that following the service I would receive many gifts from friends and family. I was more much focused on getting gifts than on attaining my manhood.

About a week before the appointed date my maternal grandmother, Ella Birnbaum, died. I certainly did not mourn her death nor, frankly, did my mother; but our family went through the customary sitting of Shiva that caused the cancellation of my Bar Mitzvah. Somehow that rite of passage never got rescheduled, and I made the transition into manhood with neither gifts nor ceremony.

The lessons I took away from not receiving gifts for faking the reading of Hebrew was (1) that I was no less Jewish; (2) that I believed in God; and (3) that I would keep religion as a private matter between me and my Maker. I have never felt any attraction to organized religion, its ceremonies or services (with the exception of the music of the Kol Nidre that I find rapturous). I have never felt the need of an intermediary—whether temple, church, synagogue, cathedral, mosque, rabbi, priest, minister or imam to commune with God. I have always prayed for God's help for others, not for myself. God always seemed to hear me.

Joan and Eric Javits with Buttons circa 1933

Lily Javits with Joan and Eric in Florida in the '30s

WESTPORT THRU COLLEGE (5)

With Sebastian Pengallo and the chickens in Westport
circa 1942

CHAPTER IV — MY EDUCATION

Three Years at Choate

In 1943 my health was so bad that my parents took me out of Bedford Junior High School in Westport to escape the harsh Connecticut winter. They sent me instead to Graham-Eckes School, a co-ed academy in Palm Beach that I attended for the next two years until June, 1945.

It was then my parents decided I should be sent off to Preparatory school. My father and I went to look at Lawrenceville, Deerfield and Choate. I liked Choate the best for its beautiful campus, impressive buildings and facilities that rivaled those of some universities. The fact that Adlai Stevenson and John F. Kennedy were Choate alumni impressed me as well.

When Headmaster George Claire St. John and his wife received my father and me on our initial visit to the school, they emanated a warmth and sincerity that conveyed the family feeling that pervaded the School. I felt no trace of prejudice despite the fact that Dr. St. John was an Episcopalian minister, and Jewish students at Choate were few. "The Head" was an imposing figure—gracious in manner, and ardent in convictions, values and faith. With flowing white hair and twinkling eyes he radiated New England's frugality, work ethic and Puritanism. Choate had an honor system that required one to write on every exam paper "on my honor" to indicate one had not cheated or witnessed cheating. I promptly applied to Choate, took a placement test and went on a waiting list before I was admitted.

In my first year, 1945-46, I lived in the Choate House. Also attending Choate at that time were Rudy Schaeffer, scion of the Schaeffer beer company who used to play great boogie woogie on the Housemaster's piano; and Ruppert Vernon, whose family owned the Ruppert Brewery in New York City.

In my Junior year I lived on the fourth floor of the Hill House with a roommate from Nashville, Tenn. The Master in charge of the floor, E. Stanley Pratt, was a leonine and dashingly handsome thespian that one would expect to meet on the London Globe's stage. He was also the school's public speaking instructor. As a former Shakespearean actor, his diction and intonation were flawless. When necessary he could amp up his volume to sound like a Roman stentorian.

Every Choate boy was required to take Pratt's public speaking course that was given in the basement auditorium of the chapel. Mr. Pratt would always sit in the last row at the back of the auditorium and have the students sit in the front row. One by one, each of us would be ordered to ascend the stage and deliver a short oration. The tension heightened within me as my turn approached. I had never spoken publicly before, and when it came Mr. Pratt immediately attacked me for any swaying, "ums" and "ers" that I might utter. Pratt would bellow "Stop swaying!" "Take your hands out of your pockets!" "Look at your audience!' "Breathe deeply!" "Think before you speak!" "Deliver with conviction!" He scared the daylights out of each student, and I was no exception. Once I had withstood his withering verbal assault, there was no longer any reason to be nervous about getting up in front of an audience, because no audience could possibly be as daunting as E. Stanley Pratt.

My weakest subject was mathematics. I always sat in the front row hoping that would help me master the material. One day, when quiz marks were about to be handed out, I saw the results sitting on the Master's desk about two feet from my nose. My curiosity got the better of me. I leaned forward a bit trying to get a peek at my mark. The Master in that course noticed it and slapped me hard across the face. He said "that's for being nosy and impolite". In those days, no one would dare question the behavior of a faculty member, so I meekly accepted my humiliation and embarrassment and absorbed that lesson in classroom decorum.

At Choate, students attended chapel twice a day. I sang in the chapel choir as an alto. We had to sing all the hymns in the Episcopalian services, and the choir leader, Duncan Phyfe, an extremely talented musician, also served as the organist. Phyfe was a refined and gracious man of slight build and aesthetic countenance who looked a bit like a choirboy himself. Nevertheless, he commanded absolute attention from his choir, while enjoying each member's friendship and respect that perhaps was due to his generous nature in accepting students in the choir (like me) who had borderline vocal ability. I enjoyed chapel for its solitude, the quiet contemplation in prayer, the beautiful music and even the sermons that The Head delivered from the pulpit.

Every Choate student had to play intramural football for at least one fall season. So as a sophomore I played in the league at my weight level—then 145-150 pounds. I played center, and was deadly accurate in hiking the ball to the ball carrier. I could send a spiral between my legs to a kicker fifteen yards back, hitting his hands over the point from which he needed to kick the ball. But I had no idea how to charge or tackle oncoming ball carriers. Consequently, I was injured a number of times when runners ran over me. After a herniated disk and a broken nose in that first football season, I switched to squash in the fall and winter semesters of the next years and to tennis in the spring, winning my "C" letter as a member of the Choate tennis team in my junior and senior years.

One big treat was to visit the Tuck Shop, Choate's own soda fountain that served ice cream, cokes, sodas, sundaes, burgers and grilled cheese sandwiches. It was housed in the cellar of a small, poorly-ventilated building that one entered by descending three steps below ground to a dimly lit space where the air was heavy with the smell of hot dogs and hamburger grease.

My closest friend at Choate was a tennis pal from Westport— "Web" Ray, whose room was directly across from mine on Mr. Pratt's floor. Mr. Nearing (whom we used to call Creeping Jesus because he always wore sneakers) was the other Master living on Mr. Pratt's floor. Radios were forbidden at Choate, so wearing his usual sneakers, Mr. Nearing would creep up and down the hall after lights out to listen for any radios. Web had a hidden radio rigged with a toggle switch that cut off automatically when his door was opened. As Mr. Nearing passed Web's room he was certain he could hear one playing. When he would throw open the door there was only silence. Mr. Nearing could never figure that one out.

After lights out Web used to climb out his fourth floor window to run along a narrow ledge to visit a friend in another room. He tried to teach me to do it, but I was afraid to even stand on the window ledge that high up. One day I decided that I was simply tired of being afraid of heights. At first, I merely dared to stand on the ledge four floors from the ground. Then, by slowly edging along, then walking it, I finally was able to run along the ledge without holding on to anything. It gave me a terrific feeling of accomplishment to overcome such a deep-seated fear.

On Saturday nights I played second violin in the school orchestra that serenaded the enormous dining hall during dinner from a loft overlooking the long room that housed more than fifty tables of ten.

One weekend afternoon in the Fall of my senior year, I decided to visit a friend in one of the cottage-style houses that served as a student dormitory. Its resident faculty member owned a small dog that had nothing but hair covering its face. One was never sure if the Master's dog could even see through all that hair. Out of boredom, I mindlessly tossed a cherry bomb out a second floor window. To my dismay I then noticed the housemaster's dog was in the vicinity. He noticed something sputtering in the grass and went over to investigate. The cherry bomb went off just as he was about to sniff it, and the result was that his facial hair was entirely gone when he looked up. Thankfully, other than a loss of hair and dignity, the dog was not affected.

That evening the Headmaster rose in the Dining Hall to announce that the entire school would be held over for Christmas vacation if the guilty party did not come forward and admit having thrown the firecracker. I could not justify making other students lose part or all of their vacation by keeping silent, so I went to the Inner Sanctum—the room where disciplinary matters were taken up—to confess. I was held over for the first few days of Christmas vacation, plus I lost my movie privileges for the rest of the year.

I also took violin lessons from the Director of the school orchestra who had the worst tobacco breath imaginable that he tried to hide with SenSen—a licorice pastel that slightly altered, but did not hide, the stench. I hated those lessons. I would try to keep my distance, but as he taught he would keep coming closer and closer to me. I would back away as I politely could. Finally I told my parents I could no longer stand it. They relieved me from having to take those cursed lessons, but not before I was to play at a recital in the school library. Recital pieces had to be played from memory without sheet music or music stand. I had not practiced enough to be sure I would perform well, and I briefly considered feigning illness or simply refusing to go through with the recital. However, realizing that was not the best option, especially in light of all the trouble I had been in, I did perform. Luckily my memory did not fail me on that occasion.

When it was time to decide to what colleges I would apply, I chose three—Princeton, Yale and Stanford. My parents did not want me to leave the East, but by then I was tired of an all-boy prep school where one had always to dress in a tie and jacket and go to chapel twice a day. Choate's grueling academic work and strict austerity were wearing on me after three years. I yearned for a fun-filled co-ed college experience where tennis was central to one's program.

David Aldrich, one of my Choate classmates, was the son of celebrated theatrical producer, Richard S. Aldrich, and the stepson of his wife, stage actress Gertrude Lawrence. David wanted us both to go to Stanford to play intercollegiate tennis. Princeton and Yale did not accept me. Both Deans of Admission said I was too young (only sixteen in my senior year at Choate); and that my grades were not good enough. My Choate average was only around C plus/B minus. The fact I had scored in the top 1% of the nation on my college boards led both college deans to presume I probably had not applied myself at Choate.

That presumption was not valid. Despite having tried my best to get better marks, I was just too immature. I either failed to read exam questions carefully enough, or did not take sufficient time to think through the answer. I shot from the hip during tests instead of reflecting before committing. So off I went to Stanford where I had no trouble getting good marks. I just needed to become a year older and a little more mature. That enabled me to take an exam without getting a case of nerves.

My year at Stanford University

As a Stanford freshman I would play tennis and experience a new freedom away from home in a co-ed school much different from the life at Choate. So at the end of August, 1948, I took the train out to California, sharing a bedroom compartment for the three night trip with another young man who lived on the West Coast. There were some other young people on the train, including an attractive blond traveling alone, but whom I had neither the savoir faire nor the nerve to approach. I later discovered that she, too, was on her way to enter the freshman year at Stanford.

When my train terminated in Oakland, on the East side of San Francisco Bay, I had to take the ferry over to San Francisco to catch a train to Palo Alto— about a forty minute ride.

Once there, I took a cab to Encina Hall, the freshman male dormitory. As I climbed Encina's front steps, suitcase in hand, and was about to enter the building, three friendly young men in T- shirts and blue jeans stopped me. They asked me where I was from and chatted with me for a few minutes. They had all graduated from public schools in California and seemed kind of sorry for me—an Eastern preppie with no idea how dudes dressed out West. They forbade me to enter the dorm in a suit and tie, and insisted I get the clothes that I would need. The four of us drove from the campus to Roos Brothers department store where they helped me buy and change into Levis, T-shirt and sneakers before driving me back to Encina, suitably attired to make my entrance.

My room assignment on the fourth floor of Encina included two roommates, one of whom brought a shiny new Plymouth sedan with him to Stanford. I envied him because I had no car, not even a bicycle. Our room was quite spacious with two windows looking out over the front of the building toward the

Stanford Stadium. Our sleeping alcove held three single beds separated by room dividers from the area that held our dressers and desks. Mark Hatfield, who later became the youngest two-term Governor elected in America and then went on to serve as Oregon's Republican United States Senator, was the well-liked, collegial graduate student who served as our resident dorm counselor.

I promptly signed up for Air Force Reserve Officer Training, as I had always wanted to be a fighter pilot. In the weekly drills I learned how to march, use a compass on bivouac and how to take down and clean an M-1 and a Colt 45. I became one of the four uniformed members of the Honor Guard that marched onto the football field at home games to present the colors while the national anthem was sung. I became quite adept at spinning my rifle and performing fancy drills.

In 1949 Stanford's tennis team was the best in America. In its match against the University of San Francisco, Stanford prevailed despite the fact that USF had Art Larsen, US national singles champion, playing number one and Sam Match playing number 2 (together they held the US national Doubles title). Because of our lineup of athletic talent, Stanford's Freshman team was even stronger than its Varsity. George Gentry played number one, Ernie Dubray played number two, Tom Lewyn played number three, Dean Brinkman played number four, followed by a group of us that were all at about the same level. Stanford's tennis coach, Elwood Bugge, was a lackluster figure with almost no knowledge of the game. I never understood how he rose to the position of coaching superb athletes when it was clear he could not contribute to improving their game. In fact when I arrived at Stanford I was still using a continental grip and stroke. That proved quite ineffective on the cement hard courts that were popular in Northern California. The ball came too low and hard to allow for a slow circular back swing. It was tutelage I received not from Mr. Bugge but from my teammates that helped me switch to an Eastern grip and a short backswing. I took pride in being recognized as one of the better doubles players, and consequently played in all the team's doubles matches to win my freshman varsity letter—a white S mounted on a handsome cardinal-red wool sweater. Athletic prowess at Stanford was adulated, and even freshmen wearing the varsity letter were envied.

Another of my close friends at Stanford was Herbert "Pete" Pulitzer, Jr., scion of the publishing family. Pete, also a classmate in the freshman year, was a childhood friend whom I had met in the fourth grade at the Palm Beach School. Pete kept a Jeep and a Czech 125cc motorcycle on campus that he let me use. We used to jump into his Jeep to go buy beer and hard beef-jerky sausage, then follow the winding roads up into the mountains where we would enjoy the view, drink beer and talk. Later Pete sold the motorcycle and got a Powell motor scooter that he also allowed me to use. After college I did not see as much of Pete as I did of his ex-wife, Lily. I heard that he built the Pulitzer Hotel in Amsterdam, Holland, and then it seemed he became a recluse on his Florida estate where he quietly grew citrus for years until his infamous divorce case from his second wife, Roxanne. That break-up brought unwelcome publicity and finally a movie that added no luster to the Pulitzer name. Lily Pulitzer, on the other hand, was much loved for her humanity and admired for her lively and colorful clothing designs that bore—and made famous—her first name.

The extensive Stanford campus was eye-poppingly beautiful with stately stucco and brick buildings that evinced a distinctly Spanish feeling with their long porticos of columned arches and red-tiled roofs. You needed more than two legs and jogging shoes to get around the campus, so by the middle of the freshman academic year I managed to convince my father that I needed a car. He generously provided several hundred dollars so I could buy a snappy 1940 Ford convertible with twin spotlights and brown metallic paint. It needed a new top, new tires, new rings, and eventually a whole new motor, but it gave me mobility, and I was able to sell it for a good price when I left the school.

If you maintained a B average, your privilege to cut class was unlimited. So having graduated from academically rigorous Choate, I felt like I had been left back a couple of grades, as many of the Stanford freshman, having come from California's public schools, could hardly write competent English. Maintaining a B average merely required some intensive effort for a few days before exam week, but in each subject a cram course was usually given by the professor in his or her home for a slight fee, and I took full advantage of that option.

After the first week or two of the Fall semester, I found class lectures added nothing to the reading assignments, so other than Drama One which was taught by a female professor who was excellent, I took liberal advantage of the cut privilege. The teaching staff in most of the freshman courses consisted of grad students serving as Teaching Assistants. Once in a while, a professor would hold a lecture in Stanford's auditorium that was so cavernous it was like sitting in the highest bleacher of a football stadium.

I quickly learned that I could get away with doing little other than playing tennis for the Stanford Freshman team 6 hours a day and then finding a movie or attacking a case of beer with some buddies. We often drove to a nearby beach where we could bury the beer cans in the cold sand and just party around a bonfire until late at night.

My two closest pals were my freshman tennis teammates, Dean "Dino" Brinkman and Tom Lewyn, both of whom I used to call "Mony"—a shortened version of Mon Ami. Tom was from Scarsdale, New York where his family belonged to the Sunningdale Country Club. I had met Tom in tournaments on the East coast where he had won the Eastern Tennis Junior championships. Tom was also an accomplished card player and magician who used his skills to earn money in his freshman year. He recruited me to assist at magic shows that he booked. My main function was either to divert attention while he did his legerdemain, or act the dummy to inject some humor. He also took me to the nearby card-house where one could play "lowball" poker. Tom was an expert at counting cards, and having me sit in as one of the players against the house increased his ability to know when to stay and when to fold. It was not long before he was able to buy a shiny new Ford sedan.

One of our classmates—a sort of Damon Runyon character—boasted to Tom and me that he had a tip on a nag called Shannon II that was certain to win in a forthcoming race at a flat track in Northern California. Drawn by his promise that it was a "sure thing" on which we could make money, we all piled into my convertible Ford and drove up to Tanforan, the Northern California race track where I put $10 "on the nose" along with my companions who also bet the Shannon II to win. Ten dollars was a small fortune in those days and doubly so for a student. What had been 3-1 odds that seemed attractive when I placed the bet, diminished rapidly as Shannon II emerged the favorite with the most money bet on it to win. It seemed everyone else who entered the pari-mutuel action had the same tip.

The race was an exciting one that ended in a photo finish between Shannon II and another horse. Back in 1948 it took quite a while for photos to be developed. While I waited, I suffered the dread of losing and a thousand pangs of remorse as I weighed the loss of $10 for the chance to make not $20, as I had hoped, but only $5 if the horse won. Finally Shannon II was declared the winner. That taught me a lesson. The angst of losing was not worth the fleeting joy of winning. After Stanford, I never again bet on cards, tennis or the outcome of any sporting event.

On Sunday nights Stanford offered free admission to a movie in its large auditorium that was normally used as a lecture hall. One Sunday I decided not to watch the movie. I wanted to ask a friend who lived on the floor above mine a question, so I went upstairs to see if he was in his room. With almost everyone at the movie, the fifth floor of the dorm was silent as a tomb. Sunday nights were particularly depressing as the weekend was over and another hectic week was about to begin. My friend lived with two other roommates so I knocked, but got no answer. The door was slightly ajar and I could see the room was dimly lit, so I pushed it open. I froze on seeing a lifeless slack-jawed student hanging from a fire sprinkler pipe, a belt looped around his neck with a stool kicked over under his feet. I turned away in shock and ran to find Mark Hatfield, the dorm monitor. I will never erase from my mind the tragic figure I witnessed—or cease wondering how hopeless he must have been to end it all.

My daily life at Stanford consisted of playing tennis all day and studying most nights. As I was rather picky I did not date very much. In fact the freshman girls were so involved in studying or getting into a sorority they were not much interested in dating either. However, in the spring trimester, I met an attractive and spirited high school girl who lived near the campus. She used to sashay around Encina Hall with one or two of her girl friends evidently hoping to meet members of the Freshman class—and given those lovely brunette curls that framed her freckled face, her small but lovely upturned nose and mischievous smile, that was likely indeed.

I dated her a couple of times and on the third date we parked by the campus lake and got into some heavy petting. She demurely told me that she loved me, and that she wanted to go further. Her intensity, her sincerity and her total trust touched me deeply. I was longing for her, as well. I asked her how old she was because I had heard that having sex in California with a girl not yet eighteen constituted the crime of statutory rape since anyone under that age was legally incapable of giving their consent. She confessed that she was just fourteen! I was shocked by her answer, though I had suspected she might be slightly under age. She certainly looked every bit of eighteen. I had visions of being thrown out of Stanford and spending my college years behind prison walls. My reaction was to abruptly drive her home and cut off all contact with her. Thereafter, whenever she saw me on campus, she glared at me with intense hatred. Whenever I recall that incident, I deeply regret the pain I must have caused her in dropping her so harshly.

At the end of the freshman year, every student was required to write a term paper in Western Civilization, a required freshman course. I had always been fascinated by the rocket bombs that Germany had developed and launched from Peenemunde toward London in WW II, so I decided to write a paper on rocket-propelled missile warfare. The largest and best library on warfare was reputedly housed in the Hoover Tower on the Stanford campus, so I ensconced myself there for a few days to do the research. My paper described the history of rocketry, the developments by Werner Von Braun and his team in Peenemunde, as well as my predictions for the future of this method of warfare.

I foresaw the development of short, medium and long-range ballistic missiles, and the difficulty of accurately guiding them to their objective. I predicted that nuclear warheads would eventually be mounted on inter-continental ballistic missiles, and the probability that such a weapon might even become a deterrent to its use, as the devastation it would cause would not leave much value for the victor, especially any would-be occupier. I also predicted the development of the anti-ballistic (ABM) missile missile. I was quite proud of my finished product when I turned it in. I was not so proud when I got back an F with the instructor's handwritten comment that said in so many words, "You studied Western Civilization to write about reality, not Buck Rodgers."

It was already May without much time to apply elsewhere, but I decided then and there to leave Stanford. I realized I would never get an education if I stayed. I would just continue to coast through and play tennis. It dawned on me that I had wasted a year of my time and my father's money. All of my closest relatives were persons of intelligence, talent and accomplishment. They were models of ambition, discipline, industry and scholarship. It was not surprising that I felt pressure to realize whatever my full potential might be. I faced the choice—stay static at Stanford, or forge ahead by trying to transfer to Yale or Columbia.

When in the summer of 1949 I got back to Westport from California, the very first thing I did after unpacking and showering, was to join my parents in our family dining room for lunch. I shocked myself, and certainly both my parents, when at some point during the meal, quite nonchalantly and from habit picked up in Stanford's cafeteria, I muttered, "Pass the fucking butter," not even prefaced with "Please!" That surely confirmed to my parents how badly spent was both my year on the Coast and their tuition payments!

Once again while I waited for admission to an Ivy League college, I prayed I would not have to go back to Stanford. Yale soon replied in the negative, but fortunately the Columbia Dean of Admissions agreed to interview me, and after we met I was put on a list to be admitted in case a vacancy opened in the sophomore class. Fortunately, by August, I heard that a place had been found for me at Columbia.

Since I was admitted at the last moment as a sophomore transfer student, I was not able to get a dormitory room on campus. They had all been assigned earlier to the entering freshman class. So my father suggested that I stay at the Hotel Adams on 86th street near Fifth Avenue. My hotel room contained just a convertible sofa, closet, bathroom, compact refrigerator and hot plate. Each day I would take the Number 4 bus up Fifth Avenue to Columbia and return after my last class, studying assiduously whenever I was not in class. Each night I would interrupt my studies only to eat a slice of bread with soup I heated up on my hot plate. My determination to get straight A's was all encompassing. My only disappointment was discovering that Columbia did not have an Air Force ROTC program. The Army and Navy had ROTC programs there, but I could not participate as both refused to give credit for my year in Air Force ROTC at Stanford.

When I entered Otis Fellows' classroom, it was to attend my very first class at Columbia. Professor Fellows was a good-looking, genial and nattily-dressed professor that taught Humanities—a required course covering great literature and philosophy of Western Civilization from, among others, Plato, Aristotle, Homer, Dante, Montesquieu, Burke, Hobbes and Locke to Voltaire and Cervantes. I was unsure of how I would do after a year of goofing off at Stanford, and I felt insecure about the academic level I would find at Columbia. I took a seat in the back row of the classroom where I tried to be as inconspicuous as possible. Only two other students sought out seats in the back row of that class. Kenneth Jones sat on my left and Michael Sovern sat on my right. I did not speak to them for the first couple of weeks but finally dared to make their acquaintance. Once we knew each other we often played intramural volleyball together in the Columbia Gym. Ken Jones was destined to become the Dean of Columbia's School of Law and Mike Sovern the President of Columbia University. However, in 1949 we three were the only students in Prof.

Fellows' class to get straight As. Later, other Columbia professors with whom I had the extraordinary privilege of studying were Boris Stanfield (Contemporary Civilization); Robert Carey (Economics); Irwin Edman (Philosophy); Mark Van Doren (English literature); Charles Frankel and C. Wright Mills (Seminar on Liberalism); Otto Wagenheim (Anthropology); and Jan Schildt (Astronomy).

The difference between Stanford and Columbia was multifaceted and stark. At Stanford almost no professors taught undergraduate classes, but at Columbia I never had a Teaching Assistant or instructor, just world-class professors! The campuses also were strikingly different. Stanford's had a rural feeling while Columbia's was clearly an urban complex. And contrary to Stanford's dress code that compelled Levis and Tee shirts on its campus, I reverted to wearing East coast attire—double-breasted business suit, shirt and tie. In preparation for the college term, I bought two suits that I wore on alternate days—one grey and one navy blue. I did not own a blazer or slacks, but my mother called me a "hoarder" because I had bought more than one suit!

At the end of my first semester at Columbia the grades of all students in each course were posted publicly on bulletin boards for all to see. I was elated to find that I had gotten all A's. That established my reputation amongst the faculty, all of whom were aware of me since my uncle at the time was their enormously respected congressman in Washington Heights, the congressional district in which Columbia was situated.

In January, I moved from the Hotel Adams up to the campus where I lived in a two-room efficiency apartment in Butler Hall on 119th Street and Morningside Park, where again I had to make my own meals. Then, in the spring of my sophomore year, I pledged to join Beta Theta Pi fraternity that had a

Columbia chapter of about fifty brothers, many of whom were WW II veterans using their veterans' benefits to get their education.

The Betas were a rough and ready bunch of "hail fellows well met." They never missed an opportunity to tap a keg and sing fraternity songs, while making life for us lowly and miserable pledges a veritable hell for weeks. Finally, after a "Hell Week" of hazing, I was initiated into the Alpha Alpha chapter as brother number 691. Thereafter, during my junior and senior years, I lived at the Beta House—an impressive four-story townhouse located on West 114th St.

On the second floor, in a back room behind the large and gracious living room, stood a full-size billiard table where the brothers played pool to relax and enjoy each other's company. I had never played pool; so I just looked on, never accepting an invitation to play because I did not want to look inept. But while I watched I studied the technique and strategy of the better players, aware that pool was an unforgiving test of skill, and I would need a fair level of competence before I played. I also came to understand that there was an unspoken respect accorded to the winners.

So late at night when my studying was done and the second floor was empty, I would go down and practice breaking massed balls, lining up difficult shots, using the bridge, putting English on the cue ball, positioning the cue ball for the next shot, etc. Finally, after many weeks of practice I felt ready and accepted an invitation to join a friendly game. Thereafter, I won my share of games of pool.

The Alpha Alpha Chapter ran a meal table on the ground floor where all the brothers would convene for lunch and dinner. We had a black chef who, in his spare time between serving us excellent meals, doubled as the neighborhood numbers runner.

At the end of my sophomore year at Columbia College, I was invited to Neuilly, France, to stay with the family of Jean Francois Saliot, a foreign student whom I had befriended and who had visited our family in Palm Beach during one of his college vacations. My aim was to speak only French during my stay with the Saliot family. Jean's grace and charm were reminiscent of a young Maurice Chevalier. Jean's dad was an automobile designer and manufacturer, and you can still see an occasional Saliot on display in antique auto shows.

The summer of 1950 had begun and my ocean liner was scheduled to sail later that June from a pier in New York City's Hudson River. When the day of departure arrived, my father offered to drive me to the ship in the family sedan. As we proceeded from Westport toward New York along the Merritt Parkway, we heard on the car radio that the North Korean army had swarmed across the 38th parallel to invade South Korea. My father insisted I should not travel until we knew what would result from that incursion. So, instead of boarding the ocean liner that was getting ready to sail, he turned the car around and I was driven back to Westport. My summer idyll in France was kaput.

As a result, I spent that entire summer in Westport, enjoying life at the Longshore Country Club and playing lots of tennis. The club's President was Pat Dougherty, an amiable Irish alcoholic. There were no Jews in the Club, at least not until Julie Baller, Mac Schwebel and Mitch Liftig, with a group of investors from New York, took it over in 1945. It was then that the Longshore Club began accepting anyone who could afford the dues, with many Jewish families from New York joining it when they came to Westport to rent a summer place.

Longshore had a sandy beach area for swimming in the Long Island Sound, as well as a large pool with a deeply-tanned swimming instructor who spent the winters teaching at an exclusive club in Hobe Sound, Florida. Longshore had a snack bar near the beachfront and a championship golf course where charismatic and handsome George Buck was the Club pro. At Longshore I met Babe Ruth, the "home run king", who came to play the Club's golf course in 1946, and Tina Louise Yeager, the teenage daughter of Louis Yeager who controlled Brazilian Traction, and his wife Betty. Tina Louise later became famous in the glamorous role of Ginger on the popular 1960's TV sitcom, "Gilligan's Island".

One balmy evening early in that summer of 1950 my parents and I went to the Longshore Club dinner dance where I could not fail to notice a strikingly tall and beautiful girl with shoulder length brown hair and bangs seated at an outdoor terrace table with a group of adults. While the band was playing incredibly danceable tunes, I went over to the table and introduced myself to its host, Larry Fisher, the New York real estate developer, and his wife who were seated with several other attractive couples. I asked the young lady to dance. She told me that her name was Stephanie Laye, and afterwards when I returned her to the table, I was introduced to her parents who had rented a summer place with the two other couples at the table that were related and in business with her mother. I was invited to join their party and spent the rest of the evening in their company. That led to a summer of innocent dating during which I learned that she would not turn sixteen until October! Stephanie was always well behaved, beautifully dressed and pleasant to be around, but there was a certain absence of emotion in her that troubled me. My inner voice was no match for her attractiveness or my sex drive so I paid it no heed. The summer seemed to end too soon when we both had to return to our studies—she to high school and I to my college junior year.

One week before the start of Columbia's fall semester I drove to New York to renovate the large front room on the fourth floor of the Beta House where I would now be rooming. It had two big windows that overlooked the Columbia campus. I bought a roll of new linoleum to cover the floor, painted the walls and ceiling and brought in some decent furniture.

During my sophomore and junior years at Columbia, I often studied in the evenings in the Butler Library on 114th Street, but because the lighting was so bad I would fall asleep. This repeated itself over many months, and I noticed many other students falling asleep over their books at the library tables. Frosted globe fixtures hanging from the lofty ceiling at generous intervals emitted only dull yellowish light. The wiring of the building was insufficient so the wattage of the incandescent bulbs was quite weak. I got hold of an instrument to measure the foot-candles of illumination that fell on the reading table surfaces and found that it was only a fourth of what it should have been for ease of reading. I made an appeal to the College Assistant Dean and to the Provost of the University to ask for better lighting, but my pleas fell on deaf ears. I was told it was not just a matter of changing the bulbs or the fixtures, it was a matter of rewiring the entire building which would be very expensive. That was a budgetary matter to be decided by the Trustees, and the University had more pressing priorities.

I decided to take matters into my own hands. After alerting the editors of the campus newspaper, The Columbia Spectator, I got hold of an enormous stepladder, at least 16 feet tall and took it into the library one evening. I opened the ladder, climbed to the top and sat with an open book directly under one of the ceiling lights. The Spectator had a photographer ready to snap a photo, and the next day's front page displayed me on the ladder with a lead article explaining what desperate students were doing to study without falling asleep in the dim lighting of Butler Library. Needless to say, the lighting of the building was improved shortly thereafter.

Having played on Stanford's freshman tennis team, I lost a year of eligibility in intercollegiate tennis competition due to the Ivy League's rules. So in the fall of my sophomore year the only tennis I played was in Columbia University's own intramural tennis tournament. One faculty member, Donald Frame, a very popular professor of French, had been the tournament's consistent winner in past years, and there were many entrants in the draw. I was unseeded and had to play quite a few rounds before I got to the finals. That year Professor Frame lost in the Semi-Final round to Ahmed Zeitoun, a student from Egypt. Zeitoun was very good but not able to edge me in the final round. The next year I was eligible to play for Columbia and earned the number one position in singles. I also played doubles in intercollegiate competition with a talented partner, Maynard Driver, who had a powerful serve. It sounded like a rifle report and came so fast even players with the fastest reflexes could barely move their racket to return the ball.

In the era of the '50s one of the popular TV entertainment shows was "Blind Date" hosted by Arlene Frances in which four young men would compete to win a blind date with an attractive young model who had to pick which one she wanted as her escort for an evening at the famed Copacabana nightclub in Manhattan. I don't remember how I got selected to be on the show, but I competed and won. Both the Copacabana and the model were disappointing. She was neither a good dancer nor a good conversationalist. In fact her looks were her only attribute. I was chagrined at the show having been seen by so many of my friends, all of whom wanted to know how the date had turned out. As much as I would have liked to, I could not bring myself to embroider the truth.

In the very early spring of my junior year I met Mabel Ashforth, a senior at Barnard College that had its dormitory across Broadway near 116th Street on the Columbia campus.

We had our first date one evening just as the last traces of winter ice were melting, and trees and crocuses lining Riverside Drive had just begun to bud. Mab, as she was called, was a regally classic beauty with an agile mind, a poetic pen, a patrician air and a timeless soul. She wore a high-collared tight-fitting Asian dress that first night, and with her thin neck, ramrod posture and gorgeous face, she stole my heart away in a second. We walked together and talked of our lives and our dreams. We both felt a deep connection forming, and the one kiss we exchanged that night sealed the bond. We did not see very much of each other for the rest of the semester, dating only occasionally as we both were very busy with our studies. Mab was preparing to graduate, and I was thinking about entering college politics.

So toward the end of my junior year at Columbia, having just been elected president of my fraternity for the next year, I decided to also run for election to the College Board of Student Representatives. The competition consisted of about a dozen candidates of which three would be chosen as "all-college" representatives, without regard to their class level, and the other six elected would represent their respective classes. When the votes were tallied, I was elected one of the three All-College representatives—surprising for a transfer student who had missed the freshman year at Columbia.

The nine-member Board, once seated, had then to select its Chairman from amongst the three All-College winners. Since I had only been at Columbia for less than two years I was competing against two others who had been there a year longer with more opportunity to become known. The infighting to elect me as Chairman ensued amongst friends and classmates, with varsity football player Charlie McCann as one of my most effective allies. I have a feeling that my supporters did not hesitate to use whatever levers were at their command. One of the perks of being the Chairman of the Student Board was the right to have a private phone in your room. Another was the privilege of having a bi-weekly private luncheon with Dean Nicholas McKnight in the faculty club dining room, but I was disappointed to find the Dean using these occasions to try to get information about student dissatisfaction or gripes. I was a non-smoker, but he never ceased trying to get me to join him in having a cigar after our meal. He preached that a collegial gentleman always enjoyed having a fine cigar with his coffee. His efforts were unsuccessful.

Soon after my election as Chairman of the Student Board I was elected a member of the Nacom Society, one of Columbia's two Senior honor society. Each was comprised of 15 leaders on campus selected at the end of their junior year to give constructive service to the College during their senior year. Among our group of Nacoms that year, all of whom distinguished themselves in later life, were Richard Capen, Jr., who became the Editor-in-Chief of the Miami Herald and later US Ambassador to Spain; Roone Arledge who revolutionized the broadcasting of sports on TV; and Richard Wald who became the head of all news broadcasting for one of the major broadcasting networks.

That summer of 1951 began on an idyllic note. I invited Mab to come to Westport to spend a weekend. I wanted my family to get to know her, and we had found precious little time for each other during the spring semester. That weekend Mab and I had a magical couple of days together in the Connecticut countryside. One balmy star-studded night on the small outdoor balcony that overlooked the gardens and lawn expanse that stretched behind our house all the way to the Long Island Sound we watched the sky, the shooting stars and the Northern Lights. Those moments were ones I will always remember.

One year had passed since the invasion of South Korea in June of 1950. The Truman Administration lost no time in swinging into action. It created an Office of Defense Mobilization to which Charles E. ("Electric Charlie") Wilson, President of General Electric Corporation, was named Chief of Defense Mobilization. Charlie Wilson was a longtime friend and law client of my father's, and almost a godfather to me, so he invited me to work in Washington during my summer vacation as an intern with a top-secret clearance. I was eager to have a meaningful work experience after finishing my junior year at Columbia College that May. Working in the war effort in such a serious role would be like a dream come true.

At the top of my list and hardest to do before I left to work in Washington was to bid farewell to Mab. She had just graduated from Barnard, and she wanted me to meet her father and grandmother, so she invited me to her family's apartment on Park Avenue. Her father, Albert B. Ashforth, was a handsome and patrician WASP who had formed the Albert B. Ashforth Company, a leading building management firm in New York City. In those years, if a young woman graduated from college and was not either engaged to marry or going steady with a likely future husband, she was considered on the brink of becoming an "old maid." In those post-World War II days waiting for the age of thirty or more to marry was unheard of.

When the appointed day and time arrived to visit Mab and meet her family, I was admitted to the building by the white-gloved doorman and sent up to the Ashforth apartment. When Mab let me in, no one else was there! Mab sat me down and explained that now that she had finished her education there was nothing more important to her than confirming the seriousness of my intentions. A cold dread came over me that both paralyzed my emotions like an icicle piercing my heart. I could not meet Mab's eyes with commitment as I had nothing to offer her. I was still in college, hoping to go to graduate school. Confronted with the urgency of her appeal and the imminence of my departure to Washington for a summer internship and then at least another year of school, I became virtually speechless and left. Days went by and I was still numb. I was unable to call Mab after that. My heart ached with the memory of her. Her insightful prose, her beautiful poetry, her elegant taste, her brilliant mind, her love of family, flowers, food, nature and life were inspirational. I felt crestfallen and crushed as I knew I could not make a commitment then.

Mab soon married her former suitor, Bo Goldman, a warm-hearted and brilliant Princeton graduate who eventually became a world-famous screen writer who wrote "One Flew Over the Cuckoo's Nest", to settle in California and raise a family. I have always regretted the way I treated Mab when we parted, and decades later I wrote Mab my apology for being so shocked and treating her so heartlessly in the way I took my leave.

During my summer internship at the Office of Defense Mobilization, I stayed with my uncle who was then serving as a member of Congress from Manhattan's 27th congressional district. Washington was experiencing a scorching summer that year, and Jack's one-bedroom ground-floor apartment on Connecticut Avenue had no air conditioning. You had to sleep in your skivvies with a noisy electric fan running all night. Getting a sound sleep was almost impossible.

The Office of Defense Mobilization in 1951 was housed in the old State Dept. Building that is now called the White House Executive Office Building. Although there were air conditioning window units in each of its offices that offered a welcome respite from the heat, if you went across the street to lunch, even in a seersucker suit, you came back drenched through jacket and shirt.

My summer assignment was to draft Mobilization Chief Wilson's quarterly report to the President. I was warned it could be no longer than two typewritten pages because I was told the President would not read more than that. The report covered a wide array of subjects, including the Nike Ajax program that was then our state-of-the-art air defense system, the floods that had ravaged the Southwest of our country and all other matters affecting US mobilization and defense preparedness. The lesson I learned during that summer internship was to edit and then re-edit my writing to strip any excess verbiage out of every sentence. It also taught me to keep things short and terse in speech as well as in prose. More than that, it afforded me a precious chance to bond with my enormously engaged and preoccupied uncle who normally would not have had time for me, but sleeping together in the same bedroom for a whole summer, and because he was so much younger than my father, Jack became more like an older brother than an uncle.

When the summer ended I returned to Columbia College as a senior to live in the same front room of the Beta house that I had previously occupied, but this time with Frank Faddis as my roommate. Frank was from North Philadelphia with a marvelous sense of humor and a very worldly-wise view of life. He loved girls, athletics and good jokes in that order. Frank had signed up for the Navy Reserve Officer Training Corps that committed him to serve for four years after graduation, in return for which he was getting his college education and eventual commission as a navy officer. Since the Betas had most of the wrestling team, much of the football team, lots of heavy drinkers but precious few serious students beyond a couple of the brothers and myself, I decided as the chapter's president that we needed to embody our fraternity's lofty ideal—"the cultivation of the intellect"—by raising the academic level of the Beta House. "Quiet Hours" after 8 p.m. were instituted and vigorously enforced to permit brothers to study without being disturbed. New respect was accorded scholastic achievement, and the chapter's grade point average zoomed immediately.

In those days the West End was a favorite watering place on Broadway where a glass of beer cost only 30 cents. We were often disturbed at night by students returning from the West End. The noise they made stumbling along the south side of 114th street toward the Phi Gamma Delta or Sigma Chi houses was usually augmented by discordant voices singing, "Let's all go and piss on the Beta House," as they tried to act that out on our front steps.

The revelry was not only at the West End. The Betas would hold beer busts from time to time where a metal keg of beer would be imported into the fraternity and tapped until empty. There were also formal fraternity galas when the house would be decorated with flowers, balloons and crepe streamers to which everyone would invite their steady girl friends that they had "pinned'.

When Stephanie who had entered Finch College that fall coyly presented me with a pair of argyle socks she had knitted for me, I began dating her again and invited her to the Beta House Fall Gala. The fraternity gala dress code was black tie. There was live music, dancing and the drinking was other than beer. The girls were not supposed to go upstairs beyond the second floor where the ladies bathroom was located, but the stairs were really steep. You don't think of accidents, dangers and risks during college revelry, but at one of those galas, Stephanie, like all the young ladies, was attired in a long gown and wearing high heels. As the evening wore on she got herself slightly pie-eyed. On descending the stairs from the second floor bathroom where she had gone to powder her nose, one of her high heels caught on her gown. She went high into the air, did a complete head over heels somersault; and as luck would have it she landed on her feet, stunned but unharmed, some twelve steps further down the stairs! Those who witnessed these acrobatics gaped in amazement. I was relieved that she survived unscathed. I got her out of there as fast as I could.

One night as I was walking back to the Beta House on the north side of 114th street I observed a car trying to park between two tightly-parked cars. The driver would first ram the one behind to make room, and then turn his wheel and ram the car ahead to push for more room. I did not consider myself especially short tempered, but when I saw this repeated several times with great force and with total disregard for any damage that might be inflicted, indignation overcame me. I reached into the driver's window that was open, grabbed the driver by the neck and pulled him completely out of the car. I said very calmly while looking him in the eye, "We do not ram cars on this block to make room to park." I set him back down on the ground and calmly walked across the street into the Beta House. I was shocked at my own fury and totally unexpected strength. I realized I probably should have only warned the driver, taken his license plate number, but not physically assaulted him. That experience certainly made me aware that I had to control my temper.

During my senior year the Meetings of the College Board of Student Representatives were held on the fourth floor of Hamilton Hall right next to the office occupied by Lou Little, coach of Columbia's football team. I had gotten to know Lou when I tried out for varsity football in my junior year to become the team kicker. I was not as good at kicking as Al Ward, and so I never got into a game. I did, however, befriend many of the players and also the coach who appreciated that I gave it the old "college try". Lou Little— whose name was originally Luigi Piccolo when he immigrated to America—was a beloved Columbia Lion with the heart of one. He had a voice that was almost as gravelly as Congressman Rangel's. Everyone on campus loved Lou Little whose Lions had beaten heavily-favored Stanford Indians in the Rose Bowl many years earlier.

One of my most meaningful college moments came at the end of my senior year. At graduation, when the lists of honors were read, my name was among those elected to Phi Beta Kappa, the honorary scholarship society. My father, who was present in the audience, cried with surprise and happiness. Another major announcement that took me by surprise was the presentation of Columbia's Lion Award to my prep school for sending our Alma Mater the outstanding member of its graduating class. Choate received a large and beautifully-sculpted bronze lion bearing an appropriately inscribed plaque. Sixty years later when my son and I were visiting Choate we saw it proudly displayed at the foyer entrance to the Choate library. I was also given—and still keep in my study—a smaller replica of that award.

Immediately after the graduation ceremony Professor Robert Carey, who had been my economics professor, walked over and put an arm around me. We were both still in our caps and gowns when he took me aside to speak to me. He explained that as the University faculty member appointed to recommend students for postgraduate study abroad on scholarship grants, he wanted to offer me the opportunity to go to England to study at Oxford or Cambridge, and he strongly urged me to consider that option. I thanked him wholeheartedly but declined, explaining that I preferred to go on that Fall to Columbia's law school to which I had already been admitted. I wanted to work with my father as soon as possible. I saw a year abroad as a delay, not an opportunity.

Columbia Law School

In the fall of 1952 when I entered Columbia Law School, I had been dating Stephanie Laye for a couple of years, and by then we had gotten engaged. As I expected, the first year of law school was the toughest. I lived on 116th St. between Broadway and Riverside Drive in a desperately bleak and cramped single room with only a bed, a small closet, a dresser and a desk. The bathroom was out in the public hall and shared by others living on the floor. I did much of my studying with my classmate and friend, Michael Freyberg, at his family's apartment on 145th Street near Broadway. Mike had been the Sports Editor of the Columbia Spectator and a member of Nacoms as well.

At Columbia Law School, the entire faculty was eminent. Just about every professor had authored or co-authored a textbook used in leading law schools around the country. I took Legal Method from Professor Harry Jones; Development of Legal Institutions from Professor Julius Goebbels; Contracts and Property from Professor Edwin Patterson; Trusts and Estates from Professor Richard Powell; Taxation from Professor Robert Anthoine; Criminal Law from Professor Herbert Wechsler; Real Estate from Professor Jerome Michael; Constitutional law from Professor Robert Dowling; torts from Professor Willis Reese; and Trade Regulation from Professor Milton Handler.

Milton Handler was a name partner in one of New York's best corporate law firms—Kaye Scholer Fierman Hays and Handler. Professor Handler had been a rival, friend and colleague in the field of anti-trust law with my father, and they knew each other well. The first day in Handler's Trade Regulation class, Professor Handler asked me if I was related to Ben and Jack Javits. I said I was, and that Ben was my father. The Professor said simply "be prepared". True to his warning, he called on me every day. I stayed well prepared, so it was no surprise when I got an A in the course. However, I got mostly Bs in my other freshman courses at the law school. I found the legal cases difficult reading and researching techniques (such as "Shepardizing" cases), tedious. I did not get the A average I needed in the freshman year to make Law Review, but I did get a lot of As in the second and third years once I had learned the legal lingo and methodology. That, however, was not in time to be elected an editor of the Columbia Law Review.

After a nine-month engagement to Stephanie Ann Laye in which I had many second thoughts and moments of doubt that I kept to myself and never discussed with my family, Stephanie and I were finally married in the Sherry Netherlands Hotel in June, 1953, with six of my closest pals as ushers dressed to the nines in top hats and tails. In retrospect, I was driven not only by a yearning for autonomy in starting a family of my own, but by some sort of karmic destiny. I certainly was not of sufficient age, maturity or experience to embark on marriage, but I certainly thought I was. I even resented the lyric of Nat King Cole's then popular hit, "They Tried to Tell Us We're Too Young".

Stephanie and her family planned the wedding and her uncle, the Cantor of the Park Avenue Synagogue, married us in the Sherry Netherlands Hotel in the presence of a hundred guests. Stephanie was gorgeous in her tiara, netting and French-lace gown with a cathedral-length veil that trailed behind her. She had never said a harsh word to me in all the time I had known her and during the months we were engaged, so I was shocked when she snarled at me as we approached the altar during our wedding because I stepped on her veil by accident.

I could understand her being tense and nervous on her wedding day, but when she promptly fell into our wedding bed, asleep before she hit the sheets, I lay awake in our suite wondering why I did not see these warnings earlier.

After our summer honeymoon that involved a lot of sightseeing, interesting days and pleasant nights in England,

Spain, Italy, France and Switzerland, I buckled down in September to begin my second year of law school. It was then we moved into our first apartment in the Glen Briar, a newly-built high-rise building that stood on the bluff of Riverdale in the Bronx looking out over the Hudson River. It was furnished with pieces that I either built and painted or managed to scrounge from my parent's attic. It had a lovely view of the towering cliffs of New Jersey on the opposite side of the river.

We slept on a convertible sofa in the living room and the apartment was not air-conditioned, but with the continuous breezes from the Hudson River, we always felt comfortable even on hot days. Happily, the rent was only $120 a month.

I used my savings to buy a beautiful black Ford Thunderbird convertible that I kept in the Glen Briar garage so we could easily get to Manhattan or drive out to my family's home in Westport. During my second and third years of law school I worked two days a week in the law firm and attended law classes during the other three weekdays. It was convenient to take the NY Central railroad from Riverdale to get either to Columbia or to Javits & Javits, the family law firm in Rockefeller Center's International Building that was headed by my father who was referred to as "B.A." At the firm I was called "Mr. Eric", and its roster included a number of other partners and associate attorneys. The Javits law firm shared a suite with the Rosenblatt firm that included lawyers offices, secretarial space, conference and file rooms, a law library, a reception area and a double telephone switchboard tended by two gals—each could field five calls at once while plugging and unplugging wires from the switchboard, while at the same time placing calls and asking for people to hold. Sol A. Rosenblatt, who headed his firm, had been a feared and formidable prosecutor before he became the leading matrimonial lawyer in New York, as well as a much-heralded trial attorney. In one of the most sensational and intensively covered murder trials in New York's history, Sol Rosenblatt won an acquittal for Ann Woodward who had been charged with first degree murder for killing her socialite millionaire husband, William Woodward, with a shotgun. Years later, Truman Capote wrote about that murder and Ann Woodward's demise in his thinly-veiled novel, "The Two Mrs. Grenville's."

My father was financially very astute. He encouraged me early on to establish a line of unsecured credit with the Bankers Trust Company. He told me to borrow $5,000, and to pay it back with interest in only ninety days. Then, a few months later he told me to borrow again—this time $10,000 and to pay that back with interest in ninety days. I did it again a few months later, borrowing $20,000 that I paid back in sixty days with interest. Following that advice I became a trusted client of Bankers Trust Company.

During my second year of law school I became interested in Moot Court competition. I won several preliminary rounds of appellate arguments to earn a place on one of the two teams in the final competition at the Harlan Fiske Stone Moot Court Honor Argument held in front of three judges from various courts at the Association of the Bar of the City of New York's magnificent building.

That year the sitting judges on the bench were Justice of the US Supreme Court Tom Clark; Federal Circuit of Appeals Judge Laurence E. Walsh; and a judge from the New York Court of Appeals. My three-man legal team had to prepare and submit a written brief and each orally argue our side of the case. A member of the opposing team, Norman Roy Grutman, was named the best speaker, but our team was declared the winner of that year's Stone Moot Court Competition. Roy Grutman later distinguished himself in trial and appellate practice, earning a national reputation for his oratorical abilities.

After finishing law school and getting admitted to the bar in 1955 my wife and I gave up the idea of continuing to live in Riverdale. We decided to move to Manhattan. The first apartment I bought was at 1025 Fifth Avenue. The price was $19,250. It had three bedrooms and three baths. It was located opposite the Metropolitan Museum between 83rd and 84th streets. The maintenance was about $250 per month plus electric and phone.

My father would teasingly call me "Mr. Fancy Fifth Avenue".

Stephanie and I were lucky to have two beautiful and intelligent children. I adored our children dearly and always gave them love and affection, but I was too busy pursuing my career to have enough time to spend with them, something I very much regret; while Stephanie was more interested in an active social life. Looking back on those years, we were both too young to be married.

After I graduated from Columbia law school in May, 1955, I immediately enrolled in an intensive study course to prepare for the two-day New York State bar examination. I was sure if I studied hard I could pass it the first time, and was especially determined to do so.

When I entered the enormous hall where the New York bar exam was given, at least a thousand other hopeful candidates were seated with large unopened envelopes in front of them containing the first day's bar exam questions. When the signal was given I opened my envelope and studied the first question that required an answer in the form of a written essay. After considering it for about five minutes I started writing. I was halfway through when my hand cramped so badly I had to stop, so I began to look around the room. Half of those sitting at desks had not yet begun to write. It was legendary that half of those taking the bar exam would fail, and I guessed that those who had not yet set pen to paper would comprise a large proportion of the failing group. I got notified in September that I had passed on my first try. I was quite proud to show up in the law office that day. I think even my father was impressed, and equally proud.

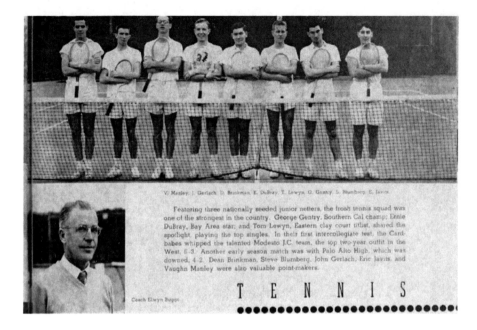

V. Manley, J. Gerlach, D. Brinkman, E. DuBray, T. Lewyn, G. Gentry, S. Blumberg, E. Javits

Featuring three nationally seeded junior netters, the frosh tennis squad was one of the strongest in the country. George Gentry, Southern Cal champ; Ernie DuBray, Bay Area star; and Tom Lewyn, Eastern clay court titlist, shared the spotlight, playing the top singles. In their first intercollegiate test, the Card-babes whipped the talented Modesto J.C. team, the top two-year outfit in the West, 6-3. Another early season match was with Palo Alto High, which was downed, 4-2. Dean Brinkman, Steve Blumberg, John Gerlach, Eric Javits, and Vaughn Manley were also valuable point-makers.

Coach Elwyn Bugge

T E N N I S

Stanford Freshman tennis team 1948 (as described in the
Stanford Yearbook)

Photo that appeared on the cover of the NY Times Sunday
Magazine of a class at Columbia College with Eric Javits
in the front row.

CHAPTER V — PASSING UP SOME EARLY OPTIONS

Growing up, and even as a college student, I had no idea what I wanted to become. I was taking a liberal arts education to get the broadest possible range of knowledge, but where would my education take me? For what would it prepare me? For what was I best suited? What would I like to do with the rest of my life? I had no answers, nor did I have the life experiences that would provide the answers.

My father would often discuss these questions with me on long walks we would take on country roads near our home in Westport. He understood how life takes twists and turns, and that one's decisions and choices determine where the journey leads. He warned that if I wanted to become rich and make a lot of money I should not become a lawyer but try to work for one of America's leading industrial or financial concerns. He explained the law was a profession, not a business, and that it provided only a comfortable living, intellectual stimulation, prestige and personal gratification.

This was true then, as lawyers were essentially servants of their clients and they had to subordinate their personal interests to those of their clients. Then, they could not solicit business or advertise, and their numbers were far smaller than now. Litigation was still the bane of the profession, as most clients would not pay for the inordinate time it would take to try a case at court, so every law firm did its best to settle a dispute, rather than litigate.

It was not until the 1960's that the American Bar Association instructed its members to keep track of their time in six-minute segments and use those time records to charge by the hour. That made litigation, as the most time intensive legal activity, the profit center of most law firms, and turned America into a litigation society in which law schools, law students, mega law firm, and enormous yearly compensation levels proliferated.

As I reached my Senior year in college I had to decide whether to go to graduate school or not (because you had to apply early if you wanted to be admitted). I figured that although I really did not yearn to be a lawyer, it would give me the most options to choose a career path thereafter. I still had no idea what I wanted to do, but I wanted to pursue more than my selfish interests. I was part of a family with distinguished members who sought to be of service in some way to others and the public. As a teen I felt no fear of failure at whatever I chose to do, nor did the eminence and success of my forbears intimidate me in the slightest. I had a drive to succeed, I thrived on competition, and since I was a better tennis player than my father or uncle, why not feel confident?

As I look back on how I eventually wound up practicing law, I realize it was despite many other opportunities, most of them attractive but all of which I declined. Each of those would have led to far different destinations on life's path.

More than one offer came during my college years. My father said he was willing to support me with a monthly stipend if I wanted to play the amateur tennis circuit. I had played for Stanford's freshman tennis team, and in the number one singles position on Columbia's tennis team after I transferred there. In those days, a tennis player on the circuit could not be a professional or play for money. At most, you would be given free rackets and strings and invited to stay in the best homes in

Southampton, Newport and Forest Hills. I was surprised that my father would offer me a chance to postpone postgraduate studies or taking a job. I didn't ask if he was merely testing me. I thanked him and declined the offer. I was eager to get my law degree and discover where my life would lead.

When I was about to graduate from Columbia Law School I flew down to Palm Beach for Spring vacation, and one day while there my father took me along with him to meet Samuel Gottesman, a family friend who owned a massive paper empire, the Eastern Corporation. He also was a controlling shareholder in the gigantic Niagara Mohawk Power Company, but he exhibited no sense of self-importance, and he seemed extremely kind. He showed me around his lovely home and questioned me about my goals in life. I said I was not certain what I would ultimately choose to do, but that I had chosen to go law school because it gave me what seemed like the widest set of options. Sam said in that case when I graduated he wanted me to come to work for him, and that as he had only daughters and no son, if I proved myself I could eventually succeed him.

At the time I had no grasp of what an opportunity Sam Gottesman was offering me. He was pleasant, jovial, and bright. I thanked him and said I would keep his offer in mind; but in truth, I could not contemplate, even for a moment, working anywhere but with my father at "J&J" as we used to call the family law firm.

Then again while I was still in my last year of law school came another unexpected opportunity to take a completely different path on life's road. One Saturday night I decided to take Stephanie to Ben Marden's Riviera, a nightclub perched atop the cliffs of New Jersey overlooking New York City from across the Hudson River. The Riviera had a reputation for excellent food and entertainment.

That weekend the Will Masten Trio was headlining the show there. The dining tables were spread out around a cavernous hall facing a raised stage on which an orchestra played dance music. Once dinner was served, the show commenced with the Will Masten Trio playing and Sammy Davis, Jr. tap dancing on stage. Finally Sammy took the microphone to sing a few of the most moving ballads of the fifties. He had a marvelous voice and captured the audience completely. Their shouts of approval and applause made him do several encores before that portion of the show ended.

During the intermission I left our table to go the bar that was in a side room off the main ballroom. While I was standing waiting to get served, Sammy came from back stage and walked over to stand beside me. We started to chat once I told him how much I enjoyed his performance. He spoke the King's English with mellifluous diction and perfect enunciation. I was fascinated to hear English spoken with such precision and purity.

I asked Sammy all about himself. He was very forthcoming and completely open. Sammy was wearing a loose-fitting satin shirt unbuttoned at the neck. I noticed that he wore the Star of David suspended from a gold chain. I had never met a black man of the Jewish faith, and I asked him if that meant he was Jewish. He replied that he was, and so was Will Masten and all of his family. I became even more fascinated when I heard that.

Then Sammy asked about me. I said that I was still going to Columbia Law School and expected to practice law at Javits and Javits, the family law firm in Manhattan. Sammy looked deep into my eyes for a long moment. He said, "I can see who you are, and what you are destined to become. I am unknown, a nobody, with no influential friends, and only my talent and ambition, but I want to be a star—not part of Will Masten's trio all my life."

107

Sammy told me that to reach his dream he wanted to find someone to work with whom he liked and whom he felt he could trust. He said he wanted a person with whom he could reach the sky. He said he already knew I was the one. Then he asked me to be his manager.

I was stunned. After only a brief encounter, he was ready to cast his lot with me. He was that decisive. I knew then nothing would stand in his way or stop him, and that he would be one of America's greatest stars. But though I expressed my gratitude for his trust, I told Sammy I would not become his manager, not because I was still in school or because I did not believe in him, but because I had different long-term goals, and that he deserved someone who espoused the goals *he* wanted. Before I returned to my table and Sammy left to go back on stage, we hugged and vowed to remain friends for life. And so we were.

I guess anyone who has ever gone to the movies or the theatre has wondered whether they could have "made it" on stage or in Hollywood. That option came along in my case as a young lawyer with less than two years experience.

In 1957 our firm represented a wealthy Canadian contractor who was a board member and the largest (5%) stockholder in MGM studios that had fallen on hard times. He, along with another dissident director, Stanley Meyer of Dragnet fame, wanted to oust the management and take over the company. The proxy battle was finally settled when my father negotiated a split board with MGM's incumbent Chairman, Joseph R. Vogel, staying on as President and picking six directors for a new board with the insurgent faction picking the same number. It was agreed that the 13th director who would serve as the Chairman was the highly respected Ogden R. Reid, President and Editor of the New York Herald Tribune.

At the signing of the settlement in MGM's executive offices in New York, I sat in to assist my father, but in reality played no role. However, once the signing of the settlement agreement had taken place, Joe Vogel turned to me and asked if I would go with him into an adjoining room to see something interesting. I turned to my father. He nodded his permission since there was no longer anything that would inhibit me from having a conversation with Mr. Vogel without his counsel present. When we went into the adjoining room it turned out to be a large gallery with enormous blow-up photos of scenes from the film, Quo Vadis, especially the chariot race in Rome's coliseum. As we walked slowly around the room, Vogel explained that they were still shooting some scenes from that movie, but he expected it to mark the financial turnaround for MGM. He asked if I had ever thought of being a movie actor, explaining that they would soon cast the lead for a movie to be called "The Young Philadelphian" about a young lawyer just starting out in practice. He said he felt I could be perfect for the role. I was quiet while he went on to say he would send me out to California for a screen test if I would be interested.

I finally responded to ask him, "Why would I want to play a make-believe lawyer on the screen when I am already a real life lawyer with actual cases?" He did not seem to have any answer so I thanked him warmly and said acting was not the career I wanted to pursue. Later, when I saw Paul Newman on screen acting in his first movie, I felt he was the perfect man for the role.

CHAPTER VI — PALM BEACH

In the late twenties Miami property boomed although it was just beginning to develop, and its beach, stretching for miles in each direction, was mostly deserted. My parents got married there in 1926, and after a brief stay drove north through Palm Beach on their way back to New York. A brand new hotel abutting Lake Worth called the Alba caught their eye. Wanting to spend the night in Palm Beach, they stopped. The desk clerk said he was sorry but the hotel had not yet received its Certificate of Occupancy.

After pleading that they were newlyweds on their honeymoon; and if they were permitted to stay just one night on their way back to New York they would never tell anyone about staying in the Alba. They became the first people to sleep in the building that is now known as the Palm Beach Biltmore Condominium. For sentimental reasons my mother bought one of the first apartments when the old hotel was converted to residential ownership in 1979.

For a number of years thereafter in the late twenties and early thirties, my parents returned to Miami for brief winter vacations, first staying at the Blackstone Hotel, and then at the Atlantis Hotel on Miami Beach. That is where my sister and I caused havoc on the crowded boardwalk with our bicycles that had no training wheels.

After 1937 my parents stopped going to Miami and began to winter vacation in Palm Beach. In those years we still traveled down to Florida by train. It was a 24-hour trip from NYC's Penn Station, and the family took a couple of Pullman sleeper-car bedrooms with upper and lower berths. The most fun part of taking the train was to sleep in the upper bunk, eat in the dining car with its linen-covered tables, or walk from car to car until you emerged from the caboose onto a small open platform where you could stand before a railing to listen to an endless clickity-clack of steel wheels on rails that seemed like music, while watching the scenery flash by on two sides at once. You almost became hypnotized staring at the rails that gradually grew thinner in the distance until they merged into a tail that slowly undulated from side to side as the train raced on. The most unforgettable part of those train trips was when I finally stepped onto the station platform in Florida to breathe deeply of the warm tropical air that carried a faint fragrance of tropical flowers and vines, in contrast to the biting cold I had left behind just a day earlier. There you could get a Negro "Redcap" to help with the luggage, and be entertained by a black minstrel trio that hoped to collect some change in their bucket on the ground. The bass notes were rhythmically plucked on twine tautly stretched from the top of a broom handle to a five-gallon drum. The percussionist strummed and tapped out the beat on an old metal washboard, and the minstrel with a mouth organ carried the tune. All three were pretty good tap dancers, too.

We first stayed at the Whitehall Hotel for a couple of years. The hotel had been erected as a high-rise annex to the magnificent mansion that railroad magnate and pioneer of Florida, Henry Flagler, had built in 1902. When hotel guests emerged from the Whitehall mansion to descend the front steps of its magnificent marble-columned portico, there were always three or four Afro-mobiles parked at the curb. These wicker carriages were large enough to seat three persons with a black driver on a bicycle seat who pedaled and steered from behind. It was a gracious era, and taking a slow carriage ride was a dignified way to enjoy the lush vegetation along Coconut Row as one rolled gently along toward Royal Poinciana Way where sentinel rows of Royal Palm trees stood guard on the way to Bradley Place.

The Whitehall Hotel owned a beachfront facility on Sunset Avenue known as the Sun and Surf Club that had two tennis courts and a large swimming pool. Guests also could use its eighteen-hole golf course situated at the North end of Palm Beach island. These amenities were for the exclusive use of the hotel's guests. At the Sun and Surf Club Dimitri Spassoff gave massages and physical therapy. In those days, Spassoff also served as the trainer for the Baltimore Colts, the professional football team owned by Carroll Rosenbloom. When the Colt's star, quarterback Johnny Unitas, snapped his Achilles tendon, it was Spassoff who brought Unitas back to play pro ball when no other player had ever succeeded in recovering from so drastic an injury. (In 1970 when I snapped my Achilles tendon on my hard-surfaced tennis court in Southampton, Long Island, it was Spassoff who brought me back from that injury, as well.)

Because our family constantly moved between Connecticut and Florida, I came to know many famous people who figured prominently in society and business circles in America, and in Palm Beach's history.[2]

My parents were founding members of the Palm Beach Country Club along with Oklahoma oilmen, Nathan Appleman and Raymond Kravis (founder of the Kravis Center of Performing Arts in West Palm Beach and the father of investment banker Henry Kravis). Other early members were Joseph P. Kennedy; oil wildcatter Jack Davis, father of Hollywood magnate Marvin Davis; New York real estate developers Martin, Larry and Zachary Fisher who amassed an office building empire; New York attorney Peter I. B. Lavan, the Senior Partner of Stroock, Stroock and Lavan; and Estee and Joe Lauder of cosmetics fame.

During WW II the beachfront road along the barrier island of Palm Beach was "blacked out". Its street lamps were extinguished at night, and any car driving along the beachfront had to have electrical masking tape on its headlights so that they could not be seen from the ocean.

German submarines were laying in wait off the coast of Palm Beach hoping to sink merchant ships coming up from the Panama canal along the East Coast of the US before they could rendezvous as part of a protected convoy for the Atlantic crossing to Europe.

Many nights I would walk up Palmo Way, the street on which we lived, to the sea wall at the beach from where I could see the torpedoed ships burning out at sea. The following morning the beaches would be black with tar and debris. Coast Guardsmen and soldiers would patrol the beachfront at night looking for rubber rafts and evidence of spies slipping ashore from submarines.

The Coast Guard cutter stationed at the north end of Palm Beach carried depth charges on its fantail. Although an underwater net was stretched across the inlet, when the Coast Guard cutter would return from its ocean patrol, the net would be lowered and under cover of darkness German U-boats could glide in unnoticed just under or behind the cutter. Once inside the inland waterway between the mainland of Florida and the barrier island of Palm Beach, the U-boat could be covertly met by opportunists, spies and sympathizers who, for gold bullion, would provide fuel and provisions, food and citrus fruit.

My sister, Joan, tells the story of one of her dinner dates during WW II with a beau whom she had met at Yale while she was a Vassar undergrad. He took her to Taboo, a popular restaurant on Worth Avenue, explaining that one of his college classmates might join them for a short while during dinner. Right on cue, a most attractive young man did appear in blazer, slacks and tie. He was introduced by Joan's date as a dear friend and his Yale roommate. However, once the visitor had eaten he excused himself politely and left. Joan's date then confided that his friend had to get back to his German U-boat in time to escape from Lake Worth while the net was dropped to allow the Coast Guard cutter to pass on its way back out to sea.

From 1944 until May 1945, I attended the Graham Eckes School in Palm Beach whose English teacher, Eugene Metz, ran a secret kangaroo court where corporal punishment was administered by some students to other students he disfavored. The penalty for his trumped-up infractions was to be beaten by a heavy wooden paddle until you lost consciousness, as I did. I always thought he had bias in his heart and a slight German accent in his speech. I found out after the war that the FBI caught him signaling German U-boats at night with a powerful flashlight from his tower bedroom in the school.

Morrison Field, the West Palm Beach airport that opened in the late thirties, began with only a couple of intersecting runways and a small shack with a wind sock on the roof. Communication was by short wave radio with Eastern Airlines' DC-3s, the only planes flying the Boston-to-Miami route. The eleven-hour flight made eleven stops carrying mail and a maximum of about twenty passengers up and down the East Coast. West Palm Beach's main commercial strip— Okeechobee Road—was only a two-lane dirt road then, totally barren on both sides except for truck farms, grazing land or untouched wilderness.

Segregation at that time in Florida was much like South Africa's. The railroad station had separate waiting rooms for Colored and White, separate water fountains and separate bathrooms. The public busses all had signs that read "Colored Passengers seat from the rear. White Passengers seat from the front". The colored district of West Palm Beach had its own "Rosemary Taxi" service, as white taxis would not serve black passengers.

Charlie Wood, the tennis pro at the Coral Beach Club, was a likeable chap who often invited me to play with movie stars and celebrities looking for a friendly game. It was on his courts that I met and played with Ginger Rogers and J. Spencer Love, the textile baron of Burlington Industries. I also was welcome at the Bath and Tennis and Everglades Clubs despite their restrictive membership policy because their tennis pros were looking for good doubles players to make interesting matches for the members.

The Kennedy home fronted on the ocean just a few blocks south of Palmo Way, the street on which we lived. I used to walk barefoot along the beach in the mornings. There I would meet Ted doing the same thing, so we would walk, talk and jog together. Our family also knew Rose and Joe Kennedy whom we would see at the Palm Beach Country Club, along with Jack and Jackie who were often golfing there. Stephanie, and I saw a lot of Emmett Hughes, JFK's military attaché, as well as actor Peter Lawford and his wife Pat Kennedy, at various social occasions. Occasionally, we were invited by Rose Kennedy to sit with her at the Everglades Club charity dinners.

I had gotten to know Jean Kennedy and her close friend, Ethel Skakel on the maiden crossing of the SS America from New York to Southampton, England in 1948. Ethel Skakel eventually married Jean's brother, Bobby Kennedy. I also was a friend of Earle E. T. Smith—Kennedy's ambassador to Cuba, and his wife "Flo" Pritchett Smith who was a longtime intimate of Jack Kennedy.

One night in 1962 when JFK was President and staying at the "winter white house" on North County Road, a call came very late for the President from a member of his cabinet. The secret service went to his first floor bedroom to wake him, but found the room empty and its window open. Needless to say, having the President go missing in the middle of the night from a house abutting the Atlantic Ocean was an unwelcome development for the Secret Service. They immediately called the Palm Beach Police to enlist their help in the search.

The next day, when the police patrol car that routinely prowled through every block of Palm Beach every hour of every day was passing our house on Palmo Way, my wife and I flagged it down. While chatting with the officer whom we knew well, he confided that the previous night he had been assigned to walk the beach, starting after midnight in front of the Kennedy house, to look for footprints or other evidence that might have been a clue to finding the President. As he walked south a few hundred feet past the Kennedy compound, he had heard a lot of laughing and splashing coming from above the seawall which towered ten feet over the beach, so he climbed up a set of stairs onto the lawn in front of Ambassador Earl E. T. Smith's home into which was set a large swimming pool.

There in the beam of his flashlight were Flo and JFK splashing about in their birthday suits, having the best of times. The President had brought just his pajamas, which he quickly pulled on to hurry back and take his telephone call. No one broke the silence that was mandatory for well-mannered Palm Beach residents and/or friends of the Kennedys, regardless of political affiliation. Most of the Palm Beach "in" crowd knew that Tommy Shevlin's wife, Durie, (a well liked and very social resident of Palm Beach) had been married to Jack Kennedy before he married Jacqueline Bouvier; but no one spoke of it, and as far as I know that marriage and annulment did not become public knowledge during Jack Kennedy's lifetime.

Sighting a UFO

Sometime in the late '60s, about 6:30 pm on a dark winter evening (and I probably have this noted in my diaries more precisely), I was driving a rented station wagon northward on Palm Beach's North County Road with five others in the car— Stephanie, my son and daughter, and two of my sister's children.

My windshield was clear as I turned just before the Palm Beach Country Club to drive up toward the ocean for about two hundred feet. In the star-studded night sky a beautiful full moon hung low over the ocean, but there beside it appeared what seemed to be a second moon of a slightly different color! I stopped the car in amazement before following the turn in the road to the left to draw parallel to the ocean sea wall. I asked if everyone in the car could see two moons, or was I seeing double. Everyone said there was no mistake, and they could see two bright orbs.

There was no traffic at that hour, so I switched off the motor and car lights and got out of the car to get a closer look. The only sounds I could hear were the waves gently breaking on the beach below the ocean road seawall, and the hissing of the water as it fell back from the sand. I noticed a red and green light flashing just at the base of the "second moon."

Suddenly the object appeared in a different position. I could not see it move there. It did not bank and accelerate, and then slow to a stop. It moved its position faster than the human eye could detect. It was just like one light going off and another appearing almost at the same time. But the red and green lights beneath it were still blinking on and off. It did this maneuver many more times over the next several minutes.

I had been an aircraft spotter in World War II, trained in identifying all the warplanes of the US and Axis forces.

Nothing on earth could dart this fast from a dead stop to another position. It clearly did not obey the laws of gravity.

Finally it took off like a rocket—and was out of sight in less than one second, leaving a trail of light as it disappeared. I got back into the car and asked if everyone had seen what I had seen. They all said they had, but that they could not discern, as I had, that it made no sound. They asked if I could tell what it was or how high it was. I replied that if it was the size of a bus, it would have been at about 2500 feet, but if it was smaller, it could have been at only 1000 to 1500 feet. I had observed cars from the fiftieth floor of buildings in New York City and from the Empire State Building's observation floor, so I had a pretty good idea of relative sizes.

Once it had vanished, I resumed driving north on County Road to my parent's home on Palmo Way where I immediately called the Palm Beach police to report the unidentified flying object I had seen. They said they had received too many calls to make an official record of my call. They suggested I call an Air Force Base in Florida near Orlando if I wanted to make an official report. I did call the base, but was told they also had too many calls to make a record of them.

Later that evening I went to a party to which I had been invited where I ran into John Randolph "Bunky" Hearst, a longtime friend from my Palm Beach childhood. I told Bunky what I had seen, and that I was still in awe about it. He said that the UFO had been over West Palm Beach for at least forty minutes that evening and had been seen by thousands of people, so he was not surprised that there was no interest in taking individual reports, as there were just too many witnesses for reports to be collected.

I eventually filed a report with the organization that collects reports of UFO sightings. I also wrote Carl Sagan, the eminent

Professor of Astronomy at Cornell, to relate my experience. He wrote back that legal proof and scientific proof of the existence of an object follow different standards, and although my sighting was quite convincing, it was not proof of the existence of UFOs. He said that our planet occupied a quite empty and remote area of the universe, and it was unlikely that we would be having space visitors, although he could not say for sure if that was the case. He implied that science would not accept the existence of UFOs until a UFO or an alien actually falls somehow into the custody of man and is examined forensically.

CHAPTER VII — LEGAL CAREER AND LIFE INTERTWINED

My career as a lawyer began officially in early December, 1955, when I was sworn in as a member of the New York Bar. My secret ambitions were exceedingly immodest: before the age 30 I wanted to author a book that got published, to be listed in Who's Who, and to have made a million dollars— which in today's money would have been at least ten times as much!!!

I often had lunch at the Mayan, a restaurant on the ground floor of our office building with an entrance on 51st street. Sometimes I was invited to accompany my father to lunch at Jack and Charlie's "21" Club, the former "speakeasy" on West 52nd street, only one block north of our office. There, the Kreindler brothers Mac, Bob and Pete, reigned supreme with co-founder Charlie Berns. Although the other founding partner, Jack Kreindler, had died, Charlie Berns and the Kreindler brothers would visit each table at which "regulars" were seated. Upstairs, the second floor dining room was an exclusive preserve where the most important figures in New York's finance, legal and business communities could be seen having chicken hash or hamburgers 21 at "power lunches" with their counterparts.

Sometime that December I ran into my childhood friend, Edward R. Downe, Jr., who was having lunch at the Mayan. Ed and I had not seen each other for quite a few years. Ed told me that he had married, and that he was about to start a mail order business in his basement, having quit as the editor of

120

Argosy magazine. I told him I had just been admitted to the NY bar, and asked if he wanted to be my first client. He agreed enthusiastically, but warned he could not pay very much. We later eventually agreed on a retainer of $50 per week.

In early 1956 while I was waiting for Ed to become my first client, my father called me into his office and told me that he had an important case he wanted me to handle. One of his friends, John Biggs, Jr., the Chief Justice of the Federal Court of Appeals for the 3rd Circuit in Delaware, had taken his wife to Italy during the Court's 1955 summer recess to tour that country in a rented Fiat automobile. Fiat was advertising heavily in America to attract tourism by including an inexpensive rental car for those who flew round-trip to Rome on Alitalia. Unfortunately, the Biggs vacation was ruined because their Fiat broke down repeatedly. Most of their days in Italy were spent being towed along country roads and waiting interminably for parts and repairs. Thus it happened that my first client was not Ed Downe, but the Delaware Chief Justice, and since most of the big corporate cases my father handled would eventually wind up in front of his court in Delaware (the most sought-after state in which to incorporate), I knew I had better get Judge Biggs satisfaction.

I realized suing Fiat in Italy would be a great mistake. The case would have to be brought in Fiat-friendly Milan, and besides the added expense, the problems of proof would so annoy Judge Biggs that he would likely drop the case. And even if we recovered a money judgment, my father did not think money would be enough to assuage his anger and frustration.

So I decided to get him an official apology from Fiat's top management, and perhaps something more that would make him feel satisfied. I started by writing the head of Fiat in the U.S. a letter, quite different from the usual lawyer's letter. It asserted no claim on behalf of Judge and Mrs. Biggs, but it recounted in painful detail each breakdown, each failure to get a prompt repair or replacement vehicle, and each less-than-luxurious accommodation the couple had to tolerate in the heat of the Italian summer, without air conditioning, while waiting to resume their tour. I concluded my letter by asking if he would kindly call me to discuss what could be done to ease the Judge's anger and allay his disappointment.

Fiat's CEO in the U.S. did call me. He offered to get an official written apology from the President or Chairman of Fiat in Italy, promising Judge Biggs that a Fiat car would be at his disposal free of charge for the rest of his life any time he came to Italy. My father later told me the Judge was quite pleased with the outcome.

During the first few years I was in practice, I was kiting around town every night to parties, restaurants, nightclubs and discos to both have fun and to expand my circle of contacts. I went often to El Morocco, the world famous nightclub that was owned by John Perona. Perona's son, Edwin, was an amusing and likeable fellow, but John Perona was a social tyrant. Entry to his club was guarded by Angelo Zucotti, the Maitre d' I befriended, who would always seat Stephanie and me in the best front row table. Zucotti's son, John, whom he put through Princeton, became deputy Mayor of the City of New York under Mayor Abe Beame, and later held important posts in government and the private sector. The area in the rear of the nightclub was derogatorily called "Siberia", where social unknowns were seated. El Morocco was a favorite watering place of society figures, movie stars, moguls and powerful CEO's such as Frank Freimann of Magnavox and Serge Semenenko of First Boston. Jerome Zerbe used to hang out there to photograph movie stars, tycoons and other important customers sitting on zebra-patterned banquettes with white plastic palm trees in the background while a six-piece orchestra adjoining the circular dance floor played popular tunes. That was where I occasionally encountered wives of high-profile couples who were considering divorcing their husbands, or whose husbands wanted to divorce them.

In my youth I had often had stayed in New York City with my parents at the Ambassador Hotel on Park Avenue, as my father was the lawyer for the hotel and he got a favored rate. Then later, when I was in law school, I would take Stephanie there to the Knight Box for dinner and dancing. Robert K. Christenberry, a prominent Republican who had run unsuccessfully for Mayor of New York City, was the president of the hotel. Prince Serge Obolensky was in charge of the Ambassador Hotel's social arrangements, and Serge, who was a social luminary in New York, brought great panache to the scene. Another celebrated émigré Obolensky was the Hotel's doorman. He cut an elegant figure in his White Russian military greatcoat and fur hat, and when he opened car doors at the front of the hotel, no other hotel could possibly have seemed as important as the Ambassador. I believe he was the original White Russian general that fled the Communists and was head of the Obolensky clan. I also knew Igor Obolensky, Alexis Obolensky and Ivan Obolensky (Obie) who was very social in Palm Beach in the '60s.

I was introduced to Westchester County's country club life in 1956 when John Rosenwald sponsored me as a member of the Century Country Club in White Plains, NY. Century was the most social and sought after of the Jewish country clubs in Westchester. It had the Lehmans, the Loebs, the Kempners and the rest of the Jewish Blue Book. I belonged to Century until 1960, when instead of once again renting a summer place in Westchester, we decided to rent in Long Island for the summer. We found an apartment in the Sandpiper overlooking the ocean at Westhampton Beach. That summer Sue and Ed Downe also took an apartment in the Sandpiper. George Hamilton, the actor, still in his late teens, was the desk receptionist at the nearby Westhampton Bath and Tennis Club where I often played tennis.

After two years at the Sandpiper, for another couple of years we went out to a club on Fire Island that was started by Frank Butler, son of the founder of Butler Aviation, and a wealthy socialite from Oak Brook, Illinois, one of Chicago's swankiest suburbs. Fire Island was a thin barrier reef island just off of Long Island and to get there, you had to take a ferry from Sayville that landed in a little beach community— either Cherry Grove or The Pines—that was peopled entirely by gay couples. The Club stood a distance away from those communities, but right on the dunes facing the Atlantic Ocean. It consisted of a small clubhouse that contained a dining room and kitchen, and a series of small cabin-like structures where rustic rooms and bathrooms were located. The clubhouse and the room structures were separated by a swimming pool surrounded by a deck with chairs. At one end of the deck, a path led up over the dune to the beach. The club manager was an old friend of mine, Miguel "Chacho" Lopez LeCube. In his youth in Argentina Chacho had been close to Gen. Juan Peron. He was very physical, magnificently muscled with a great sense of humor, joi de vivre and intuitive people skills. Because he was almost bald, he looked a little bit like Mr. Clean, the icon of the detergent by that name. He used to put Brazilian music on the loudspeaker around the pool and clubhouse and get every one drinking and dancing to the beats of samba, merengue, pasa doble and maricumbe. He would lead the entourage with both arms raised above his head, swaying to the rhythms and advancing in perfect time to the incessant beat.

Some of the guests, weekend after weekend were Howard Oxenberg, Bill and Chessie Raynor, Bill and Colette Woods,

Charles Amory, Harry Theodoracopulos, Betsy Pickering, Lenny Holzer and Baby Jane, Jerry Shields, Brownlee Currey, Mario Santo Domingo, Antonio Muñoz (a Spaniard who worked for George Moore at Citibank) and his wife-to-be Graziela, Otto Mach, Bunker Hoover, Turkish record czar Ahmed Ertegun of Atlantic Records and Motown label, his brother, and his wife Mika, Oleg and his brother Igor "Gui Gui" Cassini who wrote the Cholly Knickerbocker social columns for one of the NY daily papers and then formed Martial & Company, a public relations firm that people paid to be mentioned in his column, Clyde and Maggi McNellis Newhouse, Fernando Aguirre and David Gilmour.

Thereafter, we began to rent different houses in Southampton every summer. The first summer we rented a Dutch-style house on the beach way out on Meadow Lane. Another summer, together with my parents and sister, we rented the enormous yellow Smith house on Meadow Lane opposite the Meadow Club. It had at least twelve bedrooms and sat right atop the dunes looking at the Atlantic Ocean. It was the summer of 1967 and as idyllic a summer as one could wish. We threw a big party for the whole social scene one Saturday night to reciprocate for all the bashes, dinners and blasts to which we had been invited. All of the social set, beautiful models and members of the young international set from NY came. It was only after the party the next day that I heard what went on at the end of the evening, or should I say the early morning. A scion of an Italian wine family had gotten so drunk that when he left it was on foot prancing naked out of our driveway to find his way home.

The social schedule was always full in Southampton. Whether it was a party at the home of Angier Biddle Duke's mother, Cordelia Biddle Duke, the gracious icon of old society who loved having young people around, or the jet set parties that had every type of hippie young professional.

Finally, in 1967 I bought 2.25 acres on Gin Lane for $22,500. It was a flat piece of vacant land situated across the street from the beach and had not a tree on it. When it was not being farmed for potatoes or hay, it was overrun with pheasants and rabbits. I knew exactly the design and layout that I had in mind. I hired a local architect to draw plans for my house to my specifications. It took three years to finish construction because my contractor went bankrupt, and I had to step in as the general contractor. I kept his carpenter and subcontractors who agreed to stay on the job, knowing they would finally get paid on time. I got a twenty-year mortgage from the local bank, but unfortunately I wound up spending more than triple what I had planned to finish constructing, landscaping and furnishing the place.

We started to live there in 1970 and it was complete in 1971 with the help of a local landscape architect who made it the beautifully landscaped estate that it was. I had designed the house to be a series of small units with the French doors of each bedroom opening up on its own private garden. That is why I named it "Las Casitas" meaning the little houses in Spanish. Well hidden in the rear were a tennis court, swimming pool and pool house. I hoped it would appear unobtrusive and not worth breaking into because it sat across the street from the beach on the North side of Gin Lane, one of the nicest streets on Long Island's "gold coast."

At about the same time, Eddie Hand, a friend and trucking company magnate from Buffalo who owned 6 acres adjoining mine on the Northwest corner of Gin Lane and Little Plains Road, allowed me to land there when I flew out to view the progress on my house in a rented helicopter, instead of having to land at Easthampton's airport. In those days there still were not regulations covering noise and helicopters. Eddie's parcel was eventually sold to Carroll Petrie who, with a talented decorator and landscaper, created one of the finest residential estates in Southampton.

Las Casitas sat on Gin Lane directly opposite the Southampton Bath and Tennis Club that was owned by Southampton real estate developer, George Semergian, who was a friend of my father's pal, A. Mitchell "Mitch" Liftig. Mitch wanted me to buy the Club from Semergian in 1975 but I was simply not interested. I did not want to get involved in the social or business requirements of owning and managing a club.

We loved to go body surfing at the Little Plains beach that was no more than a minute's walk from my front door. This involved wading and then swimming out to dive beneath the towering waves to get past their breaking point, and then waiting to belly-surf a monstrous wave into shore. Usually the result was to crash onto the beach with at least some scrapes, if not bruises. But what a thrill that was between long jogs along the endless white sandy shore.

I will never forget the lovely summer day when Herbert "Bunky" Hoover III brought his speedboat to the Little Plains beach just opposite our house. It was broiling in the sun and the surf was up. After cruising parallel to the beach just offshore, but beyond the wave breakers, Bunky decided to come much closer to shore and brave getting swamped by a wave. He found a lull and came in almost to the beach. Then I noticed a giant wave starting to build about three hundred yards offshore. He noticed it only when it got within a hundred yards because people started yelling to him to get back out before he and his speedboat were swamped or even worse. He turned the prow toward the 25-foot crest just as it started to break, hit it with full throttle and launched himself and the Donzi vertically up the wave and at least thirty feet further into the air as it passed under him. He thought that was so much fun that he returned close to shore and did it again and again for the rest of the afternoon.

Bunker was an easygoing guy who loved motorcycling on his Triumph 600. I used to bike with him along the country roads on my bright red Yamaha 250cc motorcycle. Bunker eventually married Camilla Sparv, the Swedish actress who starred in the film Downhill Racer. Years later when I saw him in Florida he had been disfigured in a motorcycle accident that left him limping for life.

Though I was not a member, I used to be invited to play tennis at the Southampton Meadow Club. One of my neighbors, Carlos Nadal, was a member there and he wanted to propose me for membership. But he was told not to do so because so many members' wives disliked or felt threatened by my wife, Stephanie, for whatever reasons.

One summer I was asked to represent the Mid-Ocean Club in a team tennis tournament between some of the country clubs and tennis clubs on Long Island. I wound up in the finals of the Men's Singles against Blackie Smith, the number one player from the Meadow Club that was renowned for hosting one of the amateur tennis circuit grass-court tournaments. We played with a big audience on the Club's grass court right in front of its clubhouse porch. Blackie Smith was fast, nimble and steady. He used very smart court tactics. Nevertheless, I managed to beat him decisively and it was a satisfying victory since the Meadow Club in those days had not yet taken in any Jewish members.

Finally, in 1959 I felt we needed a still a larger apartment. My friend and client, Ed Downe, helped me sell our apartment at 1025 5th Avenue to one of his friends, so I was able to buy a 21-room co-op on Fifth Avenue between 91st and 92nd streets from Jackie Kennedy's step-brother, Hugh D. Auchincloss at the bargain price of only $64,000.

During those enjoyable early years of legal practice I handled about 100 high-profile divorces in New York. I could not attract other types of legal work since I was not yet a partner and far too inexperienced to claim I had a specialty. In most cases I would represent the wife. Usually the first step was a letter to the husband informing him that his wife had retained me with respect to their marital affairs.

In the first meeting with the husband I would assure him that the case would not be dragged through the press, and besides shielding him from publicity, there would be no overreaching—only fair and equitable treatment. I would always make clear the alternative if negotiations failed by explaining that since our firm shared office space with Sol A. Rosenblatt, New York's leading litigator in matrimonial actions; and since I was a negotiator and not a trial lawyer, I would have no choice but to turn the case over to Sol— something no husband would want to contemplate!

That was always enough to make a quietly negotiated separation or divorce possible, and it was not long before I developed into a skilled negotiator. I often came up against slippery, unethical and voracious "bombers" – the term used to denote the most infamous matrimonial lawyers. Quite surprisingly, they were the most tractable attorneys I dealt with, as they knew exactly what each case was worth.

Although I was able to keep my clients and their husbands out of the papers, I was not so fortunate myself. I had to admonish and even beg my gossip columnist friends, Igor Cassini, Joe Dever, and Aileen Mehle (better known by her pen name "Suzy"), not to mention me after my name appeared a few times in their columns about restaurants, junkets, parties and balls frequented by New York's "Jet Set". I pleaded that it hurt me with my clients if I seemed not the serious, hard-working attorney that I really was. Among the many clients I represented below the media radar in those early years of practice were restaurant magnate George Schrafft's wife

Elizabeth, watchmaking baron Ardie Bulova's wife Ileana, socialite James Harrison III's wife Barbara, Silica Glass and Sand magnate Bill Woods' wife Colette.

For members of the "Jet Set" there were frequent junkets to inaugurate new resorts like the new Hunter Mountain ski resort in New York State, or in Atlantic City where a hotel was renovated, or in Montego Bay in Jamaica where I was almost killed twice. The first close call was when Stephanie and I were vacationing in Montego Bay, and we befriended a young honeymoon couple staying at the same hotel, the Half Moon. They had rented a car to drive to Ocho Rios to sightsee, and they asked if we would like to join them. We happily said we would, and their rental car turned out to be a brand new convertible. So off we went, top down, with the newlywed groom driving with his wife in the front passenger seat. We sat in the back enjoying the scenic Jamaican countryside.

In Jamaica, cars drive on the left, not on the right as they do in the US. So as we came upon a turn in the road our host out of habit rounded the turn on the right side of the road directly into an oncoming car. When I woke up I realized I had been thrown out of the convertible by the impact and was prostrate on the road. No one was moving in either car. The husband lay crushed but breathing against the steering wheel, and his beautiful young wife had gone through the windshield. Her face looked like chop meat. I helped each of our party back to consciousness and then flagged down a passing car that took us all back to Montego Bay to a clinic run by the one doctor in town. He was a native Jamaican who, though not a plastic surgeon, of necessity stitched up the young woman's face. He must have been experienced from many road accidents and probably many knifings, too, amongst the natives, because later I learned that the young women's face hardly showed scarring.

The second time I was almost killed in Jamaica was during another of the "junkets" on which we were invited in the early '60's. It was to the opening of Carlin and Connie Dinkler's new hotel in Ocho Rios. The Dinklers, who also owned the Racquet Club in Miami, Florida, where I used to play in Pro-Am tennis tournaments, were a very popular pair on the Atlanta and Miami social scene. Stephanie and I were among the fifty or so from New York that had been invited to celebrate with the Dinklers, so after the opening ceremony and Gala Dinner, when the dancing and music had ended and the number of celebrants had dwindled, a small group of us decided to go down to the port and observe the loading of the banana freighter standing at anchor just outside Ocho Rios Bay.

In our group were Carlin and Connie Dinkler; one of the Dinkler's friends from Atlanta, Walter Troutman; Jerome Zerbe; Stephanie and me. We walked along the wharf in the port looking for a launch or motor boat that would ferry us out of the harbor to watch the flotilla of banana-laden native canoes pull alongside the freighter anchored about half a mile offshore, and see the heavy stalks passed up hand-over-hand by workers clinging at intervals to a rope latticework that dangled loosely against the hull.

We finally found an elderly native captain and his young native deckhand waiting for tourists alongside a weather beaten inboard gasoline-powered motor launch with open deck areas on the prow and fantail. It had a low windshield and roof over the cockpit that was just large enough to hold our group. After some discussion of price, we hired the captain to take us out. The deck hand untied the moorings while the captain started the motor, and we pulled away smoothly from the wharf.

It was a beautiful balmy night. The moon was full and we could see everything quite clearly from the lee side of the freighter. It was a fascinating scene to watch, but after some time one of us suggested we have the captain go around the ship and then return to port. We did not expect conditions to be different on the other side of the freighter, but to our shock once we no longer had the freighter as a shield and we rounded its stern, the wind grew cold and gusty, and the waves kicked up fiercely. I suggested we should go back since there was really nothing to see as we pulled amidships of the freighter on the ocean side. In the darkness it looked lifeless and abandoned. For some unknown reason I imagined I was in a U-boat, and that I had fired a torpedo at the mid-section of the freighter. I visualized in my mind the torpedo that I had launched, racing just below the surface and heading straight for the freighter's mid-section. In my mind's eye I could see it just about to reach the freighter and at the moment of imagined impact there was, indeed, a tremendous explosion!

The deck under my feet simply disintegrated. I was stunned. My eardrums felt like they had burst, and though I had on slacks, flames shot up both pant legs and scorched my skin and body hair. I turned around to see the whole rear deck of the launch blown open and burning fiercely. Stephanie's hair was smoldering and partially singed. No one seemed to have been hurt that badly in the explosion, but there was no place for us to stand or sit any longer, and we began discussing jumping into the water to escape the flames. I eyed the choppy black sea with fear and revulsion.

Jerome Zerbe, who was a renowned society photographer, shouted at us not to jump ship. He said he had been in the Coast Guard, and you never left a ship unless it was sinking. He said we would never make it to shore, and we would never be found. Besides the high waves, those waters were shark infested. He led us onto the gunwale, around the windshield, and made us lie down on the foredeck with the windshield glass shielding us from the flames. We saw the young native deckhand dive overboard and start to swim for shore. He was never seen again. We tried yelling to the freighter to catch someone's attention, but that ship was dark and all hands must have been on the leeward side attending to its lading, so despite the fact our launch was ablaze, no one seemed to see us.

We thought we were surely lost. Suddenly we noticed a banana canoe paddling around the stern of the freighter straight for us. When it drew alongside we all jumped down into it, including the launch's captain. He said that there must have been a leak under the deck from a gasoline line, and a spark from the engine or wiring must have caused gasoline vapors to explode. I still think I had ESP or something supernatural to anticipate the exact moment of the explosion in my mind's eye. I pray there was no causal connection between my imagination and whatever caused that explosion.

When we got to the wharf we were lifted out of the canoe and taken straight to the Montego Bay hospital to be treated for our burns and broken eardrums. The following day the story with my wife's and my picture covered the entire front page of The New York Daily News. Past entreaties to keep my name out of the society columns were of no help to me then.

My Visit to Russia in 1959

Sol Hurok, a friend of my father's and a world-renowned impresario with connections in Eastern Europe, contacted him to explain that the Soviet Union was having a big fair in Moscow in the summer of 1959, and that he had been asked to try to interest a few high level VIPs from the United States to take the Intourist tour of Moscow and Leningrad. Hurok assured my father that he could line up some high-level meetings with Russian economic and foreign policy figures, since my father was a noted economist and the political figure behind my uncle's career in the United States Congress.

It was still the height of the cold war. America's policy of containment to counter Russia's imperialistic regional domination had been in effect for quite some time, and the Soviet effort to station intercontinental ballistic missiles in Cuba that threatened world peace would take place only a few years later. However, in the summer of 1959 there seemed to be an interest on the part of the Soviet leadership to ease tensions with the United States. Perhaps that was because the policy of containment was working to their detriment.

My parents decided to go to Russia, so I flew over to France where they were vacationing, and we flew to Moscow via Aeroflot in a plane that looked like a military transport. It was outfitted with hard bucket seats and khaki canvass webbing overhead to stow luggage. There was no service of any kind on board other than a stewardess in army uniform offering warnings to truthfully declare any currency that was being brought into the Soviet Union. At Sheremetyevo airport we went through customs without incident, and after being met by our Intourist guide we proceeded to the Hotel Ukraina in Moscow.

When we checked in we were escorted up to our floor. The newly-constructed hotel at the time was the tallest building in Moscow. The floors were uneven and of unfinished hardwood. The rooms were scantily decorated with bare walls and floors, a bed, a chair, a dresser and a mirror. My room was on a corridor at the end of which a dour woman in uniform sat at a desk. She was clearly one of the "watchers" assigned to keep track of tourists. However, she went off duty at 9 pm, and our Intourist guide would leave us after we had dinner and my parents retired. That was when I would wander out of the hotel in possession of a slip of a paper that read in Russian, "I am an

American tourist staying at the Ukraina Hotel. If I get lost please help me get back there."

I would walk the quiet avenues with identical ugly high-rise buildings on either side that stretched for miles without seeing a single person, until I worked up the nerve to enter one of the apartment towers. There were no elevators so I would walk up the stairs to an upper floor and wander around hoping to meet some Russians. I finally had to knock on some doors to attain my objective, show my note, and hope that someone might speak a little English and be willing to talk to me. I did meet some very sweet people that offered me tea and cakes and tried to talk to me in Russian. There were lots of smiles, hugs and good byes, but not much English.

While in Moscow, I managed to visit Max Frankel at his apartment to chat with him. Max, a classmate of mine at Columbia College who in time would win the Pulitzer Prize and become Executive Editor of the New York Times, was then serving as its Moscow correspondent. I was guarded in my conversation with Max, even though we were in the privacy of his apartment. I worried that it could have been bugged, just as I suspected my hotel room was compromised. We chatted about college days and a little about life back in the States and Max's career with the newspaper, but not much more.

I spent a few days touring, during which I went shopping at GUM, the only department store in Moscow. There I saw plenty of cheap and shoddy merchandise that was of no interest, but did I buy one item—a mink winter hat with ear muffs for $5 worth of rubles. Now, a half century later, I still wear it against the winter weather in Sweden.

My parents and I had wonderful seats at the Moscow circus and the Bolshoi Ballet, courtesy of Intourist. Then one sunny July afternoon we went to see the Red Square. Suddenly, in a matter of minutes the weather turned bitter. Hailstones the size of golf balls hammered the paving stones. We sought shelter in the Kremlin where we viewed its jewel collection. And when we emerged the July sun was shining once again.

After we had been in Moscow for a few days we were informed that we had been given an audience with Alexei Kosygin who was destined to become the Premier, but was then Minister of Economic Planning. A lot was going on in Moscow including joint meetings of the Russian and Chinese Ruling Bodies, as well as the Moscow fair at which there was an exhibition at the American Pavilion of the Levittown-style houses being built for average American families. It was there where the celebrated Nixon-Khrushchev kitchen debate took place.

When my father and I went to see Minister Kosygin in his Kremlin office his translator was present, but our Intourist guide was not permitted to be in the meeting, and for reasons that became evident as the meeting progressed.

Kosygin was very friendly and open with us. He told us that he was in charge of all production and economic planning for the Soviet Union, and he was intimately familiar with the American economy. He claimed he knew exactly how much tonnage of steel, coal, aluminum etc. was produced by us each year, and what the figures of every industry were. He said that he was familiar with some of the books that my father had written, and they discussed some of the ideas that my father had advanced in his book, "Peace by Investment". Kosygin explained that Communism was only an interim step in their evolution to a capitalist system, That I found hard to believe, and I said so. He replied that they were "bootstrapping" their economy under Communism, but that ultimately Russia would be more capitalistic than the US, and we would be more socialistic than they would be. "We will go like this," he said as much to my amazement he took both his arms and crossed them in the air.

He then asked why we were surrounding them on all sides with military bases. He said that was not what our relationship should be. I answered that America had never fought a war of aggression, that we would never initiate an attack on Russia, and that it was the USSR that had invaded their neighboring countries, had put up an "iron curtain" and were shooting unarmed people in the back that tried to escape from their domination. He reminded us that over the centuries Russia had been invaded from every direction, with the most recent being Napoleon and Hitler. He asked if we had visited the graveyards around their cities to see the millions of their countrymen who had died at the hands of invaders. I said we had not, and he urged us to take the time to do so to gain an understanding of why it was in their psyche to be paranoid. He claimed American bases in their "near abroad" was unnerving them. He then said, "And in any event, we will have to be allies again."

"Allies against whom?" I asked. "The Chinese, of course," he replied unequivocally.

I said, "How can you tell us, Americans whom you hardly know, that we will have to be your allies against the Chinese, when their leaders are here right now in Moscow meeting with your leaders as the closest of allies?"

He responded at length. "As you know, I am the Minister of Economic Planning, and as such I am responsible for all the foreign aid that we give. Every year I allocate the absolute maximum amount of foreign aid to the Chinese that I possibly can, and every year they demand more. They will never be satisfied. All along our border with China there are incursions, disputes and incidents. You think we are running a gulag in

Siberia and sending all our dissidents and political prisoners there. It is true we are trying to populate that area, but our primary purpose is to fill it up before they take it from us."

Our meeting seemed to have come to a close, so I asked if he would allow me to take his picture with the brand new Polaroid camera that I had brought with me from America. He said that would be his pleasure, but that they had the same camera, too. I expressed disbelief, but he went on to say, "We buy everything you make in the US as soon as it comes out, and of course we study the technology and copy it if it is useful."

With the taking of a few pictures and a final plea from Kosygin that the US and Russia had to get closer to each other by such programs as exchange students, expanded tourism and increased business contact and investment, the interview ended.

At the end of the week my parents and I were slated to proceed via Intourist from Moscow to Leningrad. I could not stand the sadness I saw on the faces of the Russian people, the stench of sulfur in the air from the burning of cheap coal, and the total absence of freedom that I encountered. So I let my parents go alone to Leningrad.

I flew back to East Berlin, landing at Tempelhof and passing through the Brandenburg Gate—the only exit from East Berlin to West Berlin. Upon my return to the United States, I never told anyone in our government what Kosygin had said because I thought it was all disinformation.

Solitron Devices, Inc.

Eventually, after about five years of matrimonial cases and slaving under the tutelage of Selig J. Levitan, a brilliant

Harvard Law alumnus who mercilessly redpenciled every document I drafted, I shifted to corporate work.

The year was 1960 when I got a chance to file my first registration statement in an initial public offering ("IPO") with the Securities and Exchange Commission. Solitron Devices, Inc. had just been founded by its President, Benjamin Friedman. The underwriter was Casper Rogers & Co. of which Casper Rogers, the principal, was better known as "Arky". Wilton Jaffee was the Deus ex Machina who promised to make the Solitron offering the most successful of any in the history of the over-the-counter stock business.

"Wink" Jaffee, as he was called, was a Wall Street maven who lived in Aspen, Colo. and aspired to be Secretary of Agriculture. Wink dictated the terms of the convertible subordinated debenture offering, and I was given the job of writing the registration statement for the first $400,000 principal amount of convertible debentures. Our legal fee was set by Wink at a modest $15,000, but he permitted me to buy 20,000 shares of the company's stock at $1 per share.

I quickly discovered that Solitron's President, Ben Friedman, was a very difficult and abrasive personality, and it took all my diplomatic skills to keep Ben Friedman calm and tractable. His brother, Dr. Abraham Friedman, served as Chairman of the Board of the company although he had virtually no say in any decisions. Abe was a very soft spoken and reasonable man who could not control his headstrong brother. The bonds were "called" soon after the offering was sold, which forced bondholders to either convert into common stock or take back their investment. Since they had invested in new technology not to get their money back with a little interest, but for the possible upside, they all converted to common stock that then slowly began to climb. I sold half of my shares at prices from $3 to $7, another 5,000 shares at around $10, and the last

5,000 shares around $20. The stock eventually hit $100 from which I learned another lesson. It does not matter if you don't make the "last dollar". Almost no one does and only foolish speculators might.

In 1963, after representing Ben Friedman and Solitron for three years, I blithely went on a summer trip to Europe, thinking I could enjoy some of my newly earned wealth, and that my partner, Harold Held, would be able to take care of Solitron Devices for that period of time. It was not to be. Ben Friedman was too difficult to handle, and while I was in Europe he fired our firm and hired another. That, too, was a valuable lesson for me. I realized a professional is simply a servant who gives service. If he fails to provide it even briefly he will be discarded like a used ticket stub.

Exploring Majorca

In 1963, Stephanie and I from Madrid flew to the island of Majorca, landing in Palma to spend some days at the Hotel Formentor situated on the Bay of the same name. Reinaldo Herrera of Caracas, the father of Reinaldo Jr. who later married the famous designer Carolina, was also there at the time. Reinaldo Sr. was a friend we knew from New York and Palm Beach, and we spent some pleasant time with him, his daughter and his son-in-law. Eating 'gambas a la playa' on the Formentor beach at sunset with an evening breeze wafting in from the bay remains an unforgettable memory.

One day we decided to rent a car and drive to Palma. On the way we passed through the little village of Luckmayor where two prominent artists we knew from Palm Beach, Channing Hare and his partner, had renovated an old villa sparing no expense. They had even drilled deep wells in that parched province to provide a water supply that also fueled their lovely fountains that sprayed continuously in the hot summer days.

Luckmayor had always been dirt dry, but now glorious fountains flowed not just on the artists' private estate, but also on the village's public square. The couple showed us around their renovated villa done to the highest standard of luxury with every modern plumbing and electrical convenience.

When we finally arrived in Palma, we parked the car and started to walk along the waterfront, eventually wending our way out onto the docks of the Palma Yacht Club where many beautiful motor and sailing yachts were moored. We passed one large motor yacht where a small group sat gathered on the fantail. We smiled at them and they said hello, so we introduced ourselves and struck up a conversation that ended with our being invited aboard.

The owner of the yacht was Angelo Rizzoli, a famous Italian film producer and founder of Rizzoli Publications, Italy's biggest publishers. With him was his girl friend, Ljuba, a Slavic beauty if ever there was one. Besides an amazing physique, one could not miss the enormous diamond ring she wore on her left hand. It almost covered two of her fingers.

Rizzoli asked if we would like to take a cruise around the island of Majorca to the Bay of Formentor and have lunch along the way. Of course we accepted, and about an hour later we were cruising in the Bay of Formentor, leaning on the railing and admiring the beauty of the island.

Our tranquil cruise was suddenly interrupted by Ljuba screaming that her diamond had slipped off her hand and dropped into the Bay. Rizzoli turned a bright shade of crimson that signaled he was about to explode, but he called for the captain to come down from the bridge to discuss what to do.

The yacht was still under full power while the captain came and spoke with Rizzoli. When Rizzoli asked if there was diving equipment on board the captain replied they had not taken it along because no one had expressed a desire to scuba dive. However, he said there was a Greek crewmember below in the engine room that used to dive for pearls and coral for his living. Rizzoli agreed it was worth a try to recover the ring, so he ordered the yacht to stop, reverse engines, and hope to get back to the approximate position where the ring fell into the Bay.

The yacht had gone at least a kilometer since the ring had fallen overboard, and I did not see how we would ever find a diamond on the sandy floor of the Bay since the diamond would be almost invisible under 60 feet of water. However, after what the captain judged was the right amount of reverse engine time, we again came to a stop, shut down the engines and anchored.

There appeared from below a short barrel-chested Greek, bare to the waist with a thick matting of body hair. He was wearing only pants and sandals. He kicked off the sandals and coolly dove over the side. Minutes went by. I could not believe that any human being could stay under water for such a length of time, when suddenly after at least 5 minutes, he appeared with the ring in hand! Ljuba was ecstatic with joy at having her ring back. Rizzoli was so angry that he hardly thanked the stoker. My guess is the poor devil never even received a reward, as Rizzoli's mood was so sour that he ordered the captain to immediately head back to Palma.

Lunch was served as we cruised back, but it certainly was not accompanied by much conversation. Back in Palma, we thanked Rizzoli for the cruise, but I never saw him or Ljuba again.

Indian Trail Ranch and Indian Trail Groves

Henry Ittleson Cohn was a soybean farmer from Louisiana and a member of the prominent Ittleson family that built CIT. In the immediate aftermath of World War II he travelled to Florida to scout out an enormous tract of raw everglade and swampland lying in Palm Beach County that measured ten miles by ten miles and covered 60,000 acres.

Cohn knew farming, and what he could grow. In addition, he was a visionary who foresaw that the population of Palm Beach, a small barrier island, could not grow; and that West Palm Beach, bounded by an inland waterway, could only grow westward. He believed that he could farm this tract until, eventually, growth westward would bring development onto the property.

Cohn was so enthused with the possibility of clearing and farming the land that in 1946 he was able to convince my father and Bill Zeckendorf, a New York real estate magnate, to join in the purchase of it for $26 per acre. Ben Javits shared his investment with each of our family trusts, and he allowed Jacob Javits' trust to participate equally as well.

Henry Cohn, with his son Hank Jr., began the ambitious task of clearing the 100 square miles of jungle and mangrove swamp. They named it Indian Trail Ranch after one of the dirt roads that led into it. They could only venture onto the property in four-wheel drive Jeeps, armed with shotguns and Colt .45 automatic sidearms. The area was a haven for alligators, snakes, deer, boars, bears and panthers.

Their first bivouac headquarters office was in an army surplus aluminum Quonset hut, the walls of which were decorated with

143

giant rattlesnakes they had shot. So wide were those skins that the rattlers must have had girths the size of a strong man's thigh.

First they cleared the land using bulldozers, one 640-acre section at a time. Then came the arduous work of digging drainage ditches and dikes to drain off the swamp water into an irrigation canal system.

Cohn quickly sold a large number of cleared sections to Lion Country Safari. Other cleared sections were sold to Lefcourt Realty that began the residential community development of Royal Palm Beach. Still more sections suitable for industrial development were sold to Pratt & Whitney Corporation.

Cohn's first effort at planting crops was to grow chlorophyll that was in great demand at the time as a breath freshening agent. When demand for that crop faded Cohn turned to growing tomatoes; but just as the first section of tomatoes was ripening on the vine, a devastating tropical hailstorm destroyed the entire crop.

Eventually, agricultural setbacks and disappointments forced Indian Trail Ranch to switch to raising and grazing cattle, as meat prices were rising sharply. I remember visiting the ranch and seeing an enormous herd of cattle tended by a dozen cowboys in typical western regalia, with lassoes coiled on their saddles. Unfortunately, that did not produce a profit either, so it was back to the drawing board for the partners to decide what to do with the property that had been retained.

Zeckendorf early on sold to Charles Allen, who along with Henry Ittleson Cohn's family, eventually sold out to Sam Friedland, the Chairman and founder of Food Fair, a supermarket chain that operated all over Florida.

Sam Friedland spoke with a heavy Jewish accent. He had started his career as a butcher, in the course of which he perfected the novel idea of not cutting meat to the customer's order, but precutting and packaging it in trays covered with plastic film, labeled with the weight and price, and then displaying it to best advantage. With that innovation, he was able to develop one of the most successful supermarket chains in America.

The final decision on what to do with the remaining property was made by Sam Friedland. He opted to plant citrus. Sam, with whom I had a close working relationship, had by then become the managing partner. So in the early 1960s a separate partnership called Indian Trail Groves, Ltd. was formed and limited partners bought units to provide the capital to plant four thousand acres of all types of citrus. Citrus fruit had to be planted in sand land, not in muck land, and the newly-planted orange and grapefruit trees needed five to seven years to mature before they would yield commercial quantities of fruit.

The partnership borrowed most of the money from an insurance company to prepare the land, plant the trees and build the drainage system needed to keep water levels in the sand below the root level of the trees, else the trees would die.

Sam was enormously rich and equally generous. When the citrus partnership required additional working capital, instead of calling on the limited partners to advance the funds, Sam Friedland advanced the needed funds and debited each partner's account for his or her pro rata share. Sam expected to be repaid only if and when a profit produced enough credit in each account, after which the limited partner would again begin to share in net profits.

Once it was discovered that farming the property was unprofitable, it was decided to sell off all the muck land to help pay for the citrus development. I had formed a warm friendship with the Fanjul family that had emigrated from Cuba to Palm Beach after Castro took power in 1960. I had met Pepe Fanjul earlier in New York while he was still a student in college, and later his brother, Alfie, and their parents in Palm Beach.

The Fanjuls had been sugar barons on the island of Cuba and hoped to replicate their business in Florida, but they needed a vast amount of muck land on which to grow sugar cane. I arranged for the sale to them of many sections of the finest muck land in the entire state. The muck was so rich with nutrients, that when there was a brushfire on the property, the muck itself would actually burn! In some places the rich black muck was many feet deep.

I conducted the negotiations with the Fanjul family, resulting in the sale of thousands of acres at $350 per acre with ten years to pay—on very generous terms and secured only by a mortgage on the land itself.

Years passed before Indian Trail Groves returned money to the limited partners, and that did not last for long, as the market for citrus weakened due to competition from growers in California, imports from Brazil, trees killed by freezing weather and blight, or trees reaching the age when their production of fruit declined.

Eventually a decision was reached to liquidate Indian Trail Ranch, Inc. A partnership was formed to run the liquidation and all the assets of the corporation were transferred to it, with Sam Friedland and Sam Stein as liquidating co-trustees. Not long thereafter, Sam Stein fell ill, and I succeeded him as liquidating co-Trustee. I performed that role for almost two decades until the entire liquidation was completed.

When in 2007, Sam's son-in-law, Irving Cowan and Jack Friedland, finally sold off the last four thousand acres of Indian Trail Groves, its former partners (still including our family) shared the all-cash purchase price of $37,500 per acre.

As a young lawyer with his father at Javits & Javits.

EMJ, age 69, at the net

CHAPTER VIII — HOPES FOR A POLITICAL CAREER

The history of how our family became Republican was, for me, quite instructive. My paternal grandfather, in addition to spending most of his time in the synagogue, also served as a ward heeler on the Lower East Side for the Democratic Party's Tammany Hall machine. On election days, Morris Javits would pay neighborhood voters $2 to buy their votes for Democratic candidates.

It was not surprising then, that having witnessed their father corrupting the electoral process by bribery, the Javits sons, inspired by Fiorello LaGuardia and Newbold Morris, were drawn into the Anti-Tammany reform movement. And in 1952, though most regular Republicans were supporting Senator Robert Taft of Ohio for the Republican nomination for President, my father and uncle were supporting Eisenhower who had led the Allied Forces to victory in Europe.

That June of 1952, less than one month after my twenty-first birthday, I graduated from Columbia College. While a student I had met Eisenhower, then President of Columbia University, as a result of my having served during my senior year as Chairman of the Columbia College's Board of Student Representatives.

When later that summer, Jack, Ben and I attended the Republican National Convention that was held in Chicago, we flew together from New York's LaGuardia airport to O'Hare airport in Chicago. On the plane with us was the handsome and debonair Douglas "Tex" McCrary. Tex had made his early fortune in the oil business in Texas, and then with his svelte and beautiful wife, former Miss America Jinx Falkenberg, he hosted the successful talk show "Tex and Jinx." By 1952, Tex McCrary, Inc. was one of America's most prestigious and powerful public relations firms.

Also on the plane with our group were Alfred Strelsin, head of Cenco Scientific; William Safire, who worked for Tex's public relations firm; and David Karr, a controversial mystery man and public relations guru. Two of the Republican Party's largest Republican contributors—John Hay Whitney and Alfred Gwynn Vanderbilt, were also part of our small group that was determined to wrest the presidential nomination away from Senator Taft, who led the conservative wing of the Republican Party and who seemingly had the party's nomination virtually "locked".

"Jock" Whitney was a charismatic socialite, a serious intellectual, a wealthy investment banker and a close friend of my uncle. He was a key figure in Republican finance circles who considered himself a "liberal' Republican like Jack Javits who was liberal with respect to the role of government in such areas as housing, education, equal job opportunity and non-discrimination, but conservative on fiscal policy and defense.

Alfred Vanderbilt was another elegant social patrician of the first order. He was an exceedingly handsome and private man of vast wealth who maintained his office next to our law firm's offices on the twentieth floor of Rockefeller Center's International Building. Both my father and I consequently knew him well and saw him often. He, too, was a close friend and supporter of Jack Javits.

On arriving in Chicago, none of us had been able to get advance hotel reservations. Somehow, despite the impossibility of booking hotel rooms unless one was a Taft supporter, we managed to check into the famed Palmer House Hotel. My father hired a limousine and driver to be at our disposal to shuttle us back and forth to the convention hall. The week-long Republican convention took place in the middle of a sizzling hot summer in what was known as the Cow Palace where, instead of stockyards filled with cattle, all the seating, banners, bunting and regalia of a political get together had been installed.

One had to have convention credentials to even get into the cavernous arena. Fresh air certainly had no credentials, and smoking was commonplace and fashionable. Since there was no air conditioning, one could scarcely breathe or see for the smoke. I could not fathom how Eisenhower's forces managed to break open the tight Taft control of the Credentials Committee to allow our whole group to be credentialed; but even I wound up with an official badge that gained me admittance, not just to the Cow Palace balconies in the rafters, but to the Convention floor so that I could lobby delegates seated there!

Two brothers from New England, Sen. Henry Cabot Lodge of Massachusetts and Governor John Davis Lodge of Connecticut, were leading the Eisenhower assault and coordinating its forces. Both were dashingly attired in double-breasted bespoke white sharkskin suits. In those days if you had to urgently find someone amidst that huge mass of humanity, and you could not spot him in the crowd on the convention floor, it was hopeless. There were no cell phones or paging devices. But those two white suits stood out in that sea of humanity on the convention floor, so the Lodge brothers could always be spotted and kept in touch.

I got my first taste of political infighting in Chicago where the outcome still depended, not on state presidential primary contests, but on the "boys" in the smoke-filled back room. Despite the political theatre and the roles they played on its stage, I remained unaware of the machinations that went on behind the scenes. The experience of observing General Eisenhower's sheer popularity rolling back the tide on the convention floor until the weight of numbers overwhelmed the "backroom" deliberations of the party's power brokers allowed me to remain naïve and idealistic. The lesson that I took away from Chicago was that with a righteous cause and honorable motives, a popular insurgent could upend an entrenched incumbent.

That fall I entered my first year of law school, and at the same time I started to attend meetings of the New York Young Republican Club—a group of younger professionals that met once a month. The Club was divided into two factions—conservatives and liberal/moderates. I was in the liberal/moderate group. The other more conservative faction was led from behind the scenes by conservatism's legendary intellectual guru, Bill Rusher, and it had a very ideological agenda. There also was an older group of Young Republican alumni led by former United States Attorney General, Herbert Brownell, who still kept their membership. I eventually rose in the ranks to become a Vice President of the club, but never sought to be its President.

After graduating from law school, I continued my political activity by joining the Ninth Assembly District Republican Club that was located on East 83rd street, just a few blocks from our apartment on Fifth Avenue. I regularly attended the club's meetings, and at election time I served as a Republican captain to canvass for votes and distribute political material in our apartment building.

In 1958 I was asked to manage State Senator MacNeil Mitchell's campaign for re-election to the NY state senate from Manhattan's "silk stocking" district that took in most of the East side from 110th street down to parts of Greenwich Village. "Mac" Mitchell had been in office for more than two decades and was one of the longest serving and most powerful senators in the upper house of the NY legislature. Because his pluralities had been diminishing with each election, Mitchell was worried about getting re-elected. I agreed to run his campaign and Mitchell won—though by an unimpressive margin.

As a way of thanking me, Mitchell offered me the position of Counsel to the Affairs of the City of New York Committee of which he was Chairman. I decided to accept the job that would take me up to the state capitol in Albany one day a week to work in Mitchell's office. My duties would be to screen all legislation dealing with NYC and generally push any of "Mac's" pet projects that needed to be nudged along in legislative channels. Sen. Mitchell was also Chairman of the NY Senate Committee on Housing, so I was asked to assist its Counsel who was a full-time member of Mitchell's staff.

The Republicans, led by Senator Walter Mahoney, the Republican leader of the Senate, controlled the NY State Senate, and they comprised a very tight and firmly knit group. Joe Carlino was the leader of the Assembly, but Mahoney was clearly the "boss".

In those days, being young and idealistic, eager to get experience in state government and to do some public service, I did not want to feel like a party hack. So in negotiating the terms of my employment with Sen. Mitchell, I asked if I could hold the counsel job as an unpaid volunteer. The answer was an unmitigated no. He said there were no interns or volunteers working in the State legislature, and there would be no exceptions.

The first day I reported for work in Albany I was immediately sent to see Senator Mahoney who tried to make me feel in that five minute meeting like I was being granted a great boon to be able to earn about $10,000 for the three-month legislative session in which I would have to spend only one day a week in Albany. I already had in mind, but kept to myself, giving all the money that I earned to charity so that I could truthfully claim that I had not profited from Republican Party patronage.

So in the ensuing weeks, upon receiving my paychecks, I endorsed them to Catholic Charities, Federation of Jewish Philanthropies, Protestant Charities, the Red Cross and the Community Chest and sent them on as contributions, rather than depositing them in my own bank account.

After about two months Senator Mahoney summoned me to his office where he read me the riot act. He had heard of the return of the State's cancelled checks bearing endorsements showing I had given the money to charity, and he guessed what I intended was at some point to criticize the Republican legislature's patronage system. I refused to cower and stood my ground. I insisted it was my money, and our party should be proud that its members would support needy causes.

At the end of that year, Senator Mitchell asked me to continue serving during the next year, but I had no interest in continuing. I had become aware of how blatantly he was using his political positions to get law business. In fact, I came to view his behavior as typical of the unethical conduct of many of the Senators and Assemblymen of both parties serving in Albany. I kept my views to myself. I did not see any advantage to be gained in expressing this to MacNeil Mitchell, as I did not think he was going to change after more than twenty-five years in the New York State Senate.

Beginning in 1959 I started to work on a book about the City of New York. I had joined Citizens Union and the Citizens Budget Commission, both of which studied the issues of city life and the city budget. They also made policy recommendations and candidate selections. Consequently, I had become aware of, and familiar with, the mismanagement and problems that faced the city. One had only to look around to realize the dirt, crime, danger and discomfort for the average New Yorker. I had come to the inescapable conclusion that the city would go broke if it did not put in place a number of fiscal reforms, and that it needed many other improvements to make it livable so families would again return to urban life with their children.

My research was extensive, and with the generous help of my father's executive assistant, Gary Fairmont Filosa, I drafted a plea for action that would be entitled "SOS New York: A City in Distress!" I would work at the Javits law firm from 8:30 a.m. until 6 p.m. before returning to our apartment. Quite often Stephanie and I would go out for the evening, returning by midnight. I would try to get a couple of hours of sleep, then get up in the early hours of the morning and write for an hour or two. I would go back to bed for another few hours before the alarm clock would ring at 7 a.m.

Finally in early 1961, I had a completed draft and began looking for a publisher. My father had a friend in Palm Beach who agreed to look at the book and give advice. He read it and said that he thought George Delacorte, founder and head of Dell Publishing, might like to publish it since it was a crusading book to rally public support for improving New York. George Delacorte did like it, and he sent the book to Richard Baron, then editor-in-chief of Dial Press, who agreed to publish it.

In 1961 "SOS New York" came out to good reviews. I began to think about a political career for myself. I had turned thirty, had already made a substantial amount of money, and had been notified that I was to be listed in the next edition of Who's Who. With my three lofty goals achieved, I was still unsure about when to embark on my political career because my uncle had strongly cautioned me not to think about entering politics until I had made my name and reputation in the private sector.

So once again I sought his advice. Jack tried to discourage me from starting so soon. He told me he thought I needed more experience in the private sector and in my profession, and that I was still young enough to wait before getting into politics. I did not want to heed his advice. I was headstrong with fire in my belly, and I wanted to show my mettle in Congress or the State Senate.

Once Jack saw that I was determined to embark on a political career he recommended that I ask for the Republican nomination to run for Congress up in Harlem. I felt following his advice would mean a certain loss in my first attempt at public office. I also felt it was not a serious suggestion, and that he was just "brushing me off". I could not understand why he and Governor Rockefeller would not want an infusion of young blood in the Republican Party in New York State. Certainly, I was no threat to them. On the contrary, my goal was to be strongly supportive. In retrospect, I see that attitude as not unusual for incumbents who hold office. They are not eager for new blood or new talent to mount the stage. Why breed potential challengers to their safe and comfortable incumbencies?

I guess I inherited a bit of my father's and uncle's rebellious reform gene because in 1964 I decided to try to knock off my old friend "Mac" Mitchell in a Republican primary contest for the State Senate nomination in 1964 since it seemed unlikely that I would be offered a nomination where I would have any chance of getting elected.

I studied the Board of Elections voting results of the previous four or five elections in those assembly districts comprising the state senatorial district. They showed a continuous decline in support for Mitchell. That led me to conclude that he would probably lose the general election in 1964 if he were once more the Republican Party's candidate.

I began to assemble a comprehensive research study on all the organizations and sources of potential support in his senatorial district—a district that was comprised of three assembly districts. I did this quietly so as not to arouse any suspicion of what I might be planning and discussed the idea only with my father. Nor did I seek anyone's support for the same reason.

By the beginning of 1964 I told my father that I had definitely decided to run against Mitchell in the Republican primary election, and he did not try to dissuade me. He helped me financially by contributing personally, raising money for my campaign and getting one of his friends to let me use rent-free his vacant town house on East 56th street, just off 5th Avenue, as my campaign headquarters.

Mike Freyberg, my classmate from Columbia, agreed to be my campaign manager. A very strong finance committee was formed to help raise the necessary funds. There was plenty to do before primary election day, and little time in which to do it; but hundreds of friends and volunteers turned out to canvass, host fundraising parties, distribute literature and staff the headquarters.

Then suddenly in the midst of the campaign I was called to appear at the office of the District Attorney of NYC that was conducting an investigation of corruption and bribery in the State Liquor Authority. I had drawn the wills for two friends—Seymour and Dorothy Alter—who had been married a couple of years earlier. Sy Alter was part owner and manager of a boutique liquor store in Manhattan that had been delivering cases of wine and liquor to an elite clientele on credit, a practice not permitted by New York State law. Once that became known, the store was ordered closed by the State Liquor Authority, and Sy turned to me for help.

Never having had any experience in that area of the law, and having heard rumors about the SLA being a corrupt agency, I asked around to try to get the name of an honest and reputable lawyer to represent Sy Alter, and the liquor store he managed. I was given the name of a young attorney who had graduated from Columbia Law School. I gave the reference to Alter with the understanding that I would not have any continuing responsibility in the matter. I made it clear to both Alter and the young lawyer that I therefore did not want and would not accept a forwarding fee. I suggested to both that the correct procedure I thought should be followed was to sue the State Liquor Authority on a writ of quo warranto which is an extraordinary legal procedure asking the court by what right had the Authority acted, in the hopes that a court would find the closing of the store excessive and approve only a monetary fine accompanied by an injunction prohibiting it from selling on credit thereafter.

When I appeared at the office of the District Attorney, I explained this to David A. Goldstein, the Assistant District Attorney who interviewed me. I thought that would be the end of it. Unfortunately, it was not. I was served with a subpoena to appear before the Manhattan Grand Jury to give testimony against the Chairman of the State Liquor Authority who was rumored to have been the subject of a bribe attempt by the young lawyer representing Alter's liquor store.

On the advice of my father, I consulted with a criminal lawyer, Moses Kove, who was reputed to be one of the most able and respected criminal lawyers in New York. He advised me to ask for immunity from prosecution in exchange for testifying to the Grand Jury on all matters concerning my participation other than the truthfulness of my testimony. In retrospect, his advice was probably motivated by the fact I was a political rebel in the midst of vying for my party's nomination against an entrenched and powerful establishment incumbent who could easily get behind-the-scenes help to destroy a young opponent.

However, I told Kove that since I had done nothing wrong and intended to testify truthfully, I could see no reason to ask for immunity from prosecution on any count. Moe Kove stated he had given me his advice; but if that was my decision, so be it.

When I was sworn in to give my testimony I did not ask for immunity from prosecution. I told the Grand Jury that I had given Alter the reference to the young lawyer, but had played no part in the case except at one point I had been asked by Alter to come to a lunch meeting he had scheduled with his young attorney because of a disagreement between them to see if I could smooth it over. I did go to the meeting, but before even ordering lunch I heard what I thought was reference to a disagreement about money to be paid to someone not named. So I stood up and said to them both that I wanted no part in this matter, nor would I try to mediate anything between them. With that I walked away from the table and left the restaurant.

The Grand Jury's indictment of the Authority's Chairman eventually came down and was published. I was not named as a co-conspirator, nor was my name mentioned in the indictment. It seemed that disregarding Kove's advice had not disadvantaged me.

That should have been the end of the matter. However, the trial of the Chairman was scheduled for a Monday in June, well before primary election day. At the opening of the trial, District Attorney Frank Hogan's Deputy gave the opening statement. In it he mentioned me by name as having introduced the case to the young attorney despite the fact *my* name was not mentioned in the indictment.

With that all hell broke loose with the media asking me about my role since I was a highly publicized candidate for public office. I could never make the questions go away no matter how many times I appeared before the cameras and microphones. Marian Javits made no bones about the fact she opposed my candidacy to many friends and acquaintances privately, and I suspected, as was her practice, that she made her views known in the most uncomplimentary terms. Many years later my suspicions were confirmed when Joseph X. Dever, a journalist who wrote a social column for the NY World Telegram and Sun, told me that Marian had been an outspoken opponent during my primary fight, deprecating me to her friends, including him. I was not surprised to hear that. Marian was always fiercely jealous of Stephanie's youth and beauty and the attention that it attracted. She wanted no other Javits on the New York political scene, especially one with a more beautiful wife who might challenge her lofty position as *the* "Mrs. Javits"

Election day finally came, and although I carried the two assembly districts on the upper and middle part of Manhattan—the Ninth and the Eighth—I lost by a ten-to-one margin in the First Assembly District that covered the lower part of the Senatorial district. The primary election voting disparity was not hard to understand. Mitchell was the Republican District leader for that assembly district. He led a powerful clubhouse there with many members. He had been a state senator for 24 years. He had dispensed patronage and wielded party leadership in that area that entire time. That I lost by such an overwhelming margin in the First Assembly District easily overcame my lead in the two uptown assembly districts. Thus, I tasted defeat for the first time in my life.

I was stunned, saddened and forced to reconsider what to do with my life. $90,000 had been spent in my campaign, much of which was my and my father's money. In Mitchell's First Assembly District the firemen and police were at the polling places telling people how to vote for Mitchell, and in some cases even pulling the levers for them. There was no point in complaining about it. The press and the public would have taken it as griping by a sore loser.

What goes around comes around, and just as I predicted, Mitchell was defeated in the general election that fall by Fred Berman, an unknown young Democrat running for public office for the first time.

After the votes were tallied that night I did some hard thinking. The conclusion I reached was that I would never run for office again. It was too dirty, too dependent on money and on demonizing one's opponent. Altruism and idealism were not enough in politics. Maybe for General Eisenhower they were enough, but not for me. My father was also disappointed, but he said to me, "From defeat one gains greater strength and resolve to wage other battles".

My desire for politics, money or fame was past. I resolved to return to the practice of law, redouble my efforts to distinguish myself at the bar and look for some other means and opportunity to do public service.

A few years later, David Goldstein left the Manhattan DA's office to join our law firm as a litigator. He was a thorough and tenacious attorney who became a good friend and partner, and we had much fun working on many challenging cases together. Eventually David left our firm to work as a single practitioner. Many years went by during which we would see each other from time to time.

Then one day David confessed to me that he could never understand why, instead of following the usual procedure of the office which would have been to immediately accept the guilty plea on Friday and cancel the trial set to start on Monday, the prosecution had insisted on beginning the trial of the Liquor Authority Chairman on Monday morning by giving the opening statement to the jury (in which my name was mentioned) and only then accepting the guilty plea to cancel the trial.

It seemed to me there was only one reason for giving an opening statement in a trial that should have been cancelled three days earlier. That would be to ensure press mention of my name in the middle of my primary fight against a powerful political incumbent. The press would certainly have covered the news of a guilty plea from so prominent a defendant in any event, except my name would not have been in the story.

Sometime later, when I reminded Dave of what he had said, he denied that he had said it. I was not surprised that he would not want me to suspect what might have been a political favor done for Senator Mitchell by District Attorney Frank Hogan's office.

CHAPTER IX — LEGAL CAREER AND LIFE INTERTWINED — CONTINUED

Ivan Boesky

Ivan Boesky will be forever etched in the annals of financial infamy for his flagrant trading on inside information and for informing on Wall Street icon Michael Milken. I met Boesky in 1966 through Henry van Dam, a fellow member of the City Athletic Club who was Ivan's insurance broker. Ivan had asked Henry to recommend an attorney to represent him and his wife, Seema, in the purchase of a large Park Avenue cooperative apartment. As a result of Henry's recommendation, I was retained to handle the matter.

After the co-op purchase was successfully closed, Ivan phoned me at my law office to thank me for the work I had done. He went on to explain that he was about to leave his present employer to start his own arbitrage firm that would be called Threadneedle. He hinted that I could do some legal work for that firm, but he expected me to be "helpful". He explained that he knew I represented a number of publicly-traded companies, and if I would let him know when material events were about to happen, he would show his appreciation by paying me retainers later in other matters that were unrelated to those companies. I replied "Ivan, I sell legal services. I do not sell inside information. Your apartment closing will be the last work I do for you. We will never again have dealings with each other."

That was the last I saw or heard from Ivan Boesky. I never spoke of his unethical proposal until many years later in the '80s after he had publicly confessed to securities fraud and insider trading. In intervening years when I read of the financial success he enjoyed and the acclaim that was lavished on him for his "incisive market acumen", I knew the truth but the ethics of my profession deterred me from speaking about my former client and why I had fired him.

Creating Decent Black Housing

Long after World War II, blacks in West Palm Beach, Florida continued to live only in ghettos consisting of shacks and hovels. Everywhere in the deep south of the United States discrimination in housing could be seen from the street with the naked eye. Disrepair, neglect, and peeling paint were rampant in what the black and white communities referred to then as "colored town."

Carl Brukenfeld and his wife Helen were very dear friends of my parents, and they could always be seen at each other's parties, or out for evenings at the Patio or some other restaurant for dinner. Carl, who could swear like a trooper and often did, owned much of Worth Avenue—the town's choicest luxury shopping street that on its own had become a tourist destination. Helen Brukenfeld, who had a wry sense of humor and a heart of gold, was also a force to be reckoned with in Palm Beach. Their son, Richard, and their daughter, Jane, who was born much later, were friends of mine. Jane was nicknamed "Honey" and she was as effervescent and adorable as Shirley Temple. She never lost her childhood looks or charm as she morphed into Baby Jane, an icon of the Jet Set in the 1960s.

Carl Brukenfeld had a nose for making money, and he thought that there was money to be made in building decent housing for middle-class blacks in West Palm Beach. He started a small private company with Herbert Ralston called Equity Commercial Realty Corporation, and invited Ben Javits to join them as a partner. Ralston had some construction and business experience, and he and Brukenfeld were certain a market existed for responsible working black families wanting to live in well-built housing on a nicely-landscaped plot with Federal Housing Authority financing if the neighborhood was well maintained.

In the early '60s, they started first to build along Palm Beach Lakes Boulevard, and as they built and sold out their lots, they had to go further north around Blue Heron Boulevard in Riviera that was far removed from what was then referred to as "colored town", a run-down section of West Palm Beach. I went on the Board of Directors of Equity Commercial Realty quite soon after it was formed, and although I did not play much of a role in the company, I was proud to be involved in a valiant enterprise that was offering well-built middle-class black housing at $12,000-$15,000 per home with only $1,200-$1,500 down and a low rate of interest on a long term mortgage.

Downe Communications, Inc.

As years went by, my second client's mail order business grew. Ed Downe was incredibly astute in picking what items to sell by mail, and in buying advertising or bartering for space to promote his products. One day in 1966 he asked me to accompany him to Chicago to meet with the owner of Family

Weekly, a Sunday newspaper supplement distributed throughout the United States in which Ed had been advertising heavily, and that Ed wanted to acquire. When Ed and I met with the Publisher the meeting that began on a friendly note turned less than friendly when Ed and the Publisher got into a heated exchange. I could see the hoped-for acquisition going south, so I intervened and diplomatically pleaded to both of them to calm down. Ed credits my smoothing things over with the Publisher for his closing the deal on advantageous terms, an assessment I find too generous. Ed's plan was to combine his various assets and companies under the name Downe Communications, Inc. (DCI), and to acquire cable and broadcasting properties. In fact he acquired over 25 magazines including Ladies' Home Journal and American Home from the Curtis Publishing Company as well as the magazine group that included True Love, True Romance, True Experience, Motion Picture, Photoplay, Sport, Pageant and others.

The DCI initial public offering came out in 1968. It was very successful at its nominal offering price, but the market price quickly rose with Ed making acquisitions using DCI stock. He consummated the acquisition of Ladies Home Journal and American Home for $5.4 million in DCI stock, and also eventually acquired from McFadden/Bartell the Bartell Media assets that included several small cable systems and three AM radio stations including WADO in New York and WOKY in Milwaukee. He went on to acquire 3 FM stations and a number of larger cable systems including Canton, Ohio and Joplin, Missouri, Jules Jurgensen Watch Company, Jacquet Cosmetics, Hamilton Mint and the computer fulfillment operations of Look Magazine.

I served as a member of DCI's board of directors and was also its Secretary and General Counsel. After the stock split, I owned 60,000 shares. I never sold a single share as the price went up to $120 because Ed implored me not to, arguing that if an insider sold it would look to the public like it was time to unload. And as I recall, neither did Ed.

While the stock was rising, I felt quite rich so I bought a potato field in Southampton and began to build my country home with money borrowed from banks. Then the stock's market price declined from $120.00 all the way down to under $10.00. Control of Downe Communications eventually was sold to the Charter Company. That taught me a valuable lesson about the importance of being debt free and spending only the cash one has on hand. It took me many years to pay off the loan that had seemed no problem when I was building Las Casitas.

The Lauder Family

Estée Lauder and her husband, Joe, used to spend the winters in the '50s in Palm Beach, and they were very close friends of my parents. Estée and Joe were always invited to the parties at our house on Palmo Way, and my mother would boast about Estée's dogged devotion to her cosmetic business that she was building from nothing. Our mother thought it heroic of Estée to travel around the country to spend time behind the counter in department stores with the sales girls, teaching them how to sell and educating them about her products.

At the time, I thought that was a waste of time and energy for an independently wealthy businesswoman, but Estée's husband was her ever-patient idolizer, and he condoned whatever Estée did. So Estée would disappear on the road for long periods of time, and there were no complaints from him.

I eventually met their son, Leonard, and his wife Evelyn as a result of the family friendship. At that time Leonard was just starting to get into his mother's business. Leonard told me that their firm had decided to build a factory to produce their own products instead of continuing to use contract manufacturers as they had from the outset. Since I was a young attorney and a family friend, Leonard told me that I could do the legal work on their new plant that would be erected close to the Long Island Expressway about an hour out of New York City, and I was happy to get involved with a new client.

Soon thereafter I decided to invite Leonard and Evelyn to dinner. It was heartening to see how gracious and warm they were as a couple. They reciprocated with an invitation for Stephanie and me, and that evening during dinner Leonard explained that they had a plan to start a whole family of separate companies around different product trade names that would permit them to diversify not just their business, but spread its ownership around to younger members of the family to avoid crippling estate tax problems.

When we had finished a delicious meal and were ready to leave the table, Leonard asked me to accompany him to his bathroom. I was puzzled, but he said he wanted to show me something—to test my reaction, and to get my advice. When we got to the bathroom he took the stopper out of a small test-tube shaped vial and asked me to smell the scent that emerged, explaining that it was for a man's aftershave and cologne. It was a most agreeable and seductive aroma. I told him I liked it better than the one I used that had a smell of leather. He said that they were planning to name the new product Aramis, and would build a line of men's products around the name and the scent. When the Lauder firm needed patent and trademark counsel, I recommended Blum Moscovitz, Friedman, Blum and Kaplan, the law firm that Javits & Javits used for that specialized area of the law.

Some years later, in the early '70s when I was the General Counsel and Secretary for Downe Communications, Inc. that had bought a company in the cosmetic business, I got a call from Harold Kaplan, one of the top partners of the Blum Moscovitz law firm. He lamented that their firm found itself in a terrible predicament. He said that Estee Lauder had asked them to clear the trade name Clinique for use as a trade name. He told me their office had looked up all the registered names and had not found it as having been registered, so they had given Lauder the green light to go ahead and use the name. Kaplan explained that the Clinique line was going to be launched in about a month nationwide and all the packaging materials and advertising had been ordered and was not cancelable. Their law firm had only recently discovered that the Clinique name had been used on a product that had been sold without the name being registered in the Patent Office, but the use had established a common law trademark, and if Lauder went ahead with its launch they would be infringing that mark. He said his firm was terribly embarrassed and would be facing a malpractice suit unless something could be done to buy the rights to use the name. Since they had learned that the trade name Clinique was owned by Downe Communications of which I was General Counsel, they hoped I could help them in their predicament.

I said I would talk to Ed Downe and ask him to accommodate Leonard Lauder by selling the name to them. I explained to Ed that Leonard and his family were intimate friends of my family, and I brought Ed and Leonard together to try and arrange the sale of the Clinique mark for a fair price. Ed did so, and that was the beginning of a strong friendship between Ed and Leonard Lauder. Leonard was grateful for the favor, despite the fact that the price was the highest that had ever been paid up to that time for a common law trademark. And Blum Moskovitz, quite understandably, was enormously relieved.

There are few times in life that one can act as a trusted intermediary between two friends, and in the process do a favor for another. I felt gratified that outcome was a rare win-win for all, and no one felt unfairly treated.

City Investing Company

In 1965 our law firm had a client with a sizeable holding of shares in City Investing Company, a publicly-held New York Stock Exchange company that owned French & Company, a storied art and antiques dealer, and prime New York City real estate on Madison Avenue in which Parke Bernet's offices and auction room were located. Its Chairman and President, Robert Dowling, was a patrician figure of prominence in the business world, and although the company's net worth and market value were under $20 million, the City Investing Company and Dowling's stature loomed far larger than that.

Our client, Ernst Wolff, was an immigrant from Switzerland with a rotund physique and a "Gnome of Zurich's" brain. His wife, Ilsa, was not just a beautiful woman and a good mother to their daughters, she was aristocratic in her bearing and a shrewd businesswoman to boot. Ernst was part of a group of dissident stockholders whom he brought to our law office to discuss working together to make their holdings in City Investing more valuable. They selected my father to represent them because of his fame as a proxy fighter; but Robert Dowling's stature and clout caused the group to eventually conclude that trying to unseat Dowling would be an expensive and failed strategy; and even were it to succeed, it would not enhance their share values as much as if a new and stronger manager were to become President of the company.

City Investing had underlying financial and real estate assets worth far more than its book value reflected. The group scouted around looking for a candidate to lead the company, and eventually identified George Scharffenberger. Scharffenberger had been a rising young executive at ITT, and the group felt that if he could take over the operations of City Investing it would realize its underlying values. Conversations with Scharffenberger resulted in his willingness to take the job if it were offered. The conundrum was how to make this happen in the face of a supreme egotist like Dowling who would not want to lose control of "his" company.

City Investing Company had Davis Polk & Wardwell as their legal counsel. Davis Polk was one of Wall Street's most able and influential law firms. The partner in charge of the City Investing account was Walter Fletcher, an alumnus of Columbia College and a member of the Nacom Society whom I had befriended while I was an undergraduate. Walter had even attended the ceremony when I was inducted into that senior honor society at the end of my junior year.

I suggested to my father and Ernst Wolff that I might be able to ask Walter Fletcher to have lunch with me without stating any reason whatever, as he regarded me as a young friend and sometime protégé. I explained that I could use the luncheon to try out on Walter the idea of Dowling having a younger, capable executive come on board as his Vice-President to help him realize values of the company, and in that way avoid a proxy battle with a group of dissident stockholders that we represented.

When the lunch did take place, I assured Walter that if Dowling were willing to accept that modest help, the dissidents would be patient and allow him at least a year to evaluate the new man, and Dowling could pass the mantle only when he felt ready to do so. I told him about George Scharffenberger, and predicted that Dowling would like him as a person and feel comfortable with him as his ally and successor.

Walter agreed to try to convince Dowling to accede to the offer instead of forcing City Investing into a proxy battle. He called a few days later and said that Dowling had agreed to meet Scharffenberger in his office for an interview. The problem was that we had to convince George Scharffenberger to sign on as vice-president for a one-year trial where his promotion to President would depend entirely on Dowling willingness to step aside. We argued that Dowling's decision could be facilitated once George won Dowling's confidence, and so long as Dowling could remain Chairman of the Board.

Not much time was needed for the deal to be consummated before Scharffenberger went to work at City Investing. Within a year he was elected President with Dowling's blessing and the company scored a succession of acquisitions. In 1967 it acquired Hayes International Corp., American Electric, Inc. and Southern Financial Corporation. It also increased its ownership of General Development Corporation to 49 percent. In 1968 it purchased Rheem Manufacturing, ZD Products, Inc., Motel 6, Inc., World Color Press and the Home Insurance Company. It continued to grow under Scharffenberger's able hand and eventually was liquidated in 1984.

Saving LTV from bankruptcy

The LTV Corporation got its start in 1947 as a small Dallas-based company in electrical construction and engineering called Ling Electric Company, named after its founder, James J. "Jimmy" Ling. It grew through acquisitions and mergers throughout the 1950s— taking in such companies as Altec Electronics and the Temco Electronics & Missile Company. It continued on the prowl in the '60s, picking up Chance Vought Aircraft in an initially unfriendly takeover in 1961 to become known as Ling-Temco-Vought; and then picking up Wilson Foods in 1967 that it split into three companies—Wilson Meats,

Wilson Sporting Goods and Wilson Pharmaceuticals. In 1965 its sales were only $36 million, but by 1969 they were almost $4 billion. It used borrowed money to make acquisitions as its stock price rose. Eventually it acquired Okonite, a wire and cable manufacturer; National Car Rental; Braniff Airways; some insurance companies; and a majority interest in Jones & Loughlin Steel Company headquartered in Pittsburgh. Ling-Temco-Vought soon changed its name to LTV.

Jimmy Ling by that time had exhausted the credit of his company in making all those acquisitions, the conglomerate's combined earnings were disappointing, and its debts were mounting. Compounding the problem was the acquisition binge had triggered an investigation by the U.S. Department of Justice's Anti-Trust Division that sought an injunction to force the sale of either a) Okonite and Braniff or b) Jones & Loughlin Steel Company.

LTV was a jewel in the crown of Dallas, Texas, and it sat proudly on the head of the city's favorite son, Jimmy Ling. He had a wide group of fans and devotees in Dallas and around the country, but the economy went into decline in 1969, and shares that had sold a couple of years earlier at $167 were selling for $11. Arnold and Porter, the eminent Washington law firm, defended LTV vigorously in the federal courts, but eventually the company had to enter into a consent decree whereby it agreed to sell either Okonite and Braniff or Jones & Loughlin Steel Company by a firm deadline. And the deadline was imminent. Its petition to extend the deadline had been denied, and LTV could not complete the required divestitures in time.

It was against that background that I got a call from James Ryan, a brilliant and charming fellow, who knew LTV's President, Paul Thayer, and Paul Jennings, his then VP. He told me that he had recommended Thayer to retain me to try to get the consent decree modified to relax the deadline and to allow the sale of just Okonite without the sale of either Braniff or Jones & Loughlin. He told me that he had argued that since Arnold and Porter, the powerhouse Washington law firm had failed, only a low profile person who did not use political clout could stand a chance in softening the Justice Department's Anti-Trust Chief, Richard McLaren, an enthusiastic trust-buster, whose enmity for Ling had already resulted in removing Ling from the LTV board. Ryan said he told Paul Thayer I fit the description perfectly of what LTV needed.

I told Ryan I would be interested in meeting Thayer. The next day Thayer and Jennings flew up to New York from Dallas to discuss LTV's predicament. They told me that if they did not get the permission to sell Okonite to Jimmy Ling's new company that he had recently formed, LTV would have to file for bankruptcy in just one week. I said I would need a day to decide if I would take the case. I quickly did some research, consulted with my former anti-trust professor, Milton Handler, who felt there was nothing more that could be done legally. It was too late and had gone too far. The only chance was if the Anti-Trust Division would agree to allow a change in the consent decree. I called Thayer and told him he should send me a retainer, and I would go immediately to Washington to meet with Richard H. McLaren, the head of the Anti-Trust Division.

My meeting with Richard McLaren was one I will never forget. The United States Department of Justice is housed in an impressive building in Washington, and its interior is as cold and formal as its marble floors and unwelcoming elevators. I was ushered into a sparely-furnished and unimpressive office of modest size. McLaren greeted me graciously. He clearly was not intent on impressing me as he took his seat behind his desk and motioned for me to take the one in front of it. He struck me as a serious, business-like crusader with impressive intellect and legal skills. He had a fit physique, handsome features and not a trace of vindictiveness or malice in his expression or body language.

I told him that, despite his winning the consent decree and divestiture order, I felt his objectives with LTV had only partially been met. I thought he had wanted to 1) save the company by forcing it to a divestiture that would enable it to pay down debt (and that was failing for lack of time to find willing buyers), and 2) purge all baneful influence of Jimmy Ling from LTV by forcing him out as Chairman and President (but the Board was still heavily manned by Ling's nominees, and Ling still held his controlling block of stock in LTV).

McLaren replied that he was "fed up with Ling papering the country with worthless paper he could not repay", and it looked like a repeat performance was in the making with Ling's new company, Omega-Alpha, seeking to acquire Okonite.

I explained LTV would have to go bankrupt within a week unless he would allow a change in the terms of the consent decree to permit the sale of Okonite to Omega-Alpha. I said the company would agree to go along with a number of new provisions requiring 1) Ling, his family and trusts, etc., to divest all LTV shares; 2) all Ling-appointed directors to resign from the LTV Board; and 3) prohibiting any director from serving on both the Okonite and LTV boards.

Thus I offered McLaren the complete divorce that he sought, explaining that it was the only way to save the company and the investment of thousands of stockholders who had their precious savings at risk. McLaren said he would consider the proposal and let me know shortly. I left his office with the feeling that his decision would be fair and pragmatic. Later he phoned me and graciously agreed to the terms I had offered. I communicated the settlement terms to both Thayer, who thanked me profusely, and to LTV's outside counsel, expecting the deal to be finalized by the federal court. As far as I knew, LTV seemingly was saved from the brink of bankruptcy.

Unfortunately, the saga was not over. I soon discovered that LTV was going back into court to try to overturn the consent decree, not to amend it. The Dallas "homeboy" who was LTV's corporate secretary called me to say he was coming to New York that same day to discuss the situation. When he came into my office he imparted in a heavy Texas drawl, accompanied by strong whiffs of bourbon, that the company would not conclude the deal I had negotiated with McLaren, and that they were going back into court to get additional time and permission to sell Okonite to Ling's Omega-Alpha. As he got ready to leave he gave me his parting shot: "You Jew boys fum New Yawk ain't goin' to purge Jimmy and Jimmy's team from our cumpny".

I told him it was nice to meet him, and wished him luck with all the insincerity I could muster. No sooner had he sloshed out the door than I picked up the phone to call Richard McLaren to inform him and apologize for not being able to conclude the deal he had so graciously extended at my urging to LTV.

Within days, LTV's foray back into court had been rebuked. My receptionist announced I had a call from Paul Thayer. Thayer was abjectly apologetic. He said he could not purge Ling's acolytes without that one last effort, but he said he was now ready to implement the deal. He begged me to try to repair their gaffe and revive the arrangement. I said that I had already earned my fee, but I would *not* insist on another retainer being paid. I would nevertheless try to help him, and if I succeeded there would be no additional bill for my services. I called McLaren and asked if he would revive the arrangement despite the behavior of LTV. I explained what had transpired with Thayer at the Board of Directors, and that Thayer had to make a last stand for Ling's acolytes before he could get them all to resign. I told McLaren that I liked Thayer and felt he was a straight shooter trapped in a corporate rat's nest. McLaren was extremely gracious, and said he would adhere to the terms of our original arrangement.

I told Paul that LTV could have the deal as I had negotiated it if they implemented it faithfully, but he had to promise to spread the word around Dallas that the treatment of LTV by the "Jew boys" in New York had been more than fair. I hope he did.

Roy M. Cohn

Helen Winston and her husband were family friends in the '60s. Helen was a winsome muse of literature, theatre and the arts whose heart and head held empathy and brilliance in equal measure. Helen had been an employee at 20th Century Fox who had worked long and hard on the script for the 1967 musical film, Doctor Dolittle, based on the wonderfully imaginative children's stories by Hugh Lofting that 20th Century Fox would soon be distributing starring Rex Harrison, Samantha Eggar, Anthony Newley and Richard Attenborough.

Helen came to me bitterly disappointed when she learned that she was not going to receive screen credit for her innovative changes to the script that departed importantly from Lofting's original storyline. She had no contractual guarantee of screen credit, but she felt that she deserved at least a scriptwriter's joint screenplay credit for contributing her original creative intellectual property.

By the time Helen consulted me, 20th Century Fox had already announced its world premier for the movie would take place imminently in New York. The prints of the film had been produced for distribution, and there was precious little time for me to try to help Helen by negotiating for a screen credit. Consequently, I prepared a summons and complaint, together with a petition for a preliminary injunction, to stop 20th Century Fox from premiering the film unless and until Helen was given appropriate screen credit.

I warned Helen that it would be a long shot to get an injunction since hundreds of celluloid prints that contained screen credits without her name had already been produced and distributed; and if we were successful, the studio would have to reproduce those at great expense. It was more likely that a trial would be ordered, and if she proved her case she might get monetary damages and a screen credit on subsequent showings or reruns of the film.

When I filed the suit in the Supreme Court of the State of New York, it drew no press coverage, but caught the attention of only those people who might become aware of such matters, i.e. court functionaries, Judges and their staffs. Within a day or two, by chance I ran into Roy Cohn, the notorious lawyer, at a restaurant. We had locked horns in a number of matrimonial cases, but I was always able to settle those disputes on favorable terms without litigation because Roy Cohn loved making a quick fee without a lot of work. He was known for his brilliance, his amazing legal acumen, his complete lack of ethics and morals, his unbelievable nerve in never paying income taxes by claiming he had no income despite owning a townhouse and a yacht. He indulged in nefarious dealings in reliance on powerful connections in high places to protect him.

When I saw Roy he said he knew about the preliminary injunction that I was seeking, and that the judge to whom the case had been assigned was going to rule against my client and for 20th Century Fox; but if I wanted a favorable decision it would cost $35,000, and I could give him the money and he would take care of the rest. I told him I was not interested in fixing the case, and whatever the judge decided, favorable or unfavorable, would be the outcome. He acted like he had offered me a great favor, but he took no umbrage at my declining his offer. I was amazed that he had no compunctions about broaching bribery of a judge, or any concern that that might result in ruining his perfect record in slipping law enforcement's noose every time he was under investigation.

When, the next day, I reported this exchange with Roy to my client, I told her that if she wanted to take advantage of Roy Cohn's offer, I would withdraw and she could hire another lawyer. I said I did not consult her before declining the offer, because it would have looked like I countenanced taking the offer, and I did not.

Helen said that she was glad I had rejected it out of hand, and although she never did get the screen credit she was due, she said she would never want to get it through bribery. It is events like this that unexpectedly test one's ethics. Choices matter. There is a gratifying sense of security in knowing that guilt will never torment your life.

The Continental Steel Strike

Having difficult clients and challenging cases on which to work was what made my daily routine as a lawyer exciting. One of those came along in 1971 when Continental Steel Company's long and bitter strike with the steelworkers' union was in full swing. It was an acrimonious dispute, amidst strife and hardship in the steel industry generally, that Sidney Korshak, the renowned negotiator and Chicago labor lawyer, had tried unsuccessfully for over a year to settle.

Continental Steel was located in Kokomo, Indiana. It had operated very successfully as a producer of steel and steel products, but eventually was taken over in 1969 and became a subsidiary of and controlled by Penn-Dixie Corporation that owned and operated cement plants in many parts of the United States. Both companies were listed on the New York Stock Exchange. Jerome Castle, the Chairman of both Penn Dixie and Continental Steel, had been lending millions of dollars from Continental Steel's pension fund up to Penn-Dixie, the parent company, while at the same time extracting maximum profits from the steel subsidiary without investing commensurately in its expansion and modernization. Although this practice may have looked at the outset like a reasonable business arrangement, as the loans grew in size while risk increased, the Continental's portfolio diversification diminished. Continental Steel's workers considered this a gross abuse that endangered their life savings. They had vented their rage by burning the image of Jerry Castle on the plant wall in Kokomo, and the strike that had already lasted a year and cost each company many millions seemed like it could not be ended.

I had met Jerry Castle some time earlier at the Palm Bay Club in Miami where I was playing doubles in a pro-am tennis tournament. Castle cut a curious figure. He was slight of build, below average height despite elevator heels, with thinning curly hair and a non-descript face. He was not someone who stood out in a crowd, and no heads would turn as he walked by. Castle's paranoia extended to having bodyguards and a gun permit, and his style of living and his manner of speech gave one the feeling that he wished to emulate a younger version of mob oligarch, Meyer Lansky. I had no idea if his fears were well founded. He may have had dangerous enemies. Castle had grown up in Brooklyn with the name Kesselman that he later Americanized in preparation for the role to which he aspired— Titan of Wall Street and Industry.

Castle went from Brooklyn to business school, after which he worked in the securities industry where he somehow ingratiated himself to Ruth Axe of the legendary Axe funds. With the backing of the Axe funds he managed to take control of Penn Dixie Cement Company, and once he had gotten himself elected its President and Chairman, he stopped at almost nothing in the autocratic rule he imposed and the lavish lifestyle he comported at the company's expense. His company-owned residential suite at the fashionable Hampshire House on New York's Central Park South boasted expensive works of art from Penn Dixie's "art collection."

Castle was extremely cordial when we met. He asked if I would be willing to do legal work for the company. I agreed to do some general corporate work for Penn Dixie, but when he eventually approached me to ask if I would be willing to try to settle the strike by the workers of Continental Steel, I was very leery. I said I had to have complete latitude in structuring what I considered to be a fair resolution, subject not to the direction of Penn Dixie management, but only to ratifiation by the Penn Dixie board of directors.

I had heard that Korshak was reputed to be close to the Teamsters Union and to possibly have mob ties, and I definitely did not want to poach his client or cross swords with him. I told Jerry that I might take the case if I got Korshak's public acknowledgment that he had washed his hands of the case. Castle told me that he would talk to Korshak, and that he would have him call me.

I decided that if and when I got the commitment of the Steel Workers Union that they were ready to try in good faith to end the strike through negotiation if I mediated it, and if Korshak were willing to announce to the Union that he was washing his hands of the affair, I would take the case.

I eventually got a call from Korshak. I made it clear to him that I would not get involved unless he felt his efforts were at a dead end. He was very cordial and thanked me for not offering to take over his case without his being ready to withdraw. He said I was welcome to go ahead and try to settle the strike because he was ready to call it quits.

I also told Korshak that I was not ready to take on the case without first traveling to Pittsburgh to meet with the representatives of the national Steel Workers Union, and thereafter I might request that he hold a meeting in his Chicago law office to which he would invite representatives from both the national and the local (Indiana) Steel Workers Union. He told me he was willing to cooperate and to call on him when I was ready.

I flew to Pittsburgh to meet with the national union's leaders. It was a good meeting. They did not like Castle or the Penn-Dixie's control of Continental Steel's pension funds, but they wanted to see an end to the strike; and they felt that a new mediator might finally engender more flexibility and less ire from the Indiana steelworkers local. I told them the negotiating ground rules I would require and came away with their commitment that a negotiation once commenced would go on without interruption until the strike was settled—a commitment that I felt ensured a successful outcome.

Shortly thereafter, Korshak, as promised, held the meeting in his Chicago office at which about a dozen local and national steel union representatives were present. It took place in a large room in Korshak's law suite. Part of the room was elevated about a foot or so higher than the rest. The union representatives were seated against the windows that lined the lower level and Korshak and I stood on what seemed like a dais platform area to address them. Neither Jerome Castle, nor any Penn Dixie executive, was present.

Korshak took the floor to welcome those assembled, to graciously admit that he had been unable to achieve a mutually satisfactory outcome to the strike, and that he was washing his hands of the matter. He introduced me to those present as a person who might be willing to try to bring the parties together. He then gave me the floor.

I explained that I understood the workers and their families had suffered during the long strike. I said I would try to play a constructive role, but only if both the company and the unions pledged a good faith negotiation with no preconditions, and one that would continue around the clock without interruption—even for meals—until the strike was settled. I knew my own physical condition and capacity to work around the clock without sleep for several days, so I had confidence that I could outlast most adversaries; the larger the group the better my chances. I promised that I would be fully authorized by the parent company, and that neither Castle nor any other Penn Dixie representative would take part in our negotiations at which only Continental's VP-Labor Relations would be present from the steel company. All present agreed, and I took the case.

The meeting took place several weeks later in a motel in Kokomo, Indiana. About thirty members from the national steelworkers union from Pittsburgh and the local Indiana union were present. The ground rules I had set were to negotiate for 23 hours per day until the case was settled with one hour off from 7am to 8am each day. We would eat meals at the negotiating table that were ordered in by the motel. As promised, only Continental's Vice-President of Labor Relations was present in the motel's conference room. He sat on my right as I chaired the meeting at the head of a long, narrow conference table. He had agreed not to speak unless I asked him a question or gave him permission.

The first day I went around the table counter clockwise calling upon each one of the union men to state their position and vent their ire for as long as they wanted, and I took careful notes as I listened intently to their diatribes. Each of the men stated, at their own pace and in their own words, what they and their families had endured during the strike; how much they distrusted Castle with their pension funds; and how worried they were for their and their family's security. That process took a full twenty-three hours. There was no grumbling from the men when I dismissed the meeting at 6 am and told them we would reconvene at 7 am. There was a rush out the door to use the hour to the fullest. I thought an hour was too short to sleep, so I did stretching, yoga, and a few set up exercises, before showering, shaving and returning to the conference room.

For the entire second day I repeated in exhaustive detail what I had heard each worker say on the preceding day. I knew this was necessary to convince them that they had been, and were being, listened to. My energy or concentration did not flag for the next twenty-three hours, There was no grumbling, interruption or comment from anyone, but I did see some nodding off, and one man woke himself by snoring. Again at 6 am we adjourned for the hour of showers, catnaps and phoning home. As soon as we reconvened at 7 am we found, as we had the day before, bagels, preserves, juice and coffee waiting on the conference table.

On the third day—and it seemed to drag on endlessly—I invited dialogue, comments and suggestions from the men. I wandered off the subject, feigned confusion or contradicted myself. The first nine hours of that day were torturous. I could see the men looking at each other with anxious, even desperate stares. I noticed some notes being passed and one man's face lost all color and turned a pasty white.

Late in the afternoon on the third day the attorney who was present from the National steelworkers union raised his hand to ask if he could talk to me outside the room. I said publicly that I could not speak outside the presence of the people in the room, and that a private conversation outside the room was in violation of our meeting's ground rules. He pleaded that his request had the consent of all the union representatives present. I said that if no one objected I would meet with him outside for not more than five minutes.

As soon as we got outside and closed the door of the conference room he capitulated—stating that some of his people had completely lost patience, others had problems at home to which they had to attend, and one man was experiencing chest pain and needed to get medical attention. He begged me to end the strike by writing the settlement agreement exactly as I wanted. I asked if all the union representatives supported his request. He indicated that they were ready to end the strike and would recommend whatever I would suggest in writing.

I went back into the room and told those present that I had been asked to write out a settlement agreement for both Continental Steel and the national and local steel unions. I said that I would do my best to write it fairly, giving the unions what they needed going forward for labor peace to prevail— including Penn Dixie's agreement not to borrow further, and to repay Continental Steel's pension money over a reasonable period of years. The men unanimously agreed in their haste to leave. There was no attempt by the steelworkers' attorney to edit or revise the settlement agreement that I drafted on the spot.

Saving Penn Dixie Cement Company

Jerome Castle was so pleased with my being able to settle the Continental Steel strike that some months later he approached me again. This time he explained that Penn Dixie owed their syndicate of banks a $40 million term loan that was due in sixty days. Jerry said that he did not have the cash to pay the banks, and he had been warned they would not extend or renew the loan. Failing to pay would spell the end of his tenure in control of the company, and possible bankruptcy for Penn Dixie as well.

He said that his only chance to get the $40 million to pay off the banks was to sell the Clinchfield mill, the largest cement plant that Penn Dixie owned, to Medusa Portland Cement Company. Disposing of the Clinchfield mill that was comprised of real estate and physical assets spread over three states would be a monumental legal job that could well take more than two months. Castle said that he was afraid to go to Cleveland to negotiate the terms of the deal with Medusa because they would "smell fear on his breath" in facing such a short debt repayment deadline. He said they would not sense that on me, as he had seen me perform under stress enough times and with successful outcomes. He pleaded with me to take the case.

The challenge was exciting, but the hurdles were daunting. I would have to go out and negotiate the deal, get a contract drawn and signed by both parties, and then prepare for a closing and have the sale closed, all within sixty days. To imagine it could get done in time was simply not in the cards. I realized trying to inventory the assets of a vast cement mill, get title searches of all the real estate in three states, allow time for the buyer to perform its due diligence investigations, and set and meet the closing date was a virtual impossibility. Still I agreed. I did not even ask for a retainer, but I demanded full-time use of the company Lear jet since I had to travel without losing even an hour or two, if I had any hope of succeeding. I lost no time in heading out to Cleveland.

On the flight I took along one of my law partners, Marshall Bernstein, who I trusted for his thoroughness and draftsmanship. In the army the highest compliment goes, "He's the kind of guy I want to share my foxhole with." Marshall was that kind of partner—clear thinking, unflappable and accomplished.

The two of us went directly to the downtown office of the law firm of Squire Sanders & Dempsey who represented Medusa Portland Cement. Marshall and I entered their tower suite with corridors that seemed endless, lined with lawyers' offices. We were shown into a large working conference room where we took our seats at a majestic conference table opposite members of Medusa's management, accountants and a squad of Squire Sanders attorneys. They had no shortage of manpower, and I was impressed with the depth of knowledge, experience and ability of the ten-man team the two of us faced across the table.

Our negotiations went almost around the clock for two full days. Marshall and I struggled to remain alert and focused, while those we faced across the table were able to rotate for rest and refreshment. Our job was made more arduous by Jerry Castle's unavailability. He could be reached by phone only once each day at 3pm.

We were almost ready to conclude, having reached agreement on all issues that had been discussed, when to the dismay of the Squire Sanders contingent I suddenly raised the issue of anti-trust. They vigorously protested my raising anti-trust at the last minute since it was a possible deal killer. They had presumed my silence on that issue to that point meant I was willing to accept the risk that there might be an anti-trust problem that could prevent the transaction from being consummated. But when a cement company as big as Medusa Portland contracts to buy another major competitor's cement mill, the risk of it being challenged and delayed by the Anti-Trust division of the Justice Department is one that cannot be ignored.

I insisted that since they represented the acquirer, they had to look into and satisfy themselves—and us—on the propriety of the acquisition, with the risk of any anti-trust violation resting on them.

Fortunately, they satisfied themselves on that point, and on the third day we had a contract of sale ready for signature by the parties with a closing date set before payment of Penn Dixie's term loan was due! As Marshall and I were getting ready to leave the conference room one of the younger Squire Sanders attorneys remarked, "Eric, you are amazing! You are a regular Joe Namath."

Though totally spent by our intensive effort, that compliment lifted my spirits, as Joe Namath was then the country's foremost quarterback who completed many "Hail Mary" passes for the New York Jets. My feet were treading on feather-filled cushions as we walked down the hall to the elevator.

The partners at that Cleveland firm must have agreed with their young associate because they recommended me later for an A1 rating from Martindale Hubbell, the highest rating for an attorney in the legal profession.

Marshall and I flew back to New York with a sense of triumph but also of foreboding, since the contract provided not for a sale of stock but for a sale of assets. An enormous amount of work had to get done to catalogue and inventory the myriad assets included in the sale.

From that point on, the company's jet resembled a grasshopper, jumping around the three states involved to transport engineers, lawyers, surveyors, etc. from small airport to small airport conveniently close to each site. Thankfully, the Lear could land and take off from very short runways.

When finally the sale closed before the drop-dead due date, and Penn Dixie got the wherewithal to pay its banks, Jerry Castle once again was effusively grateful. He put me on the board of both Penn-Dixie and Continental Steel; and although he would not lose his company that year in foreclosure or bankruptcy, he was not grateful enough to behave correctly thereafter in all matters in his Chairmanship.

For a time I played the role of principled and independent outside director on his Boards exercising careful scrutiny and uncompromising judgment. Castle listened to my advice and criticism at first, but when he began to resist my admonitions I left the boards and quit as legal advisor as well. Some years later Castle was sentenced to a fifteen-month jail term for selling a tract of Florida swampland to Penn-Dixie far above its then true value.

Each client, each case, each negotiation were not just a series of episodes. They formed a ladder of learning that I climbed with diligent preparation, hard work and ethical care. In looking back, I had more than my share of difficult clients and even a few "rascals", but I managed to avoid slipping on the rungs while gaining the valuable experience that would prove helpful in my future endeavors.

CHAPTER X — WHEN LIFE CHANGED

My life changed on May 18th, 1973. My sister called from Palm Beach to tell me that our father had died of a sudden heart attack. Both he and my mother were then 78 years of age and both had experienced heart problems requiring pacemakers to be inserted to regulate their heartbeats. I told Stephanie that we would fly down to Palm Beach the next day to join my mother and sister at the funeral services there. She said that of course I should go, but she was going to remain in New York. I always thought that Ben meant a lot to her. I know that he cared for her. That she could be so callous about his death and my loss shocked me. I felt totally alone. I had never taken the time to think about my life and the emotional emptiness of it. Stephanie had decorated and run our gracious homes, capably supervised the household staff, raised well-mannered children. She was determined to take off to Gstaad for skiing and to London for shopping with her sister. Her trips grew longer by the year. I would be left alone in New York to work, but I had never allowed myself to think about leaving her or making a radical change because I felt our young children were not old enough to understand why I would leave them.

That was the moment I knew I had to face the truth about my charade of a marriage. I flew alone to Florida to comfort my mother and sister and attend the memorial service there for my father before the three of us returned to NY for the memorial service that was held in Temple Emanu-El.

Soon thereafter, I told Stephanie that I was going to move out of our apartment that Fall, and that I would inform our children of my decision when they were home from their schools for

Thanksgiving. She took the news calmly because she either did not believe I would leave her, or if I did that somehow we would eventually reconcile.

By some stroke of fate or perhaps just coincidence, on the very day my father died while visiting my friend, Marty Kimmel, one of America's leading shopping center developers at his house in the Hamptons, I met two young women who were Marty's weekend houseguests, one more beautiful than the other, and both with the same last name—Davis. Karen Davis was an aspiring opera singer who eventually married Marty Kimmel, and then much later married my friend and client, Italian billionaire, Dino Fabbri.

Kathy Davis was a successful Ford model with plenty of joie de vivre, an infectious laugh, and insatiable intellectual curiosity. I appreciated that Kathy had traditional values, loved her friends, nature and animals; and that she enjoyed the excitement of discovering what each day would bring.

As the summer wore on, I felt like one door in life had closed but another had opened. I saw more of Kathy. She frequently came out to the Hamptons where we met at discos or parties on Long Island or at Le Club in New York. That someone cared deeply for me on a romantic level was meaningful after my father's funeral. I realized that for too long I had been in denial, ignoring the painful fact of a loveless marriage by devoting myself to my work, politics and other interests. That, combined with losing my father—the family member to whom I felt closest—opened me to emotions that I might not otherwise have felt.

As promised, that Thanksgiving I told our children of my decision to leave their mother. It was then Stephanie realized I was serious and she was shocked. I packed my bags and moved down to my parents' apartment at 980 Fifth Avenue. After my father's death in 1973, my widowed mother was living in their home in Palm Beach so I had my parents' New York apartment to myself. Kathy eventually concluded that there was no future for her with me, so she made the sudden and irrevocable decision to give up her apartment and to move to California. I was deeply saddened to lose her but powerless to change her mind.

It was soon after that summer, that I started dating again. I had been separated for three years and was having a difficult time trying to negotiate a settlement and get a divorce. I did not want to litigate so I was as generous as I could be for the sake of our children, hoping to peacefully exit the marriage. However, with every concession I made, the demands grew.

It was not until I told her lawyer to go ahead and file in court that she settled. At that point, I doubted I would ever again feel anything for any one, so I stopped dating. I was firmly resolved never to marry again as the years of marriage and subsequent divorce had been torture for me.

In December, 1977 my insurance agent, Mitchell May, called to invite me to a Christmas party that he and his Swedish-born wife, Gita, a former superstar model in New York, were going to have the following Saturday night at their magnificent duplex apartment on the West Side of Manhattan. He said they were "worried about me" because I had been alone for years, and that Gita had some lovely Swedish lady friends they wanted me to meet. I replied I did not want to meet anyone, and I would pass on the party. He continued to press me. I asked if I came for only fifteen minutes, would he and his wife be upset? He said they would not, and of course I could do that.

When I showed up at their apartment expecting to have an eggnog and leave, I walked in to a packed living room, determined only to wish my host and hostess a fleeting Good Yule. I gave up the idea with my first careful look around the room so stunningly elegant and beautiful were the group of Swedish-American ladies assembled there.

My eyes locked on one particular face on the far side of the room. It was a visage of sheer loveliness, framed in blond hair, with blue eyes that glinted with spirit and cheekbones so lovely they could invite adoring pinches from perfect strangers. I made my way over and introduced myself to Dr. Margaretha Espersson. I had absolutely no recollection then of ever having met her before, but in fact we had met earlier—twice in fact.

At that moment she was the object of intense attention from two opera singers who had her surrounded—Swedish baritone Ingvar Wixell and Italian tenor, Marigay, so they were not too happy with my appearing on the scene. Mitch May had a powerful voice, loved opera and sang beautifully, so I was not surprised to see the two operatic superstars there.

As the evening wore on, Mitch began to sing to the piano accompaniment of one of his friends, and others joined in. The Swedish baritone began to sing an aria to Margaretha, but no sooner had he finished than the Italian tenor took the floor. Margaretha was beaming at the attention, while I was trying my best to maneuver her out of their clutches.

After what, for me, seemed like an eternity of arias, I got her out of there by offering to take her home and buy her the Sunday edition of the New York Times that always hit the newsstand Saturday nights.

The following morning I called to invite her to the movies. She must have realized that I was pretty taken with her, as I called so early that I woke her. She was not mistaken in that conclusion. That evening we went to a film that my friend, Earle Mack, had produced about young ballet dancers training for the Bolshoi, and that marked the beginning of a steady series of dates until I suddenly felt conflicted with memories of Kathy and the fear that another relationship might lead to another disastrous marriage.

Margaretha had earned her Masters and Doctorate in psychology and education from Columbia University entirely on her own by working for many years as Assistant Dean of Students at the School of General Studies. She was quick to discern my feelings of conflict and indecision. She told me not to call her unless I was certain about how I felt.

In a matter of weeks I called, and told her I wanted to resume our relationship. Looking back, I was "damaged goods", but Margaretha must have seen the possibilities of my once again placing trust in a female partner. She was a self-supporting, independent-minded, mature and well-educated professional who had no need to marry. She was fully my equal in education and accomplishment, Furthermore, when she said to me, "I am not your former wife. I am a different person. Not all women are the same," she made me less fearful of following my heart.

I began to stay with Margaretha at her bachelor apartment on East 57th street instead of my parent's apartment. Her studio was attractively furnished and extremely comfortable. Margaretha lived there with two Persian cats, Max and Munch. They could sense when they met me that I had an aversion to cats, so they made it their goal to seduce me. My mother hated cats. As a child, I had been warned never to have one because of the hair that would get all over everything, and at night it might lie on my face and smother me while I slept. Sure enough, Margaretha's cats loved nothing better than to jump up onto her bed and park themselves on the pillow around my head. That seemed to be their "power spot."

Max and Munch loved to chase each other so I built them a tall, carpet-covered scratching and climbing post with a branching limb high off the floor. One would gain that height advantage and eye the other down on the floor with an evil glare. Suddenly they would be dashing around the room from pillar to post trying to catch each other. It was a fun game to watch, and it was not long before they had me in their little furry pockets. As time passed, Margaretha began to experience asthmatic symptoms, and her doctor suspected the dander from her cats. She eventually gave custody of those two wonderful beings to a close and trusted friend who cared for them lovingly.

Finally, Margaretha invited me to fly over to Sweden to meet her singularly distinguished family. Her father, Kurt Espersson, was one of the most respected judges in Stockholm who, among other interests, had an uncanny ability in collecting only the finest art masterworks and 18th century furniture masterpieces. Her mother, Irja, possessed the beauty of a Hollywood siren and the soul of an angel. She had been one of the founders of the Swedish Handicrafts Center, and she had all the domestic skills and estimable values found in the women of the finest Swedish families. Margaretha's brother, Carl, with whom she was very close, served as legal counsel to the Swedish Medical Malpractice Board.

Our plane landed in Stockholm's Arlanda airport one early December morning. It had snowed the night before. It must have been a bit warmer and then turned colder because every tree looked like it was made of crystal. As our taxi drove us in toward Stockholm's center, everything was covered the purest white without a blemish. It was, indeed, an unforgettable winter wonderland that greeted me.

When we entered the palatial apartment the Esperssons owned at Lovisagatan 2, one of Stockholm's signature buildings in the city's exclusive "golden triangle," to greet her parents, I could see what a privileged life Margaretha had left behind to venture off to America and choosing to forego financial support from her family.

In Stockholm, while Margaretha slept in the mornings, I got up to join her mother who made sandwiches and coffee for just the two of us so we could enjoy wonderful private times together. Irja became someone I truly loved.

After our return to New York, the old adage, "the apple does not fall far from the tree", made me sure that however dynamic and forceful Margaretha was then, she would become with the passage of years as soft, gentle and caring as her divine mother.

The location of the spanking new apartment building Bernard Spitzer had built at 800 Fifth Avenue on the site that had been owned by a member of the Astor family was superb. It occupied the block fronting on Fifth Avenue between 61st and 62nd streets immediately north of the Pierre Hotel. Behind the building it had its own private garden with beautiful landscaping and an elegant illuminated fountain at its center. It was Bernard Spitzer's son, Eliot, who later became Attorney General and then Governor of New York State.

In years past, when I used to ride the Fifth Avenue bus down from 91st and Fifth Avenue past the ramshackle Astor mansion on my way to work at 51st and Fifth Avenue, I would think to myself that someday I wanted to live in a modern residence tower where once the Astor mansion stood.

Dreams do came to pass. I was one of the first to occupy an apartment in the spanking new 800 Fifth Ave. The living-room windows of my second floor apartment were exactly centered over the lovely rear garden and its illuminated fountain. It felt like my own private residence because only muffled city street sounds could be heard. Margaretha, whom I was seeing exclusively, helped me decorate my new "bachelor pad". She visited all the decorator showrooms and brought me samples from which I could choose fabrics, furniture and accessories to achieve a distinctly masculine look.

Finally one day when we were walking up Fifth Avenue, I got up the nerve to mutter "Maybe we should get married." Margaretha response to that equivocal remark was, "Why should we do that? I don't need to get married." All I could say was I thought we really should . . . . . and we did. We planned the wedding to take place on my and my son's birthday in May. We invited her parents to come to America to stay with us in Southampton, but we did not apprise them of the planned wedding until they arrived at Margaretha's apartment in New York. I began by saying to her father, "Kurt, I have something to ask you and something to tell you." He looked at me quizzically. "I would like to ask your permission to marry your daughter . . . . . and to tell you that the wedding is going to be on Thursday!" Kurt serious face broke into a wide smile at the news. He told me he approved. With that we all warmly hugged each other.

Our marriage took place in my mother's apartment at 980 Fifth Avenue. My friend, Judge Bentley Kassal, performed the ceremony. Those present were my mother; my children Jocelyn and Eric Jr.; my sister, Joan, and her children; Kurt and Irja Espersson; Jack and Marian Javits; and only a very few others present among whom were some of Margaretha's and my closest friends as well as my Mexican mentor, the former President of Mexico, Miguel Aleman Valdez; and Mitch and Gita May, who brought us together.

Jack Javits was there with several New York detectives in tow because the government of Iran had issued a Fatwah on his life. Margaretha was not happy to have a bunch of "suits" enter like they owned the place, but when one of them told her that he had never seen a more beautiful bride, she grudgingly welcomed them.

After the ceremony there were the usual toasts. In my toast I mentioned those loved ones who were not with us, adding "especially my father who always used to tell us that when he was gone, we should just drink a toast to him". No sooner had I finished saying those words, than Gita's right arm flew up involuntarily, tossing her champagne toward the ceiling before it fell to the carpet. Everyone turned to look, wondering what was wrong or what had happened. I thought she might have had a seizure.

Gita was mortified with embarrassment, but she managed to utter, "I am so sorry, but that was no accident". Gita had unusual psychic powers. She could read auras, and she could "see" if someone was ill, and what their ailment was even before they were aware of it themselves. She proved that once when she "saw" Margaretha at a party just after we had returned from visiting Miguel Aleman's estate in Acapulco where we both swam in the sewage-polluted bay. She told Margaretha, "Something is very wrong with your stomach. Really very wrong with your stomach! You have to be checked."

Margaretha paid her no heed until some days later she and I both started to have severe intestinal symptoms. The doctors tried everything to cure her without success, and she almost died as the amoebas ate part of her liver and through the walls of a sac encapsulating some TB germs in her lung that had been lying harmless there since her childhood. Finally, some medicine from Great Britain that had not been cleared by the Food and Drug Administration had to be specially imported to treat her; and she had to stay on other medication for a year and a half to cure her tubercular lung infection.

So when Gita swore that it was Ben who struck her arm in an upward motion just as I had finished saying we should all drink a toast to him, Margaretha, my mother and I believed her, but we may have been the only ones there who did. Gita, who had known Ben when he was alive, insisted that she actually had seen him and felt him strike her arm. My reaction was one of gratitude if Ben had, indeed, been part of the wedding party that day.

Once we were married, Margaretha redid my bachelor apartment at 800 Fifth Avenue in a less masculine décor. It made sense for us to keep our overhead low as I still had financial obligations to repay, as well as obligations arising from my divorce settlement. Even though it was just a three-room apartment, we felt it was our little haven where we could find peace and tranquility in the midst of hectic and bustling New York.

American Health Foundation

Dr. Ernst Wynder, a law client and close friend in New York from the early '60s, founded the American Health Foundation (AHF) in 1969 as a not-for-profit private research organization devoted primarily to the prevention of chronic diseases, especially cancer. Dr. Wynder had worked for many years at the Sloan Kettering Institute where, 10 years earlier, he was the first to establish the link between smoking and lung cancer.

Ernst Wynder in his prime was a bon vivant bachelor with the looks of a Hollywood actor. In fact, he was almost a double for Louis Jourdan. Ernst, with his German accent, looked more like a ladies man than a serious scientist and medical doctor. I used to see him out night after night in the best bistros and restaurants with one beautiful woman after another, but he was never late to his office the next morning, and he worked tirelessly to change America's medical system from one based on treatment of illness to one based on keeping people healthy.

Wynder loved to tell how Chinese doctors never got paid for treating the sick but collected an annual retainer as long as their patients remained healthy. He wanted to reduce the need for treating illness to a minimum. The AHF's mission was based on the concept that chronic diseases such as cancer, heart disease and stroke (which account for more than two-thirds of all premature deaths) were the result of lifestyle choices including smoking, incorrect eating, drug and alcohol abuse, sedentary lack of activity, and exposure to occupational and environmental hazards, all of which could be reduced by a rational program of disease prevention.

When Ernst decided to create the AHF he asked me to be do the legal work to form it, to serve on its board and to act as its Secretary and Counsel—all on a pro bono no-fee basis. I agreed, and from 1969 until 1989 I acted in those capacities. From its inception William Levitt, the real estate developer who built Levittown in Long Island acted as its Chairman. I had known Bill for years as an intimate friend of my uncle Jack Javits. Another key director was Mrs. Eleanor "Nellie" Dana, the wealthy widow of the industrialist Charles Dana. Nellie supported the AHF out of adoration for and friendship with Wynder. Upon her death she left a large bequest in her will for the Dana Farber medical centers. The executor of her estate, David Mahoney, who was Chairman of Norton Simon Inc., also served as Chairman and CEO of both the Charles A. Dana Foundation and of the Eleanor Naylor Dana Charitable Trust.

After Bill Levitt's death, it was David Mahoney who succeeded to the Chairmanship of the AHF Board. Other directors were Former White House Chief of Staff to Pres. Ford, Donald

Rumsfeld; David's wife, Hildegard "Hillie" Mahoney; Herbert Jacobi, Chairman of Trinkhaus and Burkhart, a leading investment bank in Dusseldorf; Admiral Elmo R. Zumwalt, the youngest man ever to serve as Chief of Naval Operations; and Marvin Traub, the Chairman and President, from 1969 to 1991, of Bloomingdale's department store.

AHF scientists were among the first to identify the relationship between colon and breast cancer and the eating habits of Americans. The AHF warned against diets high in fat and low in fiber.

Wynder was also the founder of the international journal *Preventive Medicine* that fosters worldwide exchange of information obtained from disease prevention research among professionals. The AHF also introduced and popularized various programs for informing the general public on healthy lifestyles for children and adults, with topics including health-promotion, nutrition, exercise, weight control and smoking cessation. We take all of this for granted today, but back in the '60s the general public had little or no awareness about the hazhards of an unhealthy lifestyle. The AHF's quarter-century growth from modest beginnings to a world-renowned authority in preventive medical research is a tribute to the dedication of its philosophy, its leadership, and its effectiveness.

Knowledge gained from research studies is essential, but no amount of health research, particularly in the field of prevention, can produce a positive social change without effective communication with the public.

The Foundation's achievements in effective communication involved a number of projects. Most notable, perhaps, is the well-established Know Your Body (KYB) Program. That was just an idea in Ernst Wynder's head when I left the Board of AHF to become Ambassador Designate to Venezuela in 1989.

Conceived as a complete, interactive health promotion syllabus for children and their teachers from Kindergarten through 6th grade, it is one of the most thoroughly validated programs of its type. The only truly comprehensive program in the nation, it has reached well over 100,000 students to date.

Another pioneer in the field of health was my and my uncle's good friend, Dr. William Cahan, the leading lung surgeon at Sloan Kettering Hospital. Bill often played in our tennis games on weekends when Jack and I would invite him and a fourth to meet at one of the indoor facilities in Manhattan for a friendly game of doubles. Very often Richard M. "Rich" Berman who served on Jack's Senate staff would be our fourth. Rich, was not only a terrific tennis player, but a personable and brilliant man. He is now a highly respected federal judge in the Southern District of New York. Bill Cahan's wife, Grace Mirabella, was then the editor of Vogue magazine and the Cahans, too, were my law clients.

When I noticed three lumps in a row in my neck and shoulder that seemed like they could be cancer, Bill operated on me. When he had me on the operating table and I was about to be put under anesthesia, he said he would biopsy one of my lumps, and if it were cancerous he would go on with the full operation. I woke up in my hospital room to hear Margaretha coming down the hall to see me. Fortunately, the biopsy was negative and Bill had not needed to go further. When Margaretha told me the good news I jumped out of bed, grabbed her and danced around the room with my hospital gown wide open at the back. A few passers-by in the hall got a view through my open door of more than they expected, but they watched the scene with a smile.

John Z. DeLorean

One of the automotive world's most prominent and notorious figures was the late John Z. DeLorean, a talented industrial and automotive engineer who rose from the ranks to become General Motors' golden boy by taking a sleepy Pontiac division that stirred no buyer excitement whatever back up to the pinnacle of the auto industry by launching the Pontiac GTO in 1964. It became America's first "muscle car" and a household icon. In a way, DeLorean himself—with his good looks, mod clothing and long hair—seemed to personify his GTO's flashy avant-garde design that bespoke strength, speed and style. He was a drastic departure from the typical automotive executive in Detroit who wore white shirts, dark ties and grey flannel suits. DeLorean and his GTO grabbed the imagination of younger buyers that catapulted him at age 40 to run Pontiac as GM's youngest division head ever. With that promotion he morphed from GM's golden boy to their glory guy. He compounded that success by restyling Chevrolet's Camaro into the Pontiac Firebird that became even more popular. In 1969 he was promoted again, this time to head GM's flagship Chevrolet division.

I didn't meet John Delorean until a couple of years after 1973—the year that marked for me the end of a life cycle. Concurrent with that, it was also the year that DeLorean left General Motors. By then John had earned a well-deserved reputation for being a rebel, a non-conformist, and a jet-setter who hung with the Hollywood crowd. He had formed intimate friendships with many of the biggest names in the entertainment world. As his fame and notoriety increased, he surrounded himself with the company of other celebrities and like-minded individuals who moved in "the fast lane."

It was John's young supermodel wife, Cristina Ferrare, whom I met first. Cristina was both beautiful and charming.

Her image was that of a lithe, lovely, and lissome sophisticate, but underneath was a warm-hearted, extrovert who loved to cook, loved to eat, and loved her friends and family. She had to struggle to keep the pounds off so she could maintain her svelte figure for the camera, but she did not suffer from sensory self-deprivation. I liked her for her frankness, her quick sense of humor and refusal to be politically correct.

After I separated from Stephanie and became romantically involved with Cristina's close friend, Kathy Davis, Cristina wanted me and her husband to meet because he had been trying for some time to raise the $20 million dollars to realize his dream of starting a new automotive company; and Cristina knew that I headed a prominent New York law firm, was a well-connected philanthropic and political fundraiser, and that as a sideline I had helped finance a number of private and public companies.

When Cristina, John, Kathy and I met together for the first time, it was just the four of us for dinner at a restaurant. I studied John as the two of us were introduced, while we ordered and during drinks. I was quite aware that he, too, was taking my measure. Though he was my elder by six years, he had a full head of long, jet-black hair without even a streak of grey. I suspected that he dyed it to look younger. His long, lantern-like face had an angular jaw. Fashionable at the time, his fitted jacket was cut with a definite Western flair, and his shirt collar was so long and pointed that it must have been the product of some trendy Beverly Hills designer. John seemed pleasant, and certainly intelligent enough, but my first impression was to wonder how he got his superhuman reputation.

Our dinner conversation began as mundane and superficial, but John quickly steered it to his plan to build a new car using new stronger and lighter materials. I noticed that John put everything into automotive lingo. He spoke not of his plans but of "the road map." He explained that he had hired the famous Italian auto designer, Giugiaro, to design it, and he had a first rate management team "ready to roll". All he lacked before he could "hit the gas" was the financing.

I told him that from my knowledge of the venture capital market, there was a chance to get that amount of start up money in a single tranche from only two places: either Allen & Co. or Oppenheimer & Co. John already had had many irons in the fire and had come up empty on all of them, so he knew I was knowledgeable and probably correct. I said that if I could get him the funding I would not charge a fee for raising the money but would want my law firm to be the motor company's general counsel. John agreed.

I took the deal first to Herb Allen and Stan Shuman at Allen & Co. who looked at the idea but did not think it was of interest. On my second try, my friends at Oppenheimer & Co. did like the glamour and excitement of the DeLorean project and agreed to raise $20 million dollars, using a research and development partnership to fund it. DeLorean already had a preliminary design of the car and was planning to use a revolutionary Wankel engine, but he eventually hired Lotus, the British firm, to engineer the car for him and settled on a brushed stainless steel body with an engine built by Renault. The Lotus firm had been controlled by Colin Chapman, the noted racing car figure who was a friend of John's. The person at Oppenheimer who was in charge of the public offering, Howard Phillips, was a tenacious and extremely capable investment banker. He managed to generate the interest and momentum to sell out the offering despite a series of obstacles and challenges that would have daunted many and deterred most of Wall Street's best.

Once DeLorean got his funding he asked me to serve on the motor company's board of directors and on his Executive Committee, as well as continuing to act as general outside counsel to his company. I agreed; and for about a year or two instead of raising more money from the public DeLorean sought to forge ahead, hoping to use his reputation, hype and stock to pursue all kinds of acquisitions that he felt could be synergistic for their production of transportation vehicles of one kind or another. Those he went after included Chrysler; Canada's Bombardier that manufactured aircraft, subway, and other vehicles; a privately owned Austrian bus manufacturer; a ski-mobile manufacturer; and even Lotus itself.

Well over a year was spent in trying to make these acquisitions, but none ever came to fruition. I began to get anxious about the failure to concentrate on getting the DeLorean DMC-12 automobile into production. Our office was working intensively with the Puerto Rican governmental authorities on an agreement for Puerto Rico to invest the money needed to build a plant for producing it there. I had been pressing for financial information, to be able to drive the car, and to be allowed to go to New Jersey and California to see how the car performed on the company's test tracks; but despite his promises, those requests were not honored.

Finally, after months of work, our office was ready to consummate the Puerto Rican agreement and a closing was scheduled. DeLorean said that he would have to be in Ireland at that time, but instructed us to send one of our law firm partners to Puerto Rico with a power of attorney to close it. The closing was underway in San Juan with all parties present when I got a call from our partner who said all the papers had been reviewed and approved, and the signing was imminent. He asked me to double check with DeLorean before he put pen to paper as his attorney-in-fact to close the transaction. I placed a call to John who told me to cancel the deal in Puerto Rico because he had just signed a contract to have the factory built by the British government in Northern Ireland. The British government commitment called for over $150 million to be invested in grants and loans in an effort to bring 2000 jobs to a depressed area of Northern Ireland experiencing high unemployment.

I was stunned that Delorean had simultaneously gone down a dual track on two factory sites without telling us that he had second deal in negotiation. I asked who was representing him in Ireland and he told me that Paul Weiss Rifkind Wharton and Garrison, one of New York's leading law firms had done the work there. I immediately called our partner who was poised to sign the Puerto Rican agreement and told him to walk out of the room after explaining the car factory had just been contracted to be built in Northern Ireland though another law firm without our knowledge. The government of Puerto Rico's representatives who were present at the closing became incensed, but there was nothing they or we could do.

From that point on, the Paul Weiss firm served as General Counsel for Delorean Motor Co. I felt more and more concerned about my role on the DMC board, and had increasing doubts about John Delorean's management style. His duplicity troubled me. I knew that I needed to go to Ireland and see for myself what was transpiring there. I asked for permission to make the trip and satisfy myself about the decisions that were being taken to produce and market the car. The DMC board meetings had been sketchy, and I was not comfortable with the scanty information I and the other directors were being given.

Around that time, knowing of my friendship with Henry Ford and his children, John asked me if I thought that the Ford Motor Company would be interested in acquiring the DeLorean Motor Company. He had heard that they wanted to add a hot sport car to their divisions to compete with GM's Corvette. I called Henry to broach the idea and he said he would have the President of the Ford Motor Company call me. Once I got the call, I put him in touch with DeLorean who sent him information he requested. I eventually heard back that the Ford management did not feel the DeLorean DMC-12 would fit into their line. That John would even consider selling, and that Ford would not be interested in acquiring, made me even more concerned.

Despite assurances that I would be sent to Ireland as soon as things were further along there, it never materialized. Whenever I would mention this to John, he always promised it would be arranged soon. I brought this up not just in a business setting, but also socially when we were together with Cristina and my wife, Margaretha, at John's baronial twenty-two room apartment at 834 Fifth Avenue, where the four of us would occasionally dine on Cristina's superb Italian pasta and squash flowers.

Then, quite unexpectedly, Margaretha urged me to resign from John's board and disassociate completely from him and his company. Margaretha had never before attempted to intervene in my law practice or my clients' affairs. She knew that I was dissatisfied with the limited access and scanty information I was being given by DMC, and that the amount of work our firm did had been curtailed; but when she urged me to drop John I was shocked. I told her that I was reluctant to just walk away from an important client, especially one that any lawyer in America would give his right arm to represent. At that point the name Delorean in the public mind was still synonymous with success and the launching of a revolutionary new car company.

I can still remember her words. "Eric, something awful is going to happen to that man, and when it does you will not want to be anywhere near him or have anything to do with him. Please believe me. It will be horrible!"

I had seen Margaretha intuit things that actually came to pass just as she had foreseen them. I had learned to trust her intuition, so I decided to heed her admonition as I was certainly feeling quite uncomfortable as a member of John's board of directors. The next day I called Thomas Kimmerly, a DMC Vice President and Corporate Counsel for DMC. I told him that I was not happy as a board member, having sought access and information that had not been forthcoming, so I wanted to resign effective immediately. Tom said that he understood and was sure John would as well; but since an annual Shareholders Meeting had been scheduled to take place the next month at which a new board would be elected, he was sure that John would appreciate it if I would just wait until then, at which time I would not be re-nominated. That would avoid the questions that could be raised if I resigned abruptly.

The slate that was elected a month later included John's wife, Cristina, as my replacement. From that point on, my firm and I did no further legal work for John or his company. Eventually things degenerated for the Delorean Motor Company. John had originally planned to price his car for $15,000, about the same as Chevrolet's Corvette, but by the time it was produced and launched the price was moved up to $26,000. Instead of selling 12,000 cars the first year as John had expected, the company only managed to sell 3,000 in the first six months although that was due in some measure to the recession that began in 1981 and lasted for more than a year.

These and other factors brought things to the point that in 1982 DMC had to declare bankruptcy. Much time had passed without my seeing or speaking to John, but suddenly I got a call from him. After some polite small talk, he wondered— since I had been so helpful in finding his initial funding—if I could do the same now to find the $5 million necessary to get his company out of bankruptcy. I reminded him that the first time I helped to get him financing it was without being compensated on the expectation I would enjoy a loyal long-term client relationship as a result. Since that did not occur, I said I might help him again, but not as a lawyer or for a legal fee. I said I would act as a business consultant for a percentage, in case of success, of the amount raised. He agreed, and we settled on a percentage we felt was fair.

I knew that with all of the problems that had crept into the press about his mistakes in pricing and producing the car, and his being accused by the British government of misfeasance or worse, my job would not be easy. However, I had the idea of approaching my long time friend, Peter Kalikow, a New York real estate developer, to make the investment. I had been a friend of Peter's since the early '60s when I had squired Peter and his father to Houston (with the help of a world renowned jet-setter, Italian Baron Enrico di Portanova, whose mother was a Cullen) in an effort to buy a prime piece of downtown Houston real estate controlled by the Cullen family.

That sought-for deal never materialized, but it was the beginning of a warm friendship with Peter. I remembered that Peter loved cars and especially sport cars. He was a collector of Ferraris and had even designed and built his own sport cars. I called Peter and asked if he would be interested in investing $5 million to take DMC out of bankruptcy, and he said he would. I arranged for Delorean to meet with Peter at which the outline of a deal was agreed upon between them. Peter immediately ordered his lawyers to prepare the papers. Another meeting was set for Friday of the following week at which the signing would take place. Despite DMC's bankruptcy and all the unfavorable publicity surrounding it, Peter agreed that the company could continue to bear John's name, and that he could remain its President. However, as President of the reorganized company John would own no stock, would obey Kalikow's management orders, and would get a generous salary plus a very meager expense allowance. Kalikow did not agree with John's rosy estimates of the market that existed for the DMC-12. Peter told John he would produce no more than 5,000 cars per year. In conclusion, he offered John a face saving solution but not much more.

I got a call early the next week from John explaining that he had to fly out to California for a couple of days and would still be traveling on Friday. He asked if I could get the meeting postponed. I said I would try. I called Peter who agreed to move the closing to the following week.

So it was early one October morning in 1982 while John was out in California that I opened my door to pick up my copy of the New York Times. I could not believe my eyes when I looked at the front page and read of John's arrest in a drug bust! It appeared that he was caught red-handed in a luxury hotel suite with unsavory characters that proposed to smuggle cocaine to raise money for his company. He was cuffed and carted off to jail. Even though he later won acquittal of all criminal charges by accusing the government of setting the whole thing up to entrap him, it was clear to me that once again he had surreptitiously "double dealt", just as he had in the Puerto Rico/Northern Ireland affair. He must not have been happy with Kalikow's deal and greedily took the bait of easier money and a sweeter deal.

The downward spiral continued for John. In the fall of 1983 the DeLorean Motor Company bankruptcy case turned from a voluntary debtor-in-possession proceeding under Chapter 11 into an involuntary bankruptcy under Chapter 7. A Trustee was appointed for the unsecured creditors who alleged that DeLorean, among other things, had defrauded the company of $19,000,000.

That I had distanced myself from John well before his greed and duplicity caused his downfall did not save me from the scrutiny, tribulation or the legal expenses caused by his legal entanglements—and not only in the case the bankruptcy Trustee was seeking to prove. Although ultimately DeLorean got his bankruptcy case settled and the fraud claims dismissed by paying $9,000,000, even the FBI and the US attorney investigating DeLorean eventually subpoenaed me. Since he was a former client, I had to explain that I was honor-bound by the attorney-client privilege to maintain my silence on any confidences he had imparted to me. Nevertheless, the federal authorities succeeded in getting a court order breaking the lawyer-client privilege and forcing me to answer their questions fully, and I did so. Eventually John's case went to trial in the Federal Court in Detroit where DeLorean was acquitted of all charges. The auto idol won his case but lost his Cristina who left him for a happier marriage.

I stayed out of touch with John although I did see him once in 2000 as we passed each other on an art gallery stairway without more than a nod. After John sold his apartment at 834 Fifth Avenue he moved to New Jersey where he lived quietly on a baronial Short Hills estate, still dreaming of starting another car company, until his death in 2005.

Miguel Aleman Valdez

One of the most satisfying and enjoyable client relationships of my legal career was with Don Miguel Aleman Valdez who had been the President of Mexico from 1946 to 1952. I had been representing Mexico's Tourist Council in New York for some time when my friend, "Chacho" Lopez LeCube, who worked for the Tourist Council, convinced Don Miguel, who had become its Chairman that I should represent him in the purchase of an apartment for his and his family's use in Manhattan. Chacho brought Don Miguel and his Mexican attorney to my office to introduce us.

Don Miguel was slight of build with classic Mayan facial characteristics. His easy engaging manner, charm and radiant smile camouflaged an intellect as sharp and decisive as a steel trap. Because he was a lawyer himself, he enjoyed addressing me as "Licenciado"—the Mexican salutation that accorded respect from one attorney to another. Don Miguel was a classic gentleman and courteous to a fault. We soon developed a strong and abiding fondness for each other, and our relationship deepened as we were both interested in politics and international relations. He treated me as his protégé, and placed me in a most trusted capacity by having me represent his young daughter and her mother. He also encouraged me to cultivate a friendship with his son, Mike Jr., in addition to representing the Mexican Tourist Council in the United States.

Every six years Don Miguel invited me to attend the inauguration of Presidents of Mexico as an official guest, and he would bring me to Mexico at other times so I could get to know the country better, and to meet his friends and associates. He would place his car and driver at my disposal with instructions to drive me to different parts of the country where I could see Mexico's cultural, scenic and touristic highlights.

One day in 1979 I got a phone call in my law office from Miguel Guajardo who was then the President of the Mexican Tourist Council. Mike had been the Chairman of the inaugural ceremony and festivities for Jose Lopez Portillo, the most recently elected President of Mexico, and served as Don Miguel's right hand in almost all areas. Mike told me that the Mexican government had spent a billion dollars to build a pipeline to ship their natural gas north to the United States instead of flaring it in their oil fields. He said that when President Carter refused to buy their natural gas at the price Mexico offered ($2.60 per thousand cubic feet), it was Don Miguel's desire that I become the purchaser of the natural gas from Mexico. He said Don Miguel and their party, the PRI, had always been close to America's Democratic party nationally and to the Democrats in Texas, but were now extremely angry with the Democrats and especially President Carter. He said I was the only Republican in the U.S. they liked and trusted, and that Don Miguel viewed me almost like a son.

I did not hesitate for even one moment. I told Mike Guajardo that I was deeply grateful, but I could not accept the offer. Mike could not believe it. "But it is worth hundreds of millions of dollars to you," he exclaimed. "You don't have to pay for the gas until you get paid on reselling it. We'll extend you the credit." I said "Sorry, Mike, no one would believe this is being done for me." He could not understand that I would reject that boon out of hand. I explained again that no one would believe this was done for me. They would think it was really for my uncle, a Republican and a United States Senator, and that I was just a "bag man" for him. I told Guajardo I could not do that to my uncle, and I have never regretted my decision.

Juan Carlos de Borbon, King of Spain

In 1961, Pepe Fanjul called to tell me that his close friend, Prince Juan Carlos de Borbon, was coming to Palm Beach to honeymoon with his bride, Princess Sofia of Greece. Pepe explained that Juan Carlos loved to play tennis and asked if I would play with him. The prince was then merely the protégé of Spain's dictator, General Francisco Franco, with the possibility of some day becoming King of Spain if the monarchy was restored.

I told Pepe that of course I would play tennis with Juan Carlos during his honeymoon. As I took the measure of the young Spanish prince during the course of a number of matches, I grew very fond of him. Tennis is a game that quickly reveals an opponent's personality, character and sportsmanship. Juan

Carlos was handsome, tall and fit. His radiant smile, quick sense of humor and endearing humility made me treat my new friend as just another regular guy.

I decided to throw a party at our home on Palmo Way for the newlyweds. That year the Twist was the rage in New York. I had seen Joey Dee and the Starlighters at the Peppermint Lounge on West 45th Street, so I booked the group to fly down and play at the party. Over seventy social lions of the Palm Beach party scene came, none of whom had ever done the Twist. However by the end of the evening they all had learned to energetically grind their hips to the Starlighters' hit song, "Twist Away."

When Juan Carlos was about to leave Palm Beach to return to Spain, he asked to have a few minutes with me in privacy. In that meeting, he told me how much it meant to him that I had made his holiday so enjoyable, and that he hoped our friendship would be permanent. He asked if I would keep a confidence if he told me something that had to be kept secret. He then said that at heart he was really a democrat like his father, Don Juan—Spain's monarch who had gone into exile in exchange for Franco's promise that he would raise his son to someday ascend the Spanish throne. Juan Carlos confided that if one day he did ascend the Spanish throne, he would make Spain a democracy and he would need my help. He stressed that if anyone in Spain learned his secret, he would never get to be the King of Spain. I promised to keep his secret, and to help him when that day would come. His pledge to make Spain a democracy was faithfully kept—mainly due to his conviction and courage.

That was the start of a close friendship that has lasted over fifty years during which time we have seen each other often, and each time it has been heartwarming and gratifying.

When in 1976, the King designated Adolfo Suarez as Prime Minister, I happened to have an early morning appointment for an audience with him at the Royal Palace in Madrid on the same day he was to swear in Spain's Council of Ministers. I walked across the enormous enclosed courtyard in front of the Palace and up the granite steps where I explained to the military guard at the entrance that I had an appointment to see His Majesty. I was immediately shown up a flight of stairs to the anteroom where the General Secretary ushered me through the reception room into the King's small private office. We hugged as we usually did in greeting each other, and then we began to chat about old times, memories, and the amazing journey from our tennis friendship to the culmination of Spain about to embark on its third experiment in the democratic form of government. After close to forty minutes I said I thought it be rude of me to take so much of his time. Juan Carlos said "It is not every day you come to see me, Eric. Besides, I have something important I want to discuss with you, and a favor I want to ask you."

Juan Carlos explained that his country had for many years had very favorable contracts with some Middle Eastern countries to supply oil at cheap prices, and although he wanted Spain to recognize Israel that was a democracy, he was not in a position to do so without jeopardizing those contracts. He told me Spain would recognize Israel as soon as it could afford to do so without suffering drastic economic consequences. His exact words were "I promise we will recognize Israel when we can afford to do so." He explained that he did not want a chorus of demands to do what he could not do currently, and he knew that my uncle, the Senator, might be able to pass the word to those who otherwise might put public pressure on Spain over this issue. Before I left him in his office, I did promise to discuss this upon my return to the United States.

I met with my uncle upon my return to New York and transmitted the King's request. I told of his assurance, and that I trusted his sincerity. My uncle told me he would get in touch with prominent Jewish leaders and opinion makers around the world, including members of the Rothschild family and others in the Western Hemisphere and Europe. For years there was silence on this issue. No public demands were made for Spain to recognize Israel.

Then, years later, in 1986 I got a phone call at my law office in New York from a gentleman whom I did not know. He said he was a friend of a friend who had instructed him to impart news to me so that I would be the first person in America to learn of it. He explained that not even in America's government was anyone informed that Spain would recognize Israel in the coming week. He asked me to please keep it confidential until it was officially announced. I thanked him and he rang off.

How many would bear in mind a favor for so many years? Spain was indeed fortunate to have such a thoughtful and enlightened king, and I to have such a loyal and faithful friend.

When a coup d'etat was attempted by rightists in an effort to displace Spain's young democratic government, the King of Spain donned his military uniform and called upon the army not to support the coup but to abide by Spain's new constitution. But for his immediate intervention, Spain would have reverted to autocratic rule, and its stirring example of peaceful transition from dictatorship to democracy would never have occurred.

Later on one of my trips to Spain, the King invited Margaretha and me to dinner and upon arriving at Zarzuela we were delighted to discover Alfonso Escamez, Chairman of Banco Central, and his wife were included for the dinner, as well. I had been on the board of directors of Banco Central of New

York and felt very comfortable with the warm relations that had arisen with Don Alfonso. During dinner the King related the story of how he almost disemboweled himself earlier that year when he raced from his pool terrace to answer an important phone call he had been expecting. The sliding glass door to the terrace that he thought was open was not, and he was running so fast that he shattered it completely. He had lost much blood, but fortunately he was rushed into surgery in time to survive. At that dinner I sat to the right of the Queen and directly across from us Margaretha sat to the right of the King. The fact Margaretha and I had the places of honor at the table despite the presence of the country's most important and influential banker was an indication of how esteemed was our friendship. However, the King's tale did not end with the number of stitches or transfusions that were needed. The "Peck's Bad Boy" side of Juan Carlos came to the fore as he turned to Margaretha and proudly began to unbutton his jacket and shirt to show her the scars he had sustained. Sofia shook her head with a sigh and a look of disapproval that stopped him from fully exposing scars that ran over his chest and stomach.

In 1991, my friend Earle Mack asked me to help him invite King Juan Carlos to the United States to celebrate the 500th anniversary of the expulsion of the Jews from Spain at a ceremony and Gala dinner given by Yeshiva University. I urged the king to accept the invitation; and not only did he graciously accept but he gave Spain's formal apology for the expulsion of the Jews that heralded in new spirit of tolerance between Spain's Catholics and the Sephardic Jewish community.

King Juan Carlos has been a faithful friend. He never failed to grant me an audience whenever I was in Spain. We also would see each other whenever he happened to come to America. He and Sofia even spent some private time with Margaretha and me when, in December 2004, the royal couple flew to Holland for Prince Bernhard's funeral.

When I was serving as ambassador to the OPCW in The Hague, I attended a diplomatic reception for Military attaches from various countries where I was introduced to an American admiral by Spain's ambassador, Juan Prat y Coll. The admiral asked whether Spain's king had been in Mallorca when the admiral had been in command of an American aircraft carrier there on a visit. The admiral went on to explain that a very fast powerboat had refused to keep its distance even after he warned it with a bullhorn to stay away and demanded the driver of the fast boat to identify himself. The answer came back "The King of Spain." The admiral wanted to find out if it really was the king who had yelled back to him. Ambassador Prat and I were good friends, so I said I would call the king the next day to find out. When we spoke, he admitted proudly that he had, indeed, buzzed the carrier and received a warning from its commander. I ran into the admiral again sometime later. He laughed when I told him that it really had been the king to whom he gave the warning. Considering the hole blown in an American destroyer by terrorists in Yemen in 2000, it was fortunate, indeed, that the King's playful escapade off Mallorca was nothing more than a laughing matter.

In May 2006, when I celebrated my 75th birthday in Madrid, Juan Carlos came to join Margaretha, her brother Carl, and me for an intimate dinner in a small private dining room at the Ritz Hotel where we were staying. After dinner we walked through the crowded lounge area of the lobby to accompany the King to his car. It was truly heartwarming to see the smiles, and the loving looks of respect on the faces of all the people who rose to their feet when they recognized that it was their king who was passing among their tables to leave the room.

On another occasion when I went to see Juan Carlos at Zarzuela, the palace that serves as the King and Queen's official residence in the countryside just outside of Madrid, I was driven through orchards of olive trees along its winding access road that led up to the building that resembles not a palace but a less formal country residence. After being ushered to a cozy room on the second floor, I took a seat on the sofa. While sitting there waiting to be invited in to the King's study I was gazing out at the view when I was stunned to see Queen Sofia clambering on the narrow ledge just outside the window that was at least thirty feet off the ground. I tapped on the window and asked loudly, "What in the world are you doing climbing the side of the building?" She replied that she was going to rescue her cat that had gotten up in a nearby tree and could not get down. When I asked why was she was not sending others to the rescue Sofia replied simply, "It's my cat."

One can only admire Queen Sofia's strength of character and her frank no-nonsense directness. She is a woman of intelligence, wit, charm and strong values.

The Spanish Institute Era

With the end of WW II, despite not being involved in the hostilities, Spain was indescribably poor as a result of its own destructive civil war and extended isolation from the international community.

When I visited Spain for the first time in 1948 and walked on the main shopping street of Madrid, none of the stores had their lights burning until a customer would walk in—and that was a rare event. In 1948 it cost me only twenty pesetas ($1) to take a taxi from Madrid's Barrajas airport to the Ritz Hotel in the center of the city, and the Ritz cost only 100 pesetas ($5) a night for the best double room. This desperate situation ended when America entered into a trade and military alliance with Spain as part of its Cold War containment policy toward the Soviet Union. This historic alliance between our two countries commenced with the signing of the Pact of Madrid in 1953. Spain continued emerging from isolation when it was admitted to the U.N. in 1955.

In the 60's the Spanish Institute was already known as the main cultural link between the United States and Spain. It had been founded some twenty years earlier, after the Spanish Civil War, by a few Americans who wanted to maintain contact with that country despite the reign of the country's fascist ruler, General Francisco Franco.

The Institute was housed in a beautiful land-marked townhouse at 684 Park Avenue that had been designed by the famous architect Sanford White. It had been donated to the Institute by Marquesa Margaret Rockefeller de Cuevas, a storied woman whom I knew from Palm Beach; and with whose son, Johnny de Cuevas, I went to elementary school there.

The central driving force in the Spanish Institute was its Chairman and one of its founders, George C. Moore, the President of Citibank. George was such a close friend of Jack Javits that when my uncle started his own law firm in 1956, George Moore directed all the Citibank real estate legal business to his newly-formed firm.

Once the building was donated to the Spanish Institute, George Moore realized it had to be renovated for use as a headquarters building. That meant it had to be compliant with the New York City Building Code. Knowing that would cost over a million dollars, he placed a mortgage on the building in order to borrow the necessary funds from a group of Spanish banks.

About that time he began to reduce his activity in Citibank, and as Chairman Emeritus he spent part of the year in Spain. Consequently, the affairs of the Institute began to be neglected to the point that the banks from which the Institute had borrowed were ready to call the loan and have the building sold.

Word got out that the Institute was on its deathbed. Its President at the time was Dr. Carleton Sprague Smith, an elegant and patrician intellectual of superb academic credentials, but unfortunately without the management skills and contacts necessary to raise funds.

That was the situation when I got a series of phone calls from Elizabeth Brockman, begging me to step into the picture and "save" the Institute. As a child, I had been very aware of Elizabeth Seversky, a client of my father's in her divorce from Maj. Alexander P. de Seversky. Elizabeth was an exotic, full-bosomed woman who invented elongated eyelashes and patented them but was never able to commercialize them successfully. She gave me a Doberman puppy for my thirteenth birthday that I named Ballet for its graceful athleticism. Eventually Elizabeth married David Brockman, Jack Javits' close friend and accountant, who had been widowed with two daughters and a son. David also was a real estate investor who had acquired a vast tract of property around Easthampton, Long Island, as well as an enormous virgin tract of land in the heights above Marbella, Spain. As a result of their land stake in Spain, Elizabeth courted and befriended Luis Badajoz who was married to King Juan Carlos' sister, Doña Pilar de Borbon, in the hope of somehow involving Luis in its development. Elizabeth understood well that his acumen and contacts could not only help, but would be indispensable to the future value of that property.

I was very active and engaged in the practice of law at the time, so I paid little heed to Elizabeth's pleas until she made it clear that 1) no one else was coming to the rescue, 2) that she was aware of my friendship with King Juan Carlos and how much I loved Spain, and 3) that since George Moore and Citibank were clients of my uncle's I could not sit by without trying to help avert a blemish on my uncle's friend, the Institute and US-Spain relations.

I finally relented and told her I would consider helping to save the Spanish Institute. I then called my friend, Angier Biddle Duke, who had served as ambassador to Spain and who was our neighbor in Southampton. I had known Angie for many years along with his mother who also lived in Southampton. I invited Angie to lunch at "21" and talked to him about saving the Institute. I told him that since he had been Ambassador to Spain he was indispensable to the Institute's survival, and that if he would agree to become the President, I would get involved on the Board, become Chairman of the Membership Committee, and help raise funds. Angie eventually agreed, and we entered upon the venture as a team.

Unfortunately, not long after Angie became the Institute's President, he was appointed Ambassador to Morocco by President Carter, at which point I did not want to move up to become its President, so I had to find someone to assume that role. I finally convinced George Robins who worked for one of the Spanish banks in New York to take the job. Unfortunately, he did not last long in the position, so I had to take the presidency myself. I recruited as Chairman of the Institute, John Davis Lodge, former ambassador to Spain and Governor of Connecticut who had been a family friend for most of my life. Alas, it was not long before John Davis Lodge also was appointed ambassador— this time by Ronald Reagan to Switzerland.

Eventually, Angier Biddle Duke came back from Morocco in 1981 to the Institute's chairmanship with a brainstorm. His idea was for the Institute to raise funds by throwing a Gala black tie dinner each year to be called the Gold Medal Gala at which the Institute would present its Gold Medal to someone prominent who would attract support for the Institute. Angie and I decided to give the first Gold Medal to Henry Ford II in recognition of Ford Motor Company having built an enormous plant in Spain to produce cars for Western Europe. Through the intensive efforts of Angie, myself and the Institute's Board, we raised enough money to pay off the banks and retire the mortgage on the building.

As years passed, the Gold Medal Gala became one of New York's most elegant and prestigious fundraising dinner dances. After that first Gala the Institute's Gold Medal was awarded each year to not one but two distinguished recipients. The King's sister, Dona Pilar, and Queen Sofia of Spain, often came to NY to attend the Galas, and New York's high society unfailingly turned out for the event. At every Gala always the most beautiful and expensive couture gowns and jewels were dazzlingly displayed.

Early on I realized that we needed a full-time hands-on director to run the Institute and its day-to-day cultural activities. I consulted the then Consul General of Spain in New York, Rafael Casares, for his advice. Rafael moved in many circles and knew everyone in New York that had an interest in or connection with Spain. Without a moment's hesitation Rafael hinted to me that he could make a recommendation, but he would only impart the name to me if I solemnly promised that if the Institute hired her she would be treated with the greatest consideration in every respect. After I pledged that would be the case, he suggested Inmaculada de Habsburgo for the position.

I wasted no time in seeking out and interviewing Immaculada. I saw in her all the qualities that Consul General Casares had mentioned. She was an intelligent, highly-educated and refined woman, a cousin of the King of Spain and deeply interested in Spain-US cultural relations. I could tell from the interview she would be outstanding in the Director's position, and happily she and I got along well, and she agreed to take the job.

Initially there was some sniping from one or two distinguished older members of academia who held strong opinions, like Professor Angel Alcala, who thought she was too young, that she only had her Masters of Arts degree, and, of course, was of the wrong gender. But over the next decade Inmaculada and I became the team that rebuilt the Institute. We brought on to its Board many distinguished figures from the U.S., Europe and Latin America who came from diverse fields of endeavor.

There were quite a few persons who had been interested and close to the Institute even before I got involved such as Spain's UN Ambassador Jaime de Pinies and his wife, Luz, and Jaime's brother, Dr. Felix de Pinies and his wife, Carmen (whom I had known as a Barnard student while I was an undergrad at Columbia College). The de Pinies families and especially Carmen had been important, even indispensible, members of the Institute. There also was a cadre of distinguished university professors who sat on the Institute Board that lent their cultural cachet and clout.

Some of the professors were skeptical, also, of my entry on the Institute scene. They viewed me primarily as a practicing lawyer without much background in Spain's rich culture. They were right about that, but in time they revised their view when they saw the time and support I gave to the cultural projects in which they were interested.

I oversaw the air-conditioning of the building to museum standards, and the installation of modern computer equipment, specially designed software, and a top-quality security system. I was determined that the Institute have an endowment. We could not rely, year after year, only on membership dues, contributions, fees for Spanish language classes or Gold Medal Gala ticket sales. I knew that sooner or later things would go badly, and the Institute would not be able to meet its budget.

The first step was to announce the need for an endowment. That took place at the presentation of a plaque in memory of Spain's beloved Luz de Pinies, wife of UN Ambassador Jaime de Pinies. Luz was a favorite of countless New Yorkers. Her friends responded by turning out, and many made modest donations to the Institute.

I could see that to build an endowment we needed some major gifts, as there was not a large enough circle of supporters to amass the necessary endowment from modest gifts. My and my family's close friend, Milton Petrie, was one of the most philanthropic benefactors in America at the time. I decided he might be instrumental in getting the first major gift for the Institute.

My father and I had been playing tennis doubles with Milton during lunch hours for many years on the roof of the United Parcel building on First Avenue and 38th street in New York, and Milton was one of my uncle Jack's closest friends and supporters. Milton's wife, Carroll, had also been my friend for many years around New York's social circles. Carroll had been married to Marques Alfonso de Portago, a Spanish racing car driver and heir to one of the most important titles in Spain. Carroll was no stranger to Spanish culture. I had recruited her to the Institute's Board, and eventually I proposed that she and Milton make the first major gift to firmly establish the endowment fund. They graciously responded, and we were then able to add the income from it to the annual income needed to cover budgeted expenses.

Since contributing her landmark Park Avenue town house to the Spanish Institute, Margaret Rockefeller de Cuevas had grown old, sick and lonely. She eventually married Raymundo de Larrain, an artistic and amusing member of a prominent Chilean family who was devoted and attentive to her. I had known Raymundo for many years around New York, and from time to time I had involved him in the Institute's efforts to refurbish the elegant décor of its palatial public rooms. Upon Margaret's death, Raymundo, as executor of Margaret's estate, decided to direct to the Spanish Institute a million dollar gift toward its endowment, for which we all were deeply grateful. That brought the endowment to a level greater than $2 million and ensured the Institute's ability to withstand unforeseen financial surprises.

Whenever I was in Spain I would always try to visit America's embassy in Madrid, and usually the person serving as the United States' ambassador to Spain was a friend. On a number of occasions I was able to help our ambassadors, as for instance in May 1978 when we held a luncheon at the Spanish Institute in New York in honor of Ambassador Terence Todman.

Todman had just been confirmed as Ambassador to Spain but had not left for his post. Terence was seated beside me at the lunch, and at the end of the meal he bemoaned the fact that he was going to leave shortly for Madrid, but "would have to sit all through the hot Madrid summer cooling his heels" because His Majesty was going on summer vacation right after he arrived and did not have time to afford him an audience for the presentation of his credentials.

I could not believe that the State Department could not get Todman an early date to present his credentials. Terence assured me they had tried every means but had come up short. I told him that I did not want to seem untoward, but if he had no objection I would try to see what I could do to get him the audience before the King left for Majorca. Terence said he certainly did not object. I promptly called Spain and told His Majesty that America's new ambassador was one of America's finest and most respected diplomats, that I had met him and knew that not only would he be outstanding as America's ambassador, the King would find him enormously likeable, trustworthy, forthright and frank.

The King promised me he would see Terence before leaving for his summer holiday. So upon landing in Spain Terence was able to present his credentials and go to work immediately.

On one of my trips over to Spain during Terence Todman's tenure at the Embassy, the issue of the renewal of our base treaty with Spain came up. The Pact of Madrid had been made during Eisenhower's Administration. It was the first outreach by the US to Spain during the Francisco Franco dictatorship, and by its terms it had to be renegotiated every five years. It allowed the US to have military naval and air bases on Spanish soil, but it also had two other aspects besides the military aspect—a cultural role and a scientific role. Not surprisingly, the cultural aspect of the Treaty was high on both Spain's agenda and the agenda of the Spanish Institute.

Terence told me the Treaty was on the table to be renegotiated, but I was devastated when he confided that he was about to meet his Spanish counterpart, Maximo Cajal, to negotiate renewal terms but felt ill equipped. Since Maximo and his wife Bea were close friends of Margaretha's and mine, and because Maximo was intimately familiar with my US-Spain cultural leadership at the Institute in New York, Maximo had earlier taken me into his confidence to warn me that despite Spain's close relationship with the United States, Spain would refuse to renew the treaty if only the military leg of the Treaty was under discussion for renewal.

I was not surprised when Terence confirmed at our meeting in his private office at the Embassy that he had been instructed to renew only the military aspect, not the scientific or cultural sections of the treaty. Terence realized that would kill any chance for the treaty's renewal, and the US would lose its naval base in Rota, as well as its Moron and Torrejon air bases. The loss of the naval base would be felt in the Mediterannean and the Atlantic. The loss of the airbases would be felt in diminution of air coverage over central Spain, Eastern and southern Europe, the Mediterannean, and the Spanish, Portuguese, French and North African coasts. The loss of bases would have to be made up at great expense. There was no overriding strategic or tactical reason for America dropping the scientific and cultural aspects. My guess is that the Defense Department thought them unimportant. They must not have understood the importance to the Socialist government of Spain of the Treaty's non-military aspects as a necessary sweetener to public opinion for giving control of Spain's key military bases over to a foreign power.

At the time there was widely held popular resentment in Spain against a) US fighter planes based at Torrejon, the air base near Madrid; b) against any role for Spain in NATO; and c) against any military role for Spain in Europe. The Socialists who governed Spain were certainly of that view. Once again I told Terence that I did not want to seem pretentious, but I would try to get his instructions changed to allow him to negotiate renewing all three aspects.

On my return to the United States I spoke to my uncle, then a very influential and senior member of the Senate Foreign

Relations Committee, and told him of the debacle that was about to occur if all three aspects of the treaty were not renewed. Quite soon thereafter Terence received a change of instructions and successfully negotiated renewal of all three aspects of the Treaty for another five years.

Besides being honored twice by the King of Spain with that country's Isabel La Catolica decoration, I was almost named ambassador to Spain on three occasions as I had not only been contributing to, campaigning and raising money for Republican candidates all my life and been a surrogate speaker for Ronald Reagan's presidential campaigns, but was actually well qualified to do the job. The first occasion occurred in the Reagan Administration when the Chairman of the Foreign Relations Committee, Senator Charles Percy of Illinois, told me that it had been decided at the highest level that I was going to be nominated as ambassador to Spain by the President. I was elated that I would finally get the chance to do public service. However, suddenly I was informed of a last minute glitch. Tom Enders, who headed the State Department's Latin American Affairs Bureau, had been unceremoniously dumped from that position for refusing to toe the line on Reagan's Nicaraguan Contras policy.

Such a furor arose amongst the rank and file of the State Department's career personnel resentful of White House political interference with one of the Department's favorite sons that it was decided it would be necessary to quell the rebellion by promoting Enders to some prestigious ambassadorial post to get him out of Foggy Bottom, as the State Department's office building was familiarly called. No other European ambassadorship was vacant at that moment except Spain's.

I happened to be in Spain when it was rumored that Enders would be coming as the next US ambassador. The Spanish media had heard earlier that I would be the next ambassador, so when Enders' appointment was announced the Spanish press naturally asked me to comment. I felt it was incumbent upon me to help Enders be well received. The Spanish papers carried my praise of President Reagan's appointment of Enders.

During the period when I served as the Spanish Institute's President and then Chairman, we organized groups of Board members to visit Spain as a delegation to stimulate cultural relations and support for the Institute. On these trips we were given access to places and sites that no tourist would ever be permitted to enter, feted at the residences of Spain's leading bankers, industrialists, and cultural leaders and given audiences with His Royal Majesty, the King of Spain.

Years later, when the Spanish Institute held one of its cultural trips to Spain, the organizer and leader of the touring group was Gaetana Enders, then the widow of former Ambassador to Spain, Thomas Enders, who had suddenly passed away after his return to retirement in the United States.

Margaretha and I were planning to travel to Spain at the same time as Gaetana's group, but we elected to travel alone in order to have more autonomy in our schedule than merely following the group program. We did, however, all stay in the same hotel in Madrid where we ran into members of the group daily.

Gaetana was a self-involved ball of energy, born in Morocco and just five feet tall, while her late husband had stood at least six feet four inches. In years past when the couple took the dance floor at the Spanish Institute's Gold Medal Galas, despite their great disparity in height, they danced well and with relish at any opportunity.

On that trip, my cherished friend, Placido Arango, one of Spain's wealthiest and most influential figures who had always been very supportive of the Spanish Institute's cultural programs, had graciously agreed to host a party for the Institute's visiting group. Gaetana had sent word to us, as we were not part of her visiting group, that we were not invited to Placido's party. However, unbeknownst to Gaetana, Placido himself had asked us to be there, too. When Gaetana saw us at Placido's party she glared our way as though we had crashed the party and committed some unforgivable gaffe.

And as so often happens, history repeated itself! The very next day an audience with the King had been scheduled for the tour group at the Royal Palace in Madrid. I also had requested a separate audience with the King and had been told to get there a half hour before the Spanish Institute group. When the large group walked in to the large antechamber where one waits before being invited into the Kings chambers, led by Gaetana, with Michael Dukakis' Vice Presidential candidate, Lloyd Bentsen with his wife in tow, Margaretha and I were the only other persons there. Once again Gaetana glared in our direction.

A few minutes later the General Secretary emerged to announce that Margaretha and I were to go in to meet His Majesty and the Institute's group next. Gaetana leapt up to protest that she had arranged the audience for Senator Bentsen, and that protocol demanded that they be first to see the King. The General Secretary very politely informed her that Mr. and Mrs. Javits were personal friends of the King, so Senator Bentsen and the group would simply have to wait.

There was not much Gaetana could say, but she would not give up. The next day the group had been invited to a cocktail/dinner at the home of Ignacio and Yolanda Fierro. Ignacio was a client of mine, and I had arranged for him to host the group on that occasion. However, Pepe and Emilia Fanjul had privately invited us to join them that night at private dinner they were hosting for His Majesty, members of his family, and a few friends that night at Zalacain, so I called Ignacio Fierro to explain why we could not come to his event that night. Early the next morning Gaetana caught Margaretha as she was passing through the hotel lobby. Many members of the Institute's group were standing around, including the Fanjuls, who overheard Gaetana calling out Margaretha for not showing up at Ignacio's party. Margaretha pleaded with Gaetana to lower her voice, but her pleas were ignored. Finally, Margaretha told her in a whisper that we had been dining with the King. The look on her face was priceless.

By the time the ambassadorial position in Spain came open again, Al Haig had become Reagan's Secretary of State. Both General Haig and his deputy, "Woodie" Goldberg, interviewed me at the State Department for the position. General Haig told me at the end of that meeting that I would be their candidate. Unfortunately, in 1981when Reagan was shot and General Haig made his infamous remark "I am now in control", Haig was no longer Secretary of State when the nomination of the next ambassador to Spain was made.

The third time I was almost appointed ambassador to Spain was when Donald Regan became President Reagan's Chief of Staff in 1987. Don had earlier been Chairman and CEO of Merrill Lynch where we got to know each other well as a result of my having served for many years as an Independent General Partner to both Merrill Lynch Venture Partners Funds I and II. Don assured me that he would arrange my appointment to Spain with the president, but quite soon after he got into a spat with Nancy Reagan and his tenure as Chief of Staff came to a hasty end.

Finally, in 1989, I had to resign from all boards and private engagements, including as Chairman of the Spanish Institute, upon being appointed Ambassador Designate to Venezuela by President George H. W. Bush. However, I continued to be listed as the Institute's Chairman Emeritus for some years thereafter until I joined the distinguished list of awardees of the Institute's Gold Medal when Mayor Rudy Giuliani presented me with the Institute's Gold Medal at its Gala in the fall of 1995.

In all the years of my involvement in US-Spain relations, I never exploited my position or connections in Spain for my personal, professional or commercial benefit. I kept cultural relations as my paramount concern, aware that any self-interest would sully me and the Institute. With the help of many others, I left the Institute stronger and more vibrant than I found it.

"Willow Hill"

When things became difficult financially in America in the late '70s and into the '80s, the Hamptons nevertheless became a "hot" a real estate market. Margaretha suggested it might make sense for us to rent out Las Casitas for the summers and try to find a farm or country place to buy quite inexpensively up in the Catskill Mountain area where we could also ski, so we decided to drive upstate and look around.

My back had gone out the month before keeping me in bed and not even able to walk to the bathroom. But once I could stand up, we borrowed a station wagon from a friend that Margaretha drove up to Catskill, New York, while I stretched out in the back with my knees propped up on pillows. There we met a real estate broker who took us all over the area, but we did not find any properties that interested us. Either they were too remote, too run down or too unattractive. We were impressed with the rural character and natural beauty of the area, but surprised at the disrepair, neglect and junk we saw lying everywhere. Despite that, we decided to keep trying because upstate New York was so depressed that we hoped to find an attractive place at a bargain price if we continued looking.

My sister, Joan, on hearing of our quest, told us that the best real estate broker in the Catskill area happened to be the father of her son's closest friend, Mike Price. We reached Mr. Price, Sr. who agreed to show us homes and farms he had listed for sale. A week or so later, Margaretha again drove the station wagon "ambulance" up to Catskill, and although I could barely sit or walk, the broker showed us places that were much nicer than what we had seen.

The last house he wanted to show us was the one he thought was the best buy. I was lying in the back of the wagon as it climbed up and up Cook Hill in a place called Potter Hollow. Suddenly a beautiful house appeared, and we turned into a driveway slightly covered with snow and ice. I knew the moment I saw it sitting on the side of the mountain surrounded by stately weeping willows that it would be the hideaway for us.

When we walked through the house, part of which had been built in the late 18th century, it was clear it needed to be insulated, painted, carpeted, furnished, a bathroom added upstairs and the downstairs bathroom and kitchen redone and equipped. The owner was desperate to sell, so he immediately accepted our offer for the house, its three barns and fifteen acres. The purchase price was far less than the summer rental we got for our place in Southampton. We appropriately named our new country home "Willow Hill".

We hired a German contractor from the area who was neat, honest, efficient and who finished the job quickly. We hired a bulldozer that took out a few of the many willow trees which improved the view, and at the same time dug a small pond near the house that was both picturesque and provided a water supply in case of fire.

The second summer we had to address the three attached barns that stood downhill not far from the house. They clearly needed new roofs, were leaning alarmingly downhill and looked in danger of collapsing. We hired a crew that travelled around restoring old barns. They winched and cabled the barns upright, built new supports, replaced beams and doors, put crushed shale inside on the bare ground, and added metal roofing. After a mason built a stone base around the foundations, we painted the barns ourselves.

We put gym equipment in the attic of the house that kept my back in good shape except for one winter night when I went out to fetch some firewood and slipped on some black ice that was invisible under a thin layer of newly fallen snow. That fall left me stunned with a cracked vertebrae.

We only had a few neighbors in the area. The Cook family had lived at the top of Cook Hill for generations. The family had a herd of dairy cows and several hundred acres that covered the top of the mountain and included wooded areas and fields of hay. We were a little hesitant to meet them, but we decided to drive up to their house to introduce ourselves. They were surprisingly receptive to meet the new "snakes from the city" as they called anyone from New York City. The Cook family was led by elderly Dean Cook and his wife. Their son, Walter and his wife Wilma, had two young boys, Steven and Shawn all lived together in their modest farmhouse. Dean was the farmer, assisted by his son Walter who also drove the mail for the post office and dug graves to earn extra money. The family was a staunchly Republican churchgoing clan that rose with the sun to milk the cows, cut the hay and tend their fields. We let them store hay in our barns, as they did not have enough space in their own for all the bales.

One day a filthy stray cat—starved, bruised and battered like it had survived an encounter with a fox or a coyote—came dragging itself up Cook Hill. Margaretha, hoping it would put on some weight, immediately named it Winston, after Churchill. She took it to the vet for suturing, a rabies shot and worming. We put it on a bed of blankets in the barn and fed it daily. As Winston grew strong and filled out, he would come to the kitchen door, jump up and just hang from its screen by his claws, mewing his desire to be admitted to the house. This went on for a few days until Margaretha, despite her being allergic to cats, weakened and let him in. Winston went straight to our bedroom, jumped up on the big bed and settled himself as if he owned it. As it was summer, Winston preferred to sleep under a peony bush for which Margaretha was grateful.

Winston was always with us whenever we would walk up the mountain or sit on our terrace for dinner to watch the sunset and the wild turkeys or the deer slowly come up the hill onto our property.

From the apples on our trees we made apple pies, and we always cut up some to throw out on the lawn so that herds of deer would come close to the house to find the sweet-smelling slices. We would watch them from the window and listen to their grunts as they mouthed and gummed the tasty morsels. We also had a family of raccoons—masked bandits—that used to climb up on the porch to eat Winston's leftover food. The raccoon mother was vastly overweight and could barely hoist herself up on the porch, but her babies would eagerly scramble up the high porch step to wash their hands in Winston's bowl of water before eating. They could see us watching them through the kitchen window, but it did not faze them one bit.

That was not the only wildlife on Cook Hill. We had packs of wild coyotes that could be heard howling in the woods, but the biggest shock was the night I went out to fetch some firewood and saw an animal with short beige fur, cropped ears and bobbed tail reminiscent of a boxer dog, crouching on a tree limb near the kitchen door—but dogs don't climb trees. I stared into the luminous eyes of that North American lynx until it jumped down and ran away.

As time went on we discovered that we were not alone in Willow Hill. At night when we would eat alone at the long wooden table in our big kitchen, we could hear a chorus of voices singing what sounded like hymns or church chorales. I searched without success for a possible source of the music, but there were no wires, no antennae no electronic source whatever that I could find. We found it to be very soothing and peaceful to the ears, and it never disturbed us. When we told the neighbors about "the singers" they looked at us a little strangely.

Then, one evening we discovered at dinner that we had run out of milk, so we called the Cooks to see if their son Steven (who by that time had been hired to cut our grass) could come down with a quart of milk. A few minutes later Steven showed up at the kitchen door. I told him to come in and be very quiet to see if we could hear the singers. Steven stood for a few moments while we sat back down at the dinner table. Suddenly the music and singing could be heard. Steven's hair stood straight up on his head. I had seen that happen on an animal, but never had I seen that happen to a human being. He became pale and speechless and left in a hurry.

After that, at least one of our neighbor families no longer looked skeptical when we mentioned "The Singers". But that was not the only strange occurrence at Willow Hill. Because we were finding our front door wide open when we would come up from New York, we thought someone was intruding into our house, so we had an alarm system installed with motion sensors that could detect any movement in the house at the hallways, kitchen and front entrances. We had a double deadlock installed on the front door to be sure it could not be jimmied, and we talked to the Cooks to alert them to investigate if they saw our front door open during times when we were not there, because even if the alarm was tripped, the State Police headquarters in that area was at least twenty minutes away.

One weekend we drove up on Friday and again found the front door wide open. We could not believe our eyes. We had double locked and checked the door before we left the house to return to the city. When we called the State Police to report that it was open, they said no alarm had been tripped that week.

We also found things on other weekends that seemed to have been moved from where we left them. We put those incidents down to our own bad memories.

However, soon thereafter we invited a couple of friends to come up to spend the weekend. We put them upstairs in a room next to the bathroom at the top of the staircase. The next morning at breakfast, the husband asked Margaretha why she had come up in the middle of the night to use their bathroom when she had her own bathroom downstairs?

Margaretha said she had not gone to their bathroom and had in fact slept through the night without having to get up. The husband said that they had left their bedroom door open, and he clearly heard and saw a woman in a nightgown come up the stairs go into their bathroom. He said at first he thought it might have been his wife, so he felt the bed next to his, and his wife was lying there asleep, so he assumed it had to be Margaretha.

We asked the neighbors if they had ever heard of any strange stories about our house. They finally confessed that there were rumors about a woman having been murdered in it, but they were vague on details. However, one day the "singers" just stopped singing, and after that there were no more strange events.

We sold Willow Hill when our financial situation improved, but those storybook summers and white-as-snow winters still hold a big space in our hearts.

Cleaning up United Americas Bank

In 1974, Chon Gonzalez Byass, a Spanish citizen and member of the family that controls the Gonzalez Byass sherry company in Jerez, invested over a million dollars for a minority percentage of the common stock of United Americas Bank on whose board sat some sleazy sharp types—plus Herbert Tenzer, the bank's lawyer and senior partner of the prominent law firm of Tenzer Greenblatt. Tenzer was a former Democratic member of congress who enjoyed a reputation for integrity and professionalism.

Fortunately, I had not represented Chon in the purchase of her shares in the bank, but Chon had heard of my reputation in Spain, and since she had the right to appoint one director, she called to ask me to be her representative on the board of the bank.

The United Americas Bank, formerly known as Underwriters Bank and Trust, had been taken over by a new group that changed its name in January of 1974. It quickly became apparent to me that the new group in control of the bank, together with the bank's president, had given Chon a fraudulent set of figures to induce her to invest, because soon after her purchase and my being seated on the board as her representative, the bank released a radically restated, disastrous set of figures.

Chon wanted to sue for fraud to cancel the deal, or to remove the entire board and place her trusted Spanish businessman and friend, Rafael Calleja, in charge of cleaning house and running the bank. I advised that I should first meet privately with Herbert Tenzer to see if he would split away from the group in control. In our meeting I told Tenzer that he could come over to Chon's side and work to remove the other directors, in which case he could keep his seat on the board and retain the bank's legal work, or he would be included as a defendant in the fraud case and we would seek to remove him from the board. Herbert Tenzer proved to be an honorable man. He immediately said he would work with us to change the board composition and get Calleja elected to clean up and run the bank.

We fired off a letter demanding the resignations of the "bad guys." In it we threatened suit if they did not immediately resign from their board and management positions, and stated that we were asking the Federal banking authorities to investigate the bank's affairs and their conduct. They fled like rats from a sinking ship.

It took six years to recapitalize and properly finance the bank, collect bad loans and build a portfolio of good loans for the bank—all under close scrutiny by the authorities. At first, the banking authorities were dubious about allowing Rafael and me to be in control of the bank because Rafael, despite being an experienced business executive, had never run a bank. I had never served on a bank board. Thus I, too, had no banking experience.

Facing this evident skepticism on the part of the bank examiners, I took Calleja to see my old friend, Muriel "Mickey" Siebert, who was at the time the Superintendent of Banks for New York State. I had met Mickey in 1960 when she was just a young employee at Casper Rogers and Co, the firm that underwrote the initial public offering for Solitron Devices, Inc. From our very first meeting at the N.Y. State Banking Department it was clear that Mickey Siebert liked Rafael Calleja. She must have spoken to the federal authorities to let us go ahead and rebuild the bank because the hostility and skepticism we had felt earlier suddenly evaporated.

At the end of five years of exhaustive effort, we were able to sell a healthy United Americas Bank to Banco Central of Spain. The bank's board was reshuffled, and Rafael Calleja was replaced as President by Antonio Escamez, a dashing young executive and nephew of the Spanish bank's distinguished Chairman, Alfonso Escamez

At the first meeting of the newly constituted board of the New York bank, both Don Alfonso and his nephew Antonio came from Madrid. I was pleased to meet the Chairman of Spain's leading bank. I found him to be likeable and tremendously impressive in his carriage and bearing. I had heard that he had started out as a humble sweeper of the sidewalks and front steps at the headquarters building of the bank in Madrid without education or family background to speak of, but through diligence and perseverance had, step by step, proven his dedication, work ethic, intelligence and leadership ability until he finally rose to become the head of the bank.

It pleased me that such amazing upward mobility was available not only in America. I was gratified that after meeting me, he decided I should continue serving on the board of the bank that then (1980) became known as Banco Central of New York.

Life in Sweden

By the early 1980s driving to and from Southampton on summer weekends had become an ordeal. Sitting in dense traffic on Friday and Sunday afternoons was tiring and annoying. Prices of real estate and everything else had skyrocketed as the Hamptons became the "in" place. Margaretha and I began to think about spending summers elsewhere.

Because Margaretha was aware of how fond I had become of Sweden, in 1985, one year after her mother's passing, she bought our first home there — a little "torp" about 100 years old on the island of Varmdö, forty minutes east of Stockholm by car. It was Margaretha's decision to purchase the cottage, and she bought it entirely with her own money. It was situated on a nice piece of land that included lovely oak, pear and cherry trees, lawn areas, as well as a lovely section of pine-filled virgin forest harboring patches of wild blueberries through which a winding foot path led down to a small dock on the Baltic Sea.

On the ground floor of the cottage was a tiny entrance hall with a narrow staircase to the second floor, a small bathroom, an eat-in kitchen with a wood-burning stove, a small living room and a bedroom, both with porcelain heating stoves called "kakelugnar". On the second floor was a fairly sizeable study with a desk, TV and convertible sofa, and adjoining it was a small but cozy bedroom. I was impressed that Margaretha decorated the house almost entirely with Ikea furniture. No one could have guessed that it was done on a budget of only $5,000! She papered the walls herself, used charming fabrics (bought in the U.S., England and France) to sew the curtains, and quilted others to make bedcovers and pillow shams.

Margaretha named the cottage '"Ericstorp" in the hope that I would feel it was my "home away from home". Eventually, she had a covered porch extended out from the living room so guests could eat comfortably outdoors in the summer. With her vision and talent, she made it look like a Carl Larssen illustration from a Swedish story book.

Ericstorp was located less than a kilometer from Bullandö where hundreds of the finest sail boats and motor yachts were moored. The Bullandö marina ran a small grocery store as well as an excellent restaurant that was patronized by the boating fraternity or anyone in the area desiring a delicious meal in a nautical setting.

I had to marvel at the fact that socialist Sweden had over a thousand marinas and boat basins, just this one of which easily held a billion dollars worth of boats! It was common knowledge that Swedes, like their Viking ancestors, loved the water so much that boats were the only assets not taxed under Swedish law.

For seventeen years we spent wonderful summers at Ericstorp. I could play tennis nearby at the Saltarö tennis club and swim in the Baltic after only a short walk through our forest. The Swedish archipelago was made up of thousands of islands, some of which could be seen from our small dock — some near and some far. One afternoon Margaretha and I went there to swim when I noticed that one of the distant islands had moved. I thought I was seeing things, but Margaretha discerned it was not an island but a camouflaged warship. While marvelling at the ship's disguise, we saw helicopters swooping in to hover over the water quite close to the ship. Then we noticed some frogmen diving in the water on some invisible object. After a while the helicopters, boats and divers left the area.

We learned later that the Swedish Navy had trapped a Russian sub just inside the narrow strait between two islands. In order for graduating Russian sub commanders to win permanent command of their vessel they had to traverse the treacherous rocky-bottomed Swedish archipelago to retrieve some objects left in different places and return to base undetected. The Swedish Navy merely spray painted the sub so that when the Russian returned to port, his failure would be apparent. Would that all war games were so civilized!

Whenever we drove from Ericstorp on Varmdö to stay in Stockholm overnight we were welcome to sleep at Margaretha's brother's apartment. Stockholm, an immaculate and stunningly beautiful cluster of islands and water stapled together with bridges and ferries, held endless attractions in its performing arts, its manicured parks, the Wasa ship museum and the breathtaking Millesgården art museum and sculpture garden on Lidingö, to name just a few. The city's roster of restaurants for the freshest seafood anywhere are a match for those of any major city, not to mention its clean air, pure water and gracious vivacity.

Eventually, when the opportunity arose, Margaretha decided to buy a one bedroom "pied-a-terre" in the same lovely apartment building at Lovisagatan in Stockholm's Golden Triangle where she and her brother grew up, and where he still lived, close to the bridge from Strandvägen to Djurgården island.

Margaretha and I eventually grew to feel that Ericstorp was a bit too small for us to have guests or family stay comfortably for any length of time. So in the summer of 2000 we started to look around within an hour's drive of Stockholm. It had always been Margaretha's dream to have an old classical Swedish manor house at the edge of a lake, but those were exceedingly expensive because laws prohibited the building of any new houses closer than several hundred feet from a lake or the sea.

We hoped to at least find land that would have a view of water, however distant.

By the end of the summer our efforts had been exhausted. I went back to the United States while Margaretha stayed on for some days in the hopes of still finding something. On impulse, she took a chance and called a prominent broker who specialized in country farms and estates. She described what she was looking for, never expecting to get it at a price she could afford; but the broker surprisingly said he had just the thing she wanted about one hour south of Stockholm, and she should come to see it the next day as it was going on the market the following week. Margaretha and her brother went to see "Grindstugan" (The Gate Cottage), a small manor house which had belonged to Tista Castle to which the late Count's widow would repair when her son, the new Count would marry, so that he and his bride could then take over Tista Castle.

Grindstugan was in disrepair. Margaretha emailed photos to see what I thought. Both her brother and I did not want to abandon cozy and charming "Ericstorp" for a wreck of a house that had to be completely renovated, so we both tried to discourage her. That proved impossible. She bought it that weekend, again with her own money. Margaretha then put Ericstorp on the market at a premium price, and because of its singular charm a bidding contest ensued. Her aptitude for real estate investment was validated when she realized five times what she had put into it, but then she spent two years renovating Grindstugan at a cost far greater than its purchase price.

The next summer was my first opportunity to see the house up close, so we flew from Geneva, where I was posted at the Conference on Disarmament, to Stockholm. Margaretha drove us to the house over seemingly endless deserted country roads past the Stockholm South (Skavsta) airport that had been

247

converted from a decommisioned Swedish airforce base, past Tista castle and through gorgeous tree-lined country lanes. I could not fathom how she ever found her way to such a remote place, so I asked her "How in hell did you ever find this place?" She replied with a smile "You don't call me Radarnose for nothing!"

When we arrived at Grindstugan its renovation was in full swing. Sections of the beautiful parquet flooring had been removed from the living room where the beams which had rotted needed to be replaced. The extent of the repairs was daunting, but after another year the final result was more than gratifying. The upstairs bedroom that iconic Swedish film star, Greta Garbo, had occupied during her many summer visits at Grindstugan was ready for our use. Accented with authentic Swedish and French antiques, as well as handpainted pieces that Margaretha lovingly did herself, the house had an ease and elegance that integrated beautifully with the sweeping views of the pristine lake where no other houses disturbed our view.

Despite the comfort and beauty of the new house, I was sorely missing a good tennis club nearby comparable to my tennis club at Saltarö. Margaretha started to ask around. She learned from her carpenter about a nearby estate with a beautiful clay court. She very hesitantly called up, introduced herself, and explained my availability as a tennis partner. However, in well-mannered Sweden one is expected to be properly introduced. To just cold call is unthinkable. Despite this breach of etiquette a close and wonderful friendship was formed with the owners of the Broo Gård estate, and I have never lacked for a tennis game since. In the two years that I played the Swedish National Veterans Tennis championships in Båstad, I reached the doubles final of the Men's 75s in 2010, but only the semi-final the next year when I tore a hamstring.

There have been many things to enjoy in the Swedish summers. Fishing on our lake in the evenings with our neighbor; walking through the gorgeous lush countryside; watching the young bucks and does come out of the woods to eat from our apple trees; picking chanterelles in the magnificent moss-covered forests, or going out to an 18th century drop dead charming country inn for a superb and late five-star dinner during one of the "White Nights". Since Skavsta airport had a gliding school, for my 75th birthday I enjoyed soaring over the beautiful landscapes of castle country with its forests, farms and countless lakes. Skavsta also has a skydiving club, so for my 80th birthday I took my first sky dive out of an old military bi-plane from 12,000 feet.

When we have driven in our Volvo Cross Country through other areas of Sweden such as Dalarna in the north or Skåne in the south to visit friends or family, we encountered heartwarming hospitality and endless scenic delights. Our circle of friends in the area where we live are grateful for Margaretha's restoration of historic Grindstugan, and we are grateful for their friendships and the comforts we enjoy as we spend our summers there.

Having visited Sweden for over thirty years, I am ashamed to say I still cannot speak the language, but since almost every Swede speaks English I feel right at home. Our experience each summer in the Swedish countryside has been a gentle, peaceful and restorative escape away from the frantic summer weekends in Southampton.

The Final Chapter in Jack Javits' Political Career

Jack had been a US Senator for twenty-two years when, in 1979, Margaretha and I were invited to Jack's apartment on

East 57th Street to join Jack and Marian, their son Joshua Javits and his wife, Sabina, for a family Thanksgiving lunch. Josh and Sabina had both achieved prominence in their respective fields of endeavor—Josh in labor law dispute resolution, and Sabina, who was fluent in Japanese, in Japanese commercial relations.

At that point, Margaretha and I had been together for a couple of years and married for almost six months. We were both extremely fond of, and had established a close relationship with, Josh and Sabina. The table conversation naturally turned to the question of whether Jack should run the next year for a fifth term in the US Senate.

I had been urging Jack for five years to start raising money for his 1980 race, but he never lifted a finger to get anything organized. I said I did not predict he would be defeated, but I pointed to his failure to amass a campaign war chest and his questionable health although I did not know, nor at that point did he or the family, that he had the beginnings of a serious illness. All I knew was that when we played tennis he was complaining of some weakness in his right hand. I suggested that instead of running, he might take the ambassadorship to Mexico that would place no strain on his health. It could have been his for the asking, so highly regarded was he in Mexico.

However Margaretha, with her usual candor, did not mince words. She said for his and his family's sake, at his age and without the necessary war chest, he should not run again, and that if he ran, he would lose! I sided with Margaretha in urging him not to make the race. I opined it was time for him to slow down and enjoy a bit of his later life. Jack looked shocked, but he seemed to have listened.

At the luncheon he finally conceded he did not know how to explain to his constituents that he was abandoning them after four terms in which they had given him their trust and support. I said in that case I would write his withdrawal speech. Some days later we spoke again, and he said that he would not run for reelection, and that he would announce it right after the first of the year. He reminded me that I had to draft a suggested statement for him.

The following month Margaretha and I flew over to the Palace Hotel in St. Moritz, Switzerland, to ski during the Christmas and New Year holiday. Just before year-end I called Jack from there to ask if the withdrawal statement I had drafted and sent to him was satisfactory. He said that he was still undecided but would decide soon.

A day or so later I had a call from Jack. He told me he had decided to run again. He said that an Op-Ed piece in the NY Times entitled, "Say it isn't so, Jack", convinced him not to let down his constituents. He said he wanted to give them the chance to vote him out but not to just quit on them.

When I got back to NY I learned there was to be a meeting at Jack's 57th Street apartment with his closest supporters to discuss the campaign. Alphonse D'Amato had announced that he was going to oppose Jack in the Republican primary, and there was some concern, although every expectation, that Jack could be re-nominated as a Republican.

I went touring through upstate New York with Jack's young campaign manager, meeting with upstate Republican county chairman, to try to keep them in Jack's corner. But D'Amato was more effective in cornering and nailing them down, and Jack's longtime neglect of the New York Republican Party machinery became his Achilles heel. D'Amato, a conservative, had been a County Manager on Long Island and was quite adept at machine politics. He was also popular in conservative areas of the state. D'Amato ran TV spots all over the state showing a framed portrait of Jack falling off the wall, raising people's doubts about his age and declining health and whether they could afford to keep him as their senator.

Finally primary day came, and Jack lost the Republican nomination for the US Senate. He still had the nomination of the Liberal Party, but the general election would now be a three-way race, and the Liberal Party had a much smaller registered voter base than either of the other two major parties.

Another meeting at Jack's apartment was hastily called to decide if he would remain in the race as the candidate of the Liberal Party against both Elizabeth Holtzman, a lawyer nominated by the Democratic Party, and D'Amato, the Republican candidate. There must have been more than fifty persons that gathered in Jack's huge high-ceilinged living room overlooking 57th street. Jack's campaign staff was there together with all his major supporters and closest friends.

The group was told that he had to raise $500,000 in order for his campaign ads to begin on statewide television and that was only a minimal figure. No one spoke up to offer support or pledge a donation. I could not believe the apathy and lack of support from this loyal group. Clearly they all thought it was a lost cause but were too polite to say so.

Finally Jack's public relations/press secretary broke the silence. He argued for Jack to resign the Liberal nomination, drop out of the race and throw his support to Liz Holtzman. I regarded those remarks as coming from a spineless staffer, or worse, from someone who preferred electing a Democrat instead of a Republican as New York's next United States Senator.

I rose from my seat and beckoned to two of my closest friends to follow me into another room. Leonard Lauder, Ed Downe and I went into the adjoining library and shut the door. I said the three of us could surely raise the $500,000, and once we did, the momentum would re-energize the group. I said that perhaps with enough ticket splitting by Democrats and Republicans Jack would get re-elected in a three-way race.

Leonard said that he wanted to help, but was leaving for Europe in a few days and really could not work the phones, etc., until much later on. Ed said that he, too, was leaving for Europe shortly. The two did, however, agree to lend and/or donate the campaign money to enable it to at least get started and each did lend Jack the money. That left only me to carry the burden since we had to raise donations immediately or lose the chance to demonstrate that Jack was still a viable candidate.

The three of us walked back into Jack's living room where I announced that we had agreed to raise the $500,000, and if necessary we would personally underwrite the necessary money if all or part of it had to be borrowed.

The next day I had a phone conversation with Jack in which he said he was thinking of taking his Press Director's advice! I said I wanted to see him at once. It was clear to me that if Jack pulled out, Liz Holtzman would be the next US senator because Jack's Liberal Party supporters would never vote for D'Amato and all those votes would go to Holtzman.

I hurried over to Jack's NY senate office on Lexington Avenue. When we were alone I told him that if he dropped out of the race it would be unconscionable. I told him that he, and he alone, had made the decision to run, after the family and others had advised against it, and he had said he would not. Then he changed his mind, and I reminded him that the reason he gave me was that "he could not quit on his constituents." I told him that if he quit on them now, he would be a weakling and coward in my eyes and disloyal to his faithful supporters.

It is my firm belief that I, and I alone kept him in the race with the dressing down I gave him that day. I knew it would probably mean that Alfonse D'Amato—certainly no family friend—would become the next United States Senator from New York, but I felt that was preferable to the Republican Party losing the seat.

Within days the New York Times ran an article by one of its star political reporters, Jane Perlez, casting doubt on whether Jack could even raise enough money to mount a credible campaign. Ed Downe and Leonard Lauder had already left town, and I was incensed that her article would make my job more difficult in getting donations we had pledged. So I called Jane Perlez and challenged her to come over to my office to sit beside me while I worked the phones. I have to give her credit. She did come and watch me as I raised contribution after contribution on the phone, none less than $5,000 each. That was enough for her. She wrote with less skepticism after that.

When the day of the election arrived, Jack invited Margaretha and me to the suite where, with a few friends, he watched the returns come in. As the tide turned against him and it was clear he would no longer be the Senior United States Senator from New York, I could see disappointment in his eyes but only because I knew him so well. His face showed the stoic resolve of a fatalist—no emotion, next case. I was proud of him. At least he had tried. The final tally and defeat marked the end of an era and the beginning of the decline of his health.

The Campaign to Outlaw Smoking

Knowing of my work for the American Health Foundation, Dr. William Cahan asked me one day if I would help him form the Committee to Outlaw Smoking in Restaurants and Other Public Places in New York City.

I had always been heavily allergic to smoke and had suffered greatly in restaurants, airplanes and as a board member of Banco Central because all the Spaniards at the board meetings of the bank chain-smoked in the bank's poorly-ventilated conference rooms. I thought it amazing and against all odds that one of the nation's leading lung surgeons was hoping to reduce his client base of unlucky smokers and secondary-smoke inhalers.

I had always been willing to work "pro bono" for causes I found deserving, including serving for years on the boards of the French Institute Alliance Francaise, the Spain-USA Chamber of Commerce, the Cardozo School of Law, the Javits Convention Center Operating Corporation, the Eric Javits Family Foundation—our small family foundation that donates yearly to eighty or ninety charities. So when Dr. William Cahan asked me to take up his cause, once again I enlisted. He and I were the first in the world to dare this feat. Thus was born the movement to outlaw smoking in public places that ultimately went worldwide! It all began in NYC with our brief conversation. We never dreamed it would eventually be the success it has become.

Eric Jr., Margaretha and Eric Javits, and Jocelyn Javits.
Photo by Mort Kaye Studios, Inc.

The author welcomes King Juan Carlos and Queen Sofia to the
Spanish Institute in New York (Spanish Institute photo)

The author and his wife banter warmly with
King Juan Carlos of Spain

Eric Javits with President Reagan in 1988
(photograph by Twin Lens Photo)

Reunion with my friend Mayor Rudy Giuliani

The author (front row 2nd from left) who keynoted his
fraternity's 125th anniversary on the Columbia campus

CHAPTER XI — MY DIPLOMATIC CAREER

From the time I was in prep school I understood that the privileges I enjoyed carried with them an obligation to serve. However, once I lost the State Senate primary contest in 1964, "giving back" would not be from *elective* office. What with student deferments and marrying young, I had already missed serving in the military. So any public service would have to be in an *appointive* office.

Years of practice in difficult international negotiations and building a network of contacts overseas prepared me for diplomacy; and for years I aspired to become America's ambassador to Spain. However, as my second marriage lengthened and we spent more time abroad visiting Margaretha's family, Sweden, too, became a post in which I would have felt comfortable and competent.

In an effort to *earn* rather than to "buy" a diplomatic appointment, I contributed modestly for over forty years, raised money for Republican candidates all over the country, and in that period of time worked in dozens of political campaigns, representing our party's candidates at every level.

MY FIRST APPOINTMENT

Venezuela

In 1984, I contributed for the first time to the Presidential Trust, and by so doing became a member of the Republican Eagles, a major donor program of the Republican National Finance

Committee that required an annual donation of $10,000. By 1988, when George H. W. Bush got the presidential nomination, I raised funds from friends and others in the six figures as a member of his National Finance Committee. I also served as a surrogate speaker for him in New York and its environs for which I had to prepare myself assiduously. I did well enough against difficult opposing speakers in the most hostile districts to earn the questionable privilege of having to debate again at the next tough campaign event.

When the campaign ended I wrote President-designate Bush and asked to be considered for the ambassadorship to Spain. I heard nothing for months, but finally the Office of Presidential Personnel called me to explain that the appointment to Spain had already been decided, but that the President wanted to offer me the ambassadorship to Portugal. I told them I was not looking for an ambassadorship in a country that one would consider a tourist haven with no daunting challenges.

I said I wanted a difficult post where America's interests were at stake. I asked what other countries were open that fit that description. They said Venezuela where Carlos Andres Perez, known familiarly as "CAP" had made a successful comeback by being reelected to the presidency despite his prior scandal-ridden administration and reputation for corruption as President some years earlier. Without hesitation I said that was the post I wanted.

Fortunately, I was uniquely qualified to handle the position because I had been the American lawyer for many prominent Venezuelan business figures, including Oswaldo and Ela Cisneros. Another close friend was Diego Arria, a former Mayor of Caracas and later Venezuela's UN Ambassador. I also had been the American lawyer for some of CAP's former cabinet ministers, including his former finance minister, Gumersindo Rodriguez. They had warned me about CAP, and promised they would keep an ear to the ground with their former colleagues and contacts in Venezuela to be sure CAP and his cabinet stayed corruption free, as they wanted him to restore his reputation during his comeback.

I was also the attorney in America for billionaire Spanish magnate, Ignacio Fierro, who with his brother, Alfonso, controlled Banco Central of Spain. Banco Central, in turn, controlled many of the leading banks of Latin America. I was a close friend of the two Fierro brothers, their wives and their children. Ignacio Fierro's connections in Venezuela were unequalled because he was in charge of all of Banco Central's Latin American holdings. Ignacio told me how, for decades, they had made a point of singling out, cultivating and ingratiating themselves with "comers" in Venezuela's industry and politics—even to the point of sending their children to the best schools, etc. Before my nomination was announced and while I was still free to visit Venezuela, Ignacio invited me to accompany him to Caracas where he introduced me to all the key players, including CAP—always explaining I was his U.S. attorney and close friend.

Ignacio told me about CAP's mistress, where she lived in New York City and how CAP conducted his personal and political life. He assured me that the bankers running Banco Central's subsidiary in Caracas would know of every financial transaction or misstep by CAP even before it occurred, were CAP to "go bad" for a second time.

In preparing for my appointment to Caracas I met James Campbell, my handsome, worldly and supremely accomplished CIA Station Chief-to-be, at a lunch in Washington, and we took an immediate liking to each other. We understood the importance of working closely together, the essentiality of Jim's area of responsibility and the dire consequences of not giving it the highest priority. I knew that with Jim Campbell's and his Agency's efforts and Ignacio Fierro's help, I would be privileged to get intelligence and information that no one else would have, and as the U.S. Ambassador I would have the gravitas to be able to keep CAP on the straight and narrow during his second administration as President of Venezuela.

Once I had been formally nominated as Ambassador-Designate to Venezuela by President Bush in April, 1989 I resigned from all boards and involvements, including my law firm, taking my name out of its masthead and dissociating myself completely by giving over my clients without compensation or participation in future earnings.

Margaretha and I moved down to Washington where we lived in the Embassy Suites hotel near the State Department. I began working full time as a Consultant and Ambassador-Designate while awaiting Senate confirmation.

My mornings were spent learning everything I could about Venezuela, its history, geography, government, economy, social customs and politics. My afternoons were spent with Margaretha on the other side of the Potomac in Virginia at the Foreign Service Institute studying Spanish. The State Department's Venezuelan Desk officer, Allen Yale, became my friend and my teacher. He mentored me with great care and dedication. One day when I arrived at the State Department building I was stunned to see a small group of State Department officials from whom I had been learning gathered around a cake with lighted candles to celebrate my birthday. They made me feel incredibly appreciated despite my not being a career foreign service officer. I was deeply touched.

By July I was ready to face my "murder board"—a panel of department experts who grill appointees to prepare them for their appearance before the Senate. After I had been peppered with questions by the panel for almost an hour they ended the session by telling me that I had done better than any other candidate they had ever grilled. I had expected to be confirmed and on my way to Caracas before July ended, but to my disappointment I learned that Sen. Dodd of Connecticut had put a hold on my confirmation to protest discourteous treatment of Sen. Claiborne Pell of Rhode Island, the Chairman of the Foreign Relations Committee, by certain Republican senators and by the Administration.

When September came I got a call from Chris Dodd with whom I had been friendly for some time, telling me that my confirmation hearing date had been announced and would take place the following week. He said "Eric, your hearing will be very informal, just you and me." I asked how that could be? He replied that as Chairman of the Senate Foreign Relations Committee's Subcommittee on Latin America he had the proxies of all of the members approving my appointment. I felt elated that it would be so easy, and deeply grateful for the confidence shown by members of the opposite party.

My elation did not last long. The very next day I got a call from New York to tell me that a subpoena had been left by the Regional Office of the SEC at my former law office for me to appear in a private civil investigation of three persons, two of whom were former clients of mine; and that the date and time of my appearance at the SEC's office in New York was precisely the same as my scheduled confirmation hearing in Washington, DC.

I immediately smelled a rat when I realized the investigators had waited until the very last moment to waylay me, but I immediately contacted both Abraham Sofaer, Counsel to the State Department, and Boyden Gray, Counsel to the White House, to inform them of the situation. I explained that I felt my confirmation should be postponed while I cooperated with the SEC. I also consulted an attorney for advice about the very broad demands for documents and records in the subpoena (diaries, memoranda, correspondence, etc.), realizing it would take weeks of work to prepare copies and submit what was requested.

When I appeared in the New York Regional Office of the SEC I was warned that this was a secret investigation in which no accusations had been made, and in order to protect the reputation of those being investigated I could not reveal their identities or discuss the investigation with anyone. Clearly that would cause difficulties before a Senate committee if I were asked about this investigation and could not offer a candid reply. I realized I would have to extricate myself somehow in order to have my confirmation hearing. I agreed to submit the documents they had requested at the earliest. Although I could not breach client confidentiality, I was able to answer all their questions without having to refuse any information or documents on that ground. They said they would get back to me promptly once they had reviewed the documents that I submitted.

Following my appearance, the White House Counsel's office talked to the SEC's NY Regional Office and were promised an informal "heads up" or "heads down" on me in a month or so. I eventually was called back for another session and pressed for information that would help make the SEC's case of insider trading against my two former clients. I explained that I had not represented the principal targets of their inquiry for quite some time, and that I had nothing to give them that would assist their investigation of insider trading.

By November, the SEC Regional Office still had not called the White House back as promised. As a result the White House called again to ask when the investigators would be finished with me. In response, they said that they would give their informal assessment on me by the end of the year.

In December my lawyer nudged the White House to ask where things stood. The White House counsel then called the SEC's regional office and asked if I had answered all their questions, provided all the documents requested, and if I had cooperated fully. They acknowledged that I had. They were then asked if they had any evidence that I had violated any securities laws, and they said they had none. The White House counsel then asked, since that was the case, could they not at least give a *provisional* up or down on me? The investigators apologized, saying they could not give *any* up or down signal despite their earlier promise and would not be able to do so until the entire investigation was concluded.

I presumed this was a ploy to get me to "remember" something incriminating about my former clients in order to let my nomination could go forward. However, by this time I had learned that the SEC investigation had been underway for almost a whole year! Not calling me to testify until the very day of my Senate confirmation hearing was despicable. The investigators knew that if the name of any Presidential nominee was not confirmed by the Senate by December 31st, it automatically would be sent back by the Senate, and that person would have to be re-nominated all over again to come up for Senate confirmation. They probably felt the pressure of that deadline would assure my "cooperation." However, I had no information to give them, and I certainly wasn't going to fabricate any. December 31, 1989 came and went, and the only nominee's name that was *not* sent back by the Senate was mine!

For an outgoing Senate to hold a presidential nominee over to the next year for consideration by a new incoming Senate was highly unusual. It was an indication of how much support I enjoyed from the Democratic majority that controlled the Senate at that time, and it signaled how much Senators Dodd and Pell wanted me to be confirmed. I heard the SEC regional office was stunned by that announcement. Yet when my attorney persisted in asking them in the early weeks of 1990 what disturbed them about my testimony or role, and why they could not at least give a provisional up or down, they were still not forthcoming.

I had been aware from my college days that eventually in order to do public service I would have to stand scrutiny, and that some day I might need Senate confirmation. Consequently, I knew it was important to vote in all elections, pay my taxes, pay the social security for my household employees, and I had done all of that punctiliously, even back in the '50s when no one else was paying social security taxes for their children's nannies and housekeepers.

I had been able to truthfully answer the FBI agent who questioned me for my security clearance that I did not smoke or drink, that I was not a user of drugs, and that I had no secrets that would embarrass the President if I were nominated. Never having served in the military, I felt especially obligated to render public service.

Nonetheless, I decided to resign my Ambassador-designate position rather than to keep a country waiting for me for the two years that the SEC's investigation would likely take to conclude. So, on February 2, 1990 I wrote President Bush:

> *"It is with heavy heart and deepest regret that I hereby withdraw as your Ambassador Designate to Venezuela.*

> *"In spite of assurances that it would be completed by the end of January it is now clear that the SEC's private investigation will take more time than they had forecasted.*

> *"All my life I have awaited an opportunity to serve my country and for the last ten years to serve you, and I will always be grateful to you for offering me that*

chance. I am devastated that instead of serving I have cost our nation precious time in the urgent business of husbanding our important relations with Venezuela, so I feel the way I can now best serve you and our country is to stand aside to permit the placing of an ambassador in Caracas at the earliest possible date. I am forever grateful for the trust and support you have shown me. I wish you continued success after a most impressive beginning, and assure you of my unswerving loyalty. I conclude with the hope that you will call on me at a later date if you feel I can be of service.

"Margaretha and I send you, Barbara and your family our warmest regards."

Some months later at a White House reception for the Republican Eagles, President Bush told me he regretted that I had resigned my nomination. I told him "Mr. President, they would have hated you and they would have hated me when I got there if we kept them waiting for two years for an American ambassador. I did what was right."

After almost two years the Securities and Exchange Commission wrote to me that their investigation had been concluded and had found no fault with my conduct. Since it was too late in the President George Herbert Walker Bush's first term to appoint me to another post, in his 1992 re-election bid, I again campaigned and debated as his surrogate speaker as I had four years earlier. I spoke to one very liberal audience at an event sponsored by ANTA, the American National Theatre Association, following which quite a few in the audience told me they were swayed to our candidate. Another noteworthy 1992 event in which I represented President Bush took place in Westchester County where I debated Stuart Eizenstadt, a well-known public figure who had been an adviser to President Carter. There was an audience of about one hundred for that event. The moderator was Professor James Shenton, who had been a distinguished member of the faculty and one of my professors many years earlier at Columbia College. Stuart Eizenstadt was no pushover. He was an articulate, reasoned and attractive surrogate. Professor Shenton told me later that he, and most of the audience, felt I had held the edge in that debate.

In 1991 the Republican Eagle program increased its dues to $15,000 per year. The Eagles had several hundred members in off years and five hundred or more members in Presidential election years. I would regularly attend their quarterly gatherings, two of which were held at destination resorts around the country and two in Washington, to hear from Administration and Party officials or members of the Senate or Congress. Often, if the Administration was Republican and the meeting was held in Washington, there would be a visit to the White House where the President would address the group and pose for a photo with each Eagle. The network that one developed from these gatherings was impressive. I met Michael Dell, T. Boone Pickens, Herb Kohler among many other familiar names in America's national firmament.

The Eagles had a staff of bright young people including Margaret Alexander, Kathy Phillips and Laurie Prysock, who were eager to work with Eagle members by helping them get appointments with their representatives in Washington, tickets to the gallery at the Congressional or Senatorial sessions and/or tours of the White House and the Capitol.

As I became more involved and active the staff perceived my willingness to assist in increasing the membership, and they encouraged me to call prospects on their behalf. Soon they asked me to lead recruiting efforts in New York, and I gladly obliged. Eventually they encouraged me to assume even more responsibility. They made clear that they wanted me to take a leadership role.

So in 1996, with the election of Jim Nicholson as Republican National Chairman, I was proposed by the Eagle staff—being the member with whom they had worked most closely in raising money and recruiting new Eagles—to be the group's Chairman and invited to come to Washington to meet Chairman Nicholson.

Jim Nicholson was a graduate of West Point, an Army officer, a Ranger and paratrooper who had fought in Vietnam, earning a Bronze Star and a number of other medals for outstanding service. In civilian life he had been a successful real estate developer and Republican National Committeeman from Colorado, before being elected as the Party's National Chairman in 1996. Later, in 2001, President George W. Bush appointed him U.S. ambassador to the Holy See in The Vatican City, and in 2005 Secretary of the Department of Veteran Affairs.

When Chairman Nicholson met me for the first time at the Republican National Committee (RNC) he was gracious and open, probably because the staff had put in a good word for me. Jim and I instantly liked each other, and he asked me if I would take on the leadership of the Eagles. I felt honored to be offered the opportunity. For the next three years, from 1997 through 2000 I devoted at least half of my time as a volunteer to enlarge the Eagle membership.

That first year I traveled to Washington every couple of weeks to spend a full day making calls from the RNC headquarters on First Street to prospective Eagle members around the country to get them to join or renew their memberships. We were usually able to complete a hundred calls in an eight-hour day. With her personal computer Laurie Prysock would sit across the desk from me with my Apple notebook. We would make notes of each call and conversation with names, numbers and addresses. To follow up the calls we had made, letters were prepared and sent to me in New York for my signature.

In 1997, the Eagles raised only $3 million. The next year I appointed an Executive Committee of faithful Eagles from around the country. As a result, in my first full year in office, we increased membership by more than 50% and raised $5 million. As Eagle Chairman, I made at least a couple of thousand calls each year to prospects all over the United States. I would chat with them to learn about their interests, their political priorities and gripes. I kept careful notes, often sending personal letters from time to time, and calling again if they indicated they might contribute at a later date.

As the presidential election of 2000 grew closer, the response improved. I worked closely with the officials and staff of the Republican National Finance Committee. As the presidential election season wore on, I toured all over the US with Chairman Nicholson and National Finance Chairman Mel Sembler (formerly ambassador to Australia and later ambassador to Italy) to attend fund raisers and recruit new Eagles. We flew to fundraising events in California, Arizona, Texas and Louisiana where Chairman Nicholson would make the opening remarks, and I would follow up with an appeal to renew or join the Eagles at each event. Often we would fly together in Mel Sembler's private jet to a scheduled event, and usually we were able to recruit at least a dozen or more new Eagles.

After George W. Bush won the presidency in 2000, a year in which over 2000 individuals became Eagles and members of the Presidential Trust, I visited the RNC Headquarters in Washington to thank the staff. They took me out to the large secretarial bullpen adjacent to the line of private offices and asked me to look up at the photographic portraits that lined the walls. There, among the likenesses of all the former RNC

Chairmen hung my picture. Mine was the only photo of someone who had not been a National Chairman or National Finance Chairman. They told me that they had never had a volunteer as an Eagle Chairman who did more to raise funds for the RNC, and since I had been instrumental in their raising $30 million over the preceding three years they felt my photo deserved to hang with the others. I still correspond with some Eagles and the superb RNC staffers with whom I worked over the years.

The George W. Bush Election in 2000

As the campaign of 2000 drew to a close it became harder and harder to raise money for the Presidential race or the RNC because most donors had reached their legal limit; and even if they had not, there was almost no time left for donations to be effectively spent to buy TV spots.

Toward the end of October I decided to place a call to Jack Oliver, the central figure in finance and strategy for the RNC and the Presidential Campaign. Jack was a dynamo. He kept track on his personal computer of everyone who was a fundraiser for Bush for President, how much money they raised and from whom, and he was key in deciding how to utilize people in the campaign all around the country. I spoke with him on Oct. 28th and told him that the Eagles had raised whatever money there was to be had, and that I wanted to be given the chance to go to Florida as a surrogate speaker for our presidential candidate.

I explained that I had done surrogate speaking in many prior presidential elections, but particularly this year I felt the election would be determined in Florida, the state to which thousands of New Yorkers had migrated. I explained that the New Yorkers who had moved to Florida, though Democrats, were often liberal Jews whose only Republican vote had been for Jacob Javits in his many campaigns in New York for Congress, State Attorney General and the United States Senate, and I felt they would respond to an appeal from a Javits, especially the Jewish Democratic voters that were heavily concentrated in Miami-Dade, Broward and Palm Beach counties. After hearing me out, Jack Oliver promised to call me back.

A couple of days later he called and told me that I should go down to Florida and link up with the state campaign there. He said I would be teamed during the final week of the campaign with George Schultz, who had served as Secretary of the Departments of Labor, Treasury and State, to speak to mostly Jewish audiences at synagogues, country clubs and residential communities in those three counties.

On November 2nd I was given a ride to Palm Beach on Lew and Rachel Rudin's private plane. We landed at the Signature hanger in West Palm Beach where I was met by staff members of the Florida State Republican campaign. We drove directly to the Cascades Community clubhouse in Boynton Beach for Candidate Night where I asked to speak for the Bush candidacy. Regrettably, those in charge were Gore operatives or supporters. I protested, but they would not permit me to speak. No outcry ensued as the audience seemed solidly Democratic. One would think that would not happen when a Candidate Night was held, but in highly partisan one-party areas it can and did.

The next day I was driven to Ned Siegel's office. Ned was a dear friend whom I had met in Republican Jewish circles. He was a highly successful real estate developer and a strong supporter of George W.'s who was coordinating the Presidential campaign for "W" in Florida. He had arranged for us to go to a mid-day rally featuring Bill McCollum—a candidate for Florida Attorney General—as the speaker. Ned wanted me to piggyback on McCollum's appearance to make a pitch for the presidential campaign which McCollum graciously permitted.

The next day we met again at Ned Siegel's office before going out to campaign at Boca Raton Town Center where a group of us spread out on the ground and handed out a stunningly beautiful and slickly-crafted brochure with magnificent photos and text entitled "Bush and Israel". It was a very expensive piece that had been put together by Mark Neuman, a close friend and resourceful executive for the Limited Companies, who had worked earlier in the White House for George H.W. Bush.

The brochure made a convincing case for George W. Bush as the most pro-Israel Republican presidential candidate ever, based on his first-hand knowledge and deep conviction that resulted from having visited Israel, the Golan Heights, the West Bank—and from personal meetings with Israel's foremost leaders. In the course of canvassing the Boca Town Center we ran into Rudy Giuliani who happened also to be campaigning for Bush inside the shopping mall there. He invited me into the roped-off area, introduced me and gave me a chance to reinforce his pitch for our candidate.

The next day, November 4, I left my Palm Beach apartment before dawn to drive to Miami to link up with Secretary Schultz and begin our two-man surrogate-speaking blitz. Our first appearance was at Temple Emanu-El in Miami. Secretary Schultz spoke on foreign policy, and I followed on Bush's domestic program and policy views. The audience, comprised mostly of congregants and political operatives, was polite and receptive. We spoke to some of those in attendance on our way out and were given some valuable feedback.

That first event was a warm up. I heard what Secretary Schultz had to say, and he learned what I had to say. That enabled us to fine tune our appeals at succeeding events. We got back into our cars, and the cavalcade proceeded on to the Westin Hills Country Club where a very large audience waited in an equally large assembly hall. Secretary Schulz was very convincing with his statesmanlike presentation, encyclopedic knowledge and unquestionable credibility in making the case that Bush would be head and shoulders better than Al Gore on foreign policy—and especially on America's alliance with Israel.

When Schulz finished I took the stage and asked, "How many in the audience are former New Yorkers?" Almost three quarters raised their hands. I then asked, "How many of you here voted for Jacob Javits?" Almost every hand went back up. I then introduced myself as Jack's nephew, and explained that I would speak on domestic policy. I kept it brief, pithy and very low key. I concluded by saying that I understood New Yorkers, and especially Javits voters because I had campaigned door-to-door for him in every election except his first two in 1946 and 1948 when I was still studying in Connecticut and California.

I said I realized that the audience might find it hard to vote for George W., but I concluded very emphatically, "At least don't vote for Gore. Just skip that race. Vote for your sheriff, your judges, your congressman, your state officials, but please do not vote for Gore." I repeated this at every stop, every event and in every speech. Each time I saw many heads nodding in agreement.

On Tuesday, November 7th, I voted in New York with Margaretha and then we took the afternoon shuttle to Washington, DC where the leadership of the Bush Finance Team and Victory 2000 assembled at the St. Regis Hotel to watch the returns come in on giant TV monitors.

When the networks "called" Florida for Gore quite early in the evening, I knew that something was amiss. The heavily Republican area of Florida is concentrated in the panhandle that stretches from the north end of the Florida peninsula westward toward Louisiana and Texas. My friend and college roommate, Frank Faddis, who lives in Pensacola had told me how solid that area of the state was for Bush. And since the Panhandle was in a different time zone—an hour behind the rest of Florida—its polling places were still open when the rest of the state's voting places had closed. I immediately announced in the room where the returns were being watched on a big TV monitor that either the Network must have been mistaken, or there was dirty work afoot to have the state called for Gore before all the polls in Florida had closed. I knew many Floridians in the Western part of the state would hear the news, get discouraged and either not go out to vote or leave the polling places to go home for supper.

The results finally tallied on election night gave 246 electoral votes to Bush and 255 to Al Gore, but New Mexico's (5), Oregon's (7), and Florida's 25 were all too close to call that evening. Florida's 25 electoral votes became the key to the election, despite the fact that both New Mexico and Oregon were soon declared in favor of Gore.

The next day, November 8th, I flew back to NY. The word went out that there was to be a recount battle in three of Florida's counties and that a vast number of Democratic operatives and attorneys were already ensconced in Florida to secure the state for Gore. I quickly called a few lawyer pals to urge them to join the team that would fly to Florida to ensure that the election was not stolen away from Bush. One young friend, New York attorney John Ballan, agreed to fly down to work with the Bush Team.

On Friday, November 8th, John and I landed in West Palm Beach. That evening we attended the Fort Lauderdale Town Meeting that was held in the Sun Sentinel Building. We had to listen to the fulminations of Alcee Hastings and a great deal of disinformation and posturing by Democrats at that meeting, combined with accusations that many Democratic voters had been unfairly prevented from voting at certain polling places.

The next morning John Ballan and I reported to the Palm Beach County Courthouse where the Bush team that would act as "Observers" of the count received a briefing by John Bolton in preparation for the counting, by hand, of the Palm Beach County ballots.

The scene was a zoo. The ballot counting took place in a soundproof glass-enclosed area on the Municipal Building's ground floor. Inside the enclosure sat the Canvassing Board— composed of three officials that examined the ballots—while two or three Observers from each presidential campaign stood watch behind them. Judge Charles E. Burton presided as the Chairman of the Canvassing Board along with Carol Roberts and Theresa LePore, all three of whom were members of the Democratic Party. While the ballot counting went on in the glass enclosure no one was admitted or could exit from it until a recess was declared in the counting. Observers on duty could only be replaced during a recess.

Just outside the glass enclosure throngs of newsmen and TV cameramen stood behind a forest of cameras on tripods, all aimed at the counting process that was happening inside, all shouldering each other for elbowroom. As their camera lenses zoomed in and out on the counting of the ballots, the lens cases would bang up against the glass partitions. It was impossible for anyone standing outside the enclosure to attract the attention of someone inside because there was constant knocking on glass from all sides.

I was not part of the first shift of Observers working inside the glass enclosure, so I stood outside one of the windows to keep watch on what was happening inside. I saw that the counting of ballots began with Carol Roberts who would hold the butterfly-shaped ballot up to the ceiling light to see if there had been denting or a partial separation of a "chad"—that small separable circle that a voter would punch out to indicate his or her preference for President. Roberts would then pass the ballot to Chairman Burton seated to her right, stating her view of whether it was a vote for Bush or a vote for Gore. He would then examine the ballot and pass it to Theresa Le Pore on his right for her to view before he would decide how to count that vote. I noticed that when Chairman Burton was busy talking to Ms. Le Pore on his right those two were totally concentrated on the ballot they were holding up to the ceiling's light. Ms. Roberts, unnoticed by them would then furtively lower the ballot she was holding below the worktable that stood before them.

Although I could not see exactly what she was doing, her arm and body motions were consistent with her making an effort to punch out, dent or loosen a chad. I banged furiously on the glass partition to try to catch the attention of our Bush Observer team in the enclosure, but to no avail. I had to wait until there was a recess to get a message inside as to what was happening. Once Chairman Roberts was apprised of what was going on, he made the two women trade places so that he could examine each ballot before it reached Carol Roberts. I was greatly heartened by the integrity of the Chairman, as opposed to the flagrant partisanship of Ms. Roberts who later was quoted as saying she was "willing to go to jail if that is what it took to get a recount."

The following morning John Ballan and I promptly got to work on the legal case headed by lead attorney Ben Ginsberg. We were instructed by Joe Albaugh to take a call from attorney Kevin Martin, Esq., in the Tallahassee headquarters to give him our "take" on the preceding day's events at the Canvassing Board. We suggested that our team of lawyers subpoena all TV tape recordings of the hand count taken by the networks and cable stations. We were told to go to the Carlton Fields law firm in West Palm Beach to prepare and help finalize the affidavit that John Ballan would submit in the litigation. There we met lawyers who were working independently on the case. John Ballan and I took a call from Tim Flanagan, a member of the Tallahassee legal team working to seek injunctive relief asking that we send them copies of the Press Pool reports.

That afternoon Ballan and I went to the rally that was staged outside the Municipal Building in West Palm Beach. It was mostly street theatre to boost the morale of the Bush forces and to try to lower the morale of the Gore forces. There we ran into pollster Frank Luntz and real estate developer Kevin Foley, as well as other key figures in the Bush campaign. I took calls on my cell phone in the midst of the crowds from Jim Nicholson and Joe Albaugh to report on what was happening and to hear about the national effort on the popular vote elsewhere. That night we caught a late flight back to New York.

The battle in the two recounts of only the three southernmost counties—one requested by Al Gore, the other ordered by the Florida Supreme Court—went first to the Florida Supreme Court, and then all the way to the United States Supreme Court. It took more than a month before the Florida dispute was resolved in Bush's favor.

History has now recorded that the election was hotly contested but not stolen, and that Bush won Florida and the presidency by only 537 votes from Dade, Broward and Palm Beach counties—the very same and only counties in which George Schultz and I toured as Bush's Surrogates.

Many pundits tried to explain the absence of voting at the top of the ticket for either Bush or Gore as being attributable to confused or doddering voters who did not know how to punch out chads, but they never could explain how they were able to easily punch them out for other races on the same ballot. I like to think those pleas to Jewish audiences in those three counties not to vote for either Presidential candidate were the reason. Indeed, that may have been the deciding difference in Bush's favor.

The Bush Transition Team went to work immediately after the Electoral College named George Walker Bush as President of the United States. Time was of the essence in getting the transition moving as much time had been lost while the recount battles had raged.

To those aspiring to be appointed in the new Bush Administration, word went out that everyone had to apply on the internet with an accompanying resume and expression of preference for the position one sought. Everyone was cautioned not to apply in any other way. I submitted my digital resume and application, explained my qualifications, and requested the ambassadorship to Spain or Sweden. I got no response, and for months heard nothing about my application.

Nevertheless, in January I began writing Senators and other prominent figures I knew to ask for their support or recommendation to the President for me to be appointed. Among those who gave their support were Senators Orrin Hatch, Dick Lugar, Chris Dodd, Trent Lott, Chuck Hagel, Alan Simpson, Frank Murkowski, Pete Domenici, Jesse Helms, and General Colin Powell, Governors George Pataki and Tom Ridge and Donald Rumsfeld.

Former Secretary of State, James A. Baker, to whom I had written and under whom I had served in 1989 as Ambassador-

Designate to Venezuela, told me that he had supported only those very few seeking appointments who he felt deserved his highest recommendation, and I was one of those. He told me that I could use his name if needed. I was, and still am, deeply grateful for his confidence.

The inaugural festivities for the President began on January 17, 2001, three days before the inauguration ceremony at which the President would take his oath of office, and a jam-packed three days ensued. I can remember how excited Margaretha and I felt as we flew to Washington to check into the Grand Hyatt. That evening the entire Republican Eagles Executive committee dined with Jim Gilmore and RNC Chairman Jim Nicholson. The next day there was a joint lunch for the Presidential Trust and Republican Eagles at which Andy Card was the featured guest of honor. I had met Andy in Boston at a Presidential Trust fundraising event that he organized when I was touring the country as Chairman of the Eagles and surrogate speaking for the Bush candidacy. That night we attended a Victory 2000 Leadership Party (I was on its National Executive Committee), an Empower America event featuring Jack Kemp and Donald Rumsfeld, and a fireworks display followed by a candlelight dinner featuring Governor Pataki. The next day there was a serious business breakfast for the Victory 2000 National Finance Committee, followed by a Republican Jewish Coalition and AIPAC lunch at which Paul Wolfowitz and Haley Barbour spoke, and that evening we attended a gala dinner with entertainment by the Pointer sisters and the Beach Boys.

Finally on Saturday, Jan. 20th, after a brunch hosted by Empower America's Bill Bennett, Jack Kemp and Vin Webber, we all went to the swearing in of the 42nd President of the United States in front of the Capitol and then watched the Inaugural Parade as it moved from 7th to 17th Street NW.

Late that afternoon, Paul Rodzianko, a friend whose forbear in Russia had been deposed as head of the Duma during the Russian revolution, reached me on my cell phone as I was reviewing the Eagle staff's preparations at Union Station for the Inaugural Galas to be held that night. Rodzianko told me that a group of about eight Russians who were members of Russia's Unity party had come to Washington to attend the inauguration of George W. Bush, but had been unable to get tickets to any inaugural events. He asked if I could get them into one of the many Gala celebrations. When I heard that Boris Gryzlov, Chairman of the Unity Party was in the group (he later became the head of the Russian State Duma), I asked the Eagle staff if they had any extra tickets. Luckily, I was able to provide the group with the access they craved. I could just imagine the bragging rights they took back to Moscow with them, but when I noticed them later that night huddled together amidst the rejoicing crowd in Union Station, gawking at the festivities in progress but not participating, I felt sad that their country did not yet enjoy the full panoply of freedoms and civil rights that we Americans enjoyed.

Then on Sunday before flying back to New York, Margaretha and I enjoyed an early brunch with my cousin, Joshua Javits, his wife Sabina and their children, after which we dropped by publisher Tom Phillips' country place in MacLean, Virginia, where he hosted a gathering in honor of Suzanne and Jim Nicholson.

Appointments were being announced every day and having heard nothing regarding my candidacy, I finally decided to call Karl Rove. He said that the President was well aware of my capability and qualifications, but that he and the president felt I should not be appointed to a country because my experience conducting difficult international negotiations made me far better suited for a multilateral post. He said the President wanted to offer me my choice of a number of multilateral ambassadorial posts, including United Nations-Vienna, Organization of American States in Washington, Conference on Disarmament in Geneva, or a post at the United Nations-New York. I expressed my preference to be appointed as the United States Permanent Representative and Ambassador to the Conference on Disarmament in Geneva.

Things moved quickly after that. Once again, I had to immediately resign from every Board, organization and committee to which I belonged. I withdrew from my law firm, and, as before, turned over all my clients for which I received no remuneration except for work already done.

Thereafter, I went through some months of intensive FBI investigation before my nomination was formally sent up to the Senate Foreign Relations Committee on which Senator Joseph Biden was serving as Chairman. Since the Democrats controlled the Senate, Sen. Biden's staff and the Democratic Majority's staff on Foreign Relations conducted my interviews. Republican Foreign Relations Committee staffers only sat in as observers.

As one who had lived through the Cold War years with the threat of nuclear anihilation from the tens of thousands of nuclear warheads and delivery systems in the Russian and American silos, submarines and launching platforms, I understood the importance of non-proliferation, disarmament and arms control.

Before my confirmation by the full Senate I spent many months as Ambassador-Designate working in the State Department to learn the ropes and to familiarize myself with the treaties, the vocabulary, procedures, rules and regulations that would govern my service. Having had no prior experience in disarmament treaties or arms control issues prior to my nomination for the position, my preparation at State consisted of reading all the treaties and explanatory treatises, learning all the acronyms that were commonly used, fully understanding the issues with which I would be dealing, as well as America's vital interests and redlines in the disarmament field. Those included preserving the ability of America to defend its homeland, its allies, and the freedom to navigate the world's seas while at the same time progressing to reduce the world's nuclear arsenal, the bargain agreed to encourage and perpetuate the Non Proliferation Treaty by which its member nations agreed to forego nuclear weapons This took a good half year during which time I moved around the State Department's many divisions, as well as other Federal agencies with which I would be working once I got to Geneva, meeting officers I needed to know and with whom I might have to consult.

During those months of preparation I worked most closely at State with Bob Mikulak, Pierce Corden and Donald Mahley to prepare for my confirmation hearing before the Senate. When the day came for me to appear before the Senate Foreign Relations Committee, I was accompanied by Pierce Corden up to the Hill where Margaretha and my cousin, Joshua Javits and his wife, Sabina, were waiting in the Senate Hearing Room. Senator Barbara Boxer of California sat as the Chairman of my hearing, accompanied by Senators Richard Lugar of Indiana and Joseph Lieberman of Connecticut.

In the State Department vehicle that drove us to the hearing, Pierce Corden had warned me that usually there was one difficult question that would be asked. I said I already knew what it would be. "How can you be so sure?" he asked. I replied that I would be asked why the Bush Administration was not supporting the Comprehensive Test Ban Treaty because that is what the Democrats presumed would be the most difficult and embarrassing question for me to answer.

When that very question was posed by Barbara Boxer I replied, "If and when the Senate finds me fit to become a member of the Bush Administration and confirms my appointment, and after I have a chance to familiarize myself with the merits and with the Administration's reasons, I will gladly offer a response, but at this point I must respectfully decline because I am not qualified to give an authoritative answer." Senator Boxer smiled and said, "Good answer."

From that point my confirmation hearing became a warm and friendly affair. Complimentary and supportive statements made by Senators Dodd, Lieberman and Lugar were heartening. Not long after my hearing, my nomination was sent to the floor of the Senate where I was confirmed by unanimous vote.

The author with White House Chief of Staff Andy Card

With President and Mrs. Bush in Philadelphia at the
Republican Convention, Summer of 2000

Eagle Chairman Javits in 2000 with the RNC's Eagle staff. L
to R Jeanette Corcoran, Laurie Prysock, Paige Marriott, Paige
Lance, Mimi Hedgecock

Amb. Javits with Secretary of State Colin Powell circa 2003
(photo by Dept. of State)

A couple of retirees with their wives Florida in 2012

Marine Gunnery Sgt. Scott upon my departure from The
Hague, presenting me the flag and wishing me "Fair winds and
following seas"

CHAPTER XII — THE CONFERENCE ON DISARMAMENT

When December 6, 2001 was fixed as the date for my swearing-in ceremony I learned that I would be sworn in by Richard Armitage because Secretary of State, Colin Powell, was out of the country. I felt a little disappointed that I would not be sworn in by Secretary Powell, a man I admired greatly, but once I had met Deputy Secretary Armitage, with his barrel chest, military demeanor and warmth, I felt no regrets whatever.

On the appointed day, Margaretha and I held a private lunch on the seventh floor of the State Department for a small group of close friends and family, and then we moved to the large reception room to greet all of those invitees who had come from around the country and the Department to see me sworn in. My uncle's widow, Marian Javits, who felt she was always the central figure, made her grand entrance with the announcement to all present: "Good afternoon. *I* am Mrs. Javits." Margaretha smiled and said "No, Marian. Not today, you're not."

Before I was to depart for Geneva, I was asked to have a meeting with the then Under Secretary of State for Arms Control and International Security, John Bolton. I went up to his office on the 7th floor where I was asked to check my cell phone with the receptionist. Fred Fleitz, who sat in on our meeting, ushered me in. John was very cordial. He felt that he could confide in me because he knew my political credentials for "W" were impeccable. He did not spend a lot of time going over my portfolio, but since I was to be the Ambassador to the Conference on Disarmament (the "CD") where treaties were negotiated, he wanted to impress on me that I should not defer or be obedient to the "career" people in the Department who he felt were too soft and wobbly on foreign policy with respect to treaties, multilateralism and security. He made it clear that he did not trust treaties to protect the security of the United States, as they conveyed a false sense of security for the "willing-to-be-deluded." I said that I was aware of the pitfalls and would avoid being arrogant or overbearing while trying to lead with America's interests and objectives as my compass. He wished me luck.

Margaretha and I left the next day for Palm Beach to establish our Florida personal residences, get our drivers licenses and register to vote. We had already given up our New York apartment in which we had lived for over twenty years, and I had already resigned from all boards and other involvements. We had sold our mountaintop "Willow Hill" in upstate New York, and "Las Casitas" in Southampton. After a lifetime of being a New York lawyer involved in many aspects of New York City with a family name that was strongly identified with the New York law, politics, and civic affairs, I was off to commence a new career as an American diplomat in Europe.

When Margaretha and I landed at the Geneva airport, Maria Jesus King, my secretary-to-be, was there to meet us. Maria was a career civil service employee who had worked for decades at State. She was an accomplished linguist—fluid in English, French, Spanish, German and Italian. She was incredibly thoughtful, loyal and kind, with the competence, skill sets, tact and total knowledge needed to ensure "her" Ambassador could function with minimal stress and maximum efficiency.

Maria's husband, John King, had been a key figure as Deputy Chief of Mission for prior ambassadors at the CD delegation. John was a highly respected, even-tempered, soft-spoken and deeply-thoughtful advisor that I agreed to keep on staff as a consultant during my term of service. In all my years, I had never experienced any secretary with Maria's skill levels. And our personalities were a perfect match. She and her John made each day at work a pleasure. I am not sure I reciprocated, as I would work but not notice the flowers she would buy with her own money to place prominently on my desk. That prompted a much-deserved dressing down from Margaretha for my obliviousness.

Nor did my good fortune in staff end with Maria and John King. I was lucky to have Sherwood McGinnis as my Deputy Chief of Mission. He was conscientious, knowledgeable, a workaholic and well liked by our colleagues. He made me feel supported in every area. I showed my confidence in him by letting him guide the agenda and discussion in the morning staff meetings that I interrupted with only occasional questions, comments or directions.

Our ambassadorial residence was a full-floor apartment at the top of a building on one of Geneva's most fashionable streets, Quai Wilson. When we first arrived, its décor looked more like a Holiday Inn than an ambassadorial residence ready for representational hospitality. Margaretha tastefully redid its décor with support from the Department of State and the help of a talented member of the Geneva Mission. Its small balcony looked out over Lake Geneva with its lovely Peace Jet Fountain, and on a clear day you could see Mont Blanc off in the distance. Once we had unpacked, settled in, hung our paintings and met our staff we felt securely ensconced in our new home. Our chef, who lived across Lake Geneva in France, was very talented, but we had to admonish him for relentlessly berating the female household staff. Once when we were discussing the importance of non-proliferation of nuclear weapons, he commented, "Wizzout zee bumb, Frahns wud be nuzzing!"

My first official lunch upon arriving in Geneva was a shocker. I was driven to the residence of H.E. Lazlo Horvath, the Hungarian Ambassador, who received me quite coolly. There were about fourteen other ambassadors standing around who politely introduced themselves or were introduced by my host. After about fifteen minutes we repaired to the dining room where a long table was set with my Hungarian host at the head. I was seated midway on the side facing the strong glare from windows that lined the entire opposite wall. No sooner had I begun the appetizer than I was excoriated over America's decision to "kill" the additional protocol to the Biological and Toxin Weapons Convention that had been under negotiation for years. Endless work had been done by the negotiators in its drafting.

The Protocol was intended to provide the same kind of supervisory regime for biological weapons as had been provided for chemical weapons by the Organization for the Prohibition of Chemical Weapons with headquarters in The Hague. Many countries had staked their hopes on having a security monitoring and enforcement mechanism for bio-weapons. The United States had led them to expect that an addendum was in the offing, and that the intention to conclude one was shared by all. So, when John Bolton, without any warning whatever, cut off all further negotiations, the eruption of rage was daunting.

I was not surprised when Iran's Ambassador, Ali Asgar Soltanieh, excoriated my country in a quite precise discourse for having torpedoed, without warning and contrary to everyone's expectations, an invaluable instrument for world security. However I was surprised when even Britain's ambassador David Broucher ripped into me. One after another they read the riot act to me. The tone of the lunch was dismal. I felt like I was their entrée de jour.

I decided to keep my calm and let everyone talk until they had run out of steam. I finally asked if they would like me to reply. I began by saying that I was a newcomer to diplomacy, unfamiliar with the Biological and Toxin Weapons Convention, or the negotiations for an Additional Protocol that would have created an international organization to enforce it. I said I had played no part in what had happened, but I could understand their chagrin and disappointment. I solemnly promised that as long as they might deal with me, they would never be blindsided or misled by me to believe something that they could not rely upon.

I told them I could only guess the cause for America's sudden about face. I presumed it was because of the inability to allow international inspections of American biological laboratories, and at the same time protect the proprietary knowledge of the companies under inspection. I explained that development of new drugs cost billions of dollars, and you had only to sneeze and blow your nose during an inspection of a laboratory or a production facility while inconspicuously rubbing your Kleenex against a wall or counter. The secrets that had been developed in that lab would exit with the Kleenex, and millions or billions of high tech research and product development value would be lost. I explained that every effort must surely have been made to try to overcome that glaring vulnerability, but finally the realization that it could not be overcome must have caused the decision to abort trying to get an additional protocol.

I sensed that my very sincere expression of sympathy for their frustration and anger, my explanation of what I guessed was the reason for the abrupt reversal of policy, and my pledge never to blind side or disappoint without plenty of advance warning changed the mood of the meeting. I left the Hungarian ambassador's residence with a sense that they had sized me up and decided to give me a chance.

Soon after that memorable luncheon I attended a big reception in the Palais de Nations given by the Chinese delegation. China kept two Chinese ambassadors in Geneva— one, their Permanent Representative to the UN office in Geneva and other International Organizations in Switzerland—Ambassador Sha Zukang, and the other, their Permanent Representative to the Conference on Disarmament—Ambassador Hu Xiaodi.

Ambassador Sha was known for his having trained and mentored many of the younger arms control "rising stars" in China's foreign service, and also—to put it politely—for his extreme self assurance. He would tell anyone who would listen, "I am best ambassador. I have best phone number in Beijing, nothing but number fours. I am best negotiator" etc.

Ambassador Hu, on the other hand, had a reputation for being a modest, kind and sensitive person whose decency was quite apparent. As I entered the Palais' enormous reception room I spotted Sha holding court in the center of the floor surrounded by a bevy of admiring onlookers. We had not yet met, and I decided this would be the ideal place to have our first encounter. I strode right up to Sha and said that I would like the honor not just of meeting him but of giving him a warm embrace, as I had heard so many wonderful things about him that a handshake would not suffice to show my respect and admiration. I then got him in a bear hug from which he could not escape. People around us were astonished, but when I released him he was beaming and looked as pleased as punch.

Sha and I had many occasions to get to know one another well, and although he was an outspoken hawk who ranted at America supplying arms to Taiwan, he also took it well when I lectured him on the senselessness of China threatening Taiwan militarily. He confessed that he had been a leader in China's Cultural Revolution who organized bands of violent youths, but then betrayed them when it was politically expedient to do so. That is how he saved himself and began his spectacular rise in their Foreign Service. I asked him once why he hated the Japanese so fervently. He told me that he watched his mother die right before his eyes, bayoneted in the stomach by a Japanese soldier. He also seemed to enjoy browbeating and demeaning his compatriot, Amb. Hu. He loved to brag how he insisted that he and Hu swim together across Lake Geneva at its narrowest point, but as often happens on that lake, the weather changed when they were midway. Suddenly, gale force wind and waves kicked up, making it truly treacherous to cross. They both made it to the far shore, but Hu was gasping for air and almost drowned in the process. Sha then told Hu he could walk or bum a ride back to the Geneva side of the lake, but that he, Ambassador Sha, best ambassador, would swim back, and he actually did!

On another occasion when I was still getting to know and hoping to build a working relationship with Amb. Hu, he told me how angry he and Sha were with America sending modern interceptor aircraft and anti-aircraft ground-to-air missiles to Taiwan. He told me that China was going to massively strengthen its nuclear missile force and would not be deterred by America's nuclear arsenal. It was obvious to me that Sha had ordered Hu to give me this dressing down, so I politely heard him out. Then I asked him if he thought the best way for a man to woo a woman was to carry her off by force. Or was it better to send her flowers, treat her kindly, exhibit patience and be kind to her friends and family? He had to admit that force was not the better option for a long-term relationship. I told him that building up artillery batteries directly opposite Taiwan and threatening it would not bring it into China's arms, but would give the US Congress cause to continue sending Taiwan military hardware to defend itself. I pointed out that only defensive weaponry was being sent to Taiwan. I concluded by saying, "If you continue to threaten her, all you will get in the end will be a hot rock, not a bride." Somehow, I hope that message, or similar ones from other Westerners, may have gotten through. China's evolving moderation toward Taiwan has been a welcome development.

The Conference on Disarmament was established in 1979 as the single multilateral international forum for the negotiation of disarmament treaties. It started with 40 nation members and has grown to 65 Member States at the present time. Its annual sessions are divided into three segments consisting of ten weeks starting in January, seven weeks in May and June and seven weeks usually in August and September. The Director General of the UN Organization of Geneva acted as the Secretary-General of the Conference on Disarmament, and its sessions were presided over by the Member States on a rotating basis with each country holding the chair for a period of four weeks.

Its initial task was to agree on a program of work. Since it operates on the basis of consensus, all members must agree on the agenda of work it will do that year. If it fails to agree during the first ten weeks, very little takes place for the rest of the year. If it does agree, but does not finish its work by the end of the third segment, then it must resolve by consensus to continue again in the following year. From the Conference on Disarmament and its predecessors have emerged the Non Proliferation Treaty, the Seabed treaties, the Chemical Weapons Convention, the Biological and Toxin Weapons Convention and the Comprehensive Nuclear-Test-Ban Treaty.

The Conference on Disarmament is, in fact, an exclusive club. Most of the Ambassadors were former Foreign Ministers or experienced and respected veterans of their respective Ministries of Foreign Affairs. Each week at least two or three lunches would be hosted in Geneva's finest restaurants or at embassy residences by ambassadors who were members of the Western European and Other Group of countries to discuss the deadlock that had gripped the Conference on Disarmament for at least six years, even before I arrived, in the hope of reaching consensus on a work program before another year was frittered away.

The most viable work program option seemed to be a Fissile Material Cut-off Treaty negotiation, but the Russians and the Chinese preferred to negotiate a treaty covering weapons in space; and also to get some discussion, if not negotiations, started on nuclear non-proliferation. The insidious practice referred to as "linkage" was the means by which consensus on a work program could be sabotaged. If there were competing work projects backed by rival groups of countries, the likelihood of getting all to agree within the first ten weeks of each year was little to none because it only took one Member State's dissent to block work from going forward. And usually the price demanded by each group for agreeing to work on any item was to simultaneously link working on that with working on something else they favored.

A Fissile Material Cut-off Treaty had long been the aspiration of the European Union and some of the most responsible Member States of the Conference on Disarmament. Efforts had been made year after year to start work on that project, but each time those efforts had faltered by failing to garner consensus support. At every lunch the host would always say immediately upon the guests being seated and the appetizer course being served, "There are no free lunches", often followed by, "I now call upon the Ambassador of the United States (or some other Ambassador) to tell us how he sees the situation, and how we can get away from demands for linking issues so as to break the deadlock in the CD."

I would generally defer to whoever sat beside me so that I could speak after all others had spoken. I felt obligated to be consistently optimistic in my remarks because if the United States appeared otherwise, the mood of frustration and hopelessness would be even more compounded.

Work in the Conference on Disarmament, as in the United Nations itself, was discussed within five regional groups[3] of Member States. Among the Western Group country ambassadors, the Ambassadors of France and of Italy were the most notable. France's ambassador never failed to put his foot in his mouth whenever he spoke. It was amusing to see the incipient smiles of the Group in anticipation of the inevitable faux pas on faces around the table whenever he asked to be recognized. And he rarely disappointed. Some who knew his wife thought she should have been the French ambassador. She was acerbic, incisive, and quite unapproachable unless she liked and respected the object of her attention. But her husband's appointment as an ambassador was made, as far as I could tell, on his three strong assets—a good name, a good school and a good tailor.

As for my dear friend, Mario Maiolini, the Ambassador of Italy, he was short in stature but effusive in warmth. He also had the distinction of being the most erudite, educated and articulate of all our colleagues. He had studied at Columbia and other universities, and he knew his literature, history and philosophy better than most professors. Nor did he shrink from revealing his knowledge and his opinions—in great detail and length at Western Group meetings—much to my delight and the chagrin of many. He had the most delightful wife, Vivi, who used to jovially complain, "I spend-a my whole-a life-a running behind-a Mario with the pasta!"

It came to my attention in 2002 that an American spokesman was being sought to speak at a forthcoming conference on the subject of Weapons in Space where representatives of Russia and China would advocate the commencement of negotiations for a new Treaty on Weapons in Space and present their proposals for what that treaty should provide. The two countries had published a working paper entitled, "*Possible Elements for a Future International Legal Agreement on the Prevention of the Deployment of Weapons in Outer Space and the Threat or Use of Force Against Outer Space Objects.*" I inquired who would represent the U.S., and was told that no one in the Departments of State or Defense was willing to undertake that role.

I could not believe that America would allow such an important venue to take place without having someone present to counter the propaganda that would be spewed by America's adversaries. It did not seem like a case of bureaucratic oversight, but more like the bureaucracy not feeling confident it had the right spokesperson to do battle there. I immediately made it known that I would like to be America's spokesman at the Conference on Future Security in Space that was to be held in New Place, England in May, and possibly for lack of any other bidders I was given the green light to present America's position.

To that conference, Russia and China sent two of their most authoritative and prestigious figures. They were first on the program to speak in favor of their joint proposal. When it was my turn to speak, I contended in part, "The United States remains committed to the peaceful exploration and use of outer space by all nations, as declared in the 1967 Outer Space Treaty . . . We fully understand that maintaining international peace and security is an overarching purpose that guides activities on earth as well as in outer space, but in the final analysis preserving national security is likewise necessary and essential. For these reasons, the United States sees no need for new outer space arms control agreements and opposes negotiation of a treaty on outer space arms control."

I explained that there already existed an extensive and comprehensive system for limiting the uses of outer space to peaceful purposes that provided a framework for legitimate military uses of outer space. I cited the Limited Test Ban Treaty, the Committee on the Peaceful Uses of Outer Space and the Outer Space Treaty. I went on to say, "We believe that the existing multilateral arms control regime adequately protects States' interests in outer space and does not require augmentation." Rather, the problems that need to be addressed are right here on earth—the need for effective implementation of, and full compliance with, key regimes that tackle the very real threat of weapons of mass destruction" for which I cited the Nuclear Nonproliferation Treaty, Chemical Weapons Convention, and Biological Weapons Convention. I described as "groundless" concerns that missile defense might upset strategic stability and lead to a new arms race. I said the strategic arms reduction agreement signed by the U.S. and Russian presidents in Moscow on May 24, 2002, "demonstrates that pursuit of missile defense and the demise of the Anti-ballistic Missile Treaty are not an impediment to further reductions in nuclear weapons, or to increased U.S.-Russian cooperation." My remarks—followed by discussion with the audience in which I stressed the looming threat of objects in orbit that constituted "space garbage"—won the day against the spokesmen from Beijing and Moscow.

I got to know Sweden's Ambassador to the Conference on Disarmament quite well at numerous Western Group meetings and luncheons. Henrik Salander was bright and sincere. We first met in Stockholm where we lunched together before I arrived in Geneva. I learned that he had attended the same high school in Stockholm as my brother-in-law, and that in his youth Henrik had formed a musical group called "The Monkeys" that had become idols to Sweden's teenagers. The Monkeys at their height had even cut a gold record, "The Lion Sleeps Tonight."

So when Henrik Salander told me that Anna Lindh, Sweden's Foreign Minister, would be coming to Geneva to meet the UN Director General, I felt very honored Henrik wanted me included in their meeting. He explained the discussion would be those subjects of interest to Sweden and to UN international organizations.

The Lindh meeting took place in a private room at the UN headquarters with only about 8 others in attendance. After the Director General's welcoming statement and other appropriate formalities, she seized the opportunity to turn the meeting into a Swedish confrontation with the U.S. on the many policy issues where we had differences. I liked her frankness, her demeanor and her willingness to engage. I let her talk for almost half an hour until she finally grew silent. I was very careful to begin my reply by stating that I appreciated the chance to meet her, to hear her views and to begin a dialogue that might bring us closer. I began by asking her to imagine herself seeing the world through the eyes of the U.S. foreign minister. Then, point by point, I drew a word picture of what I thought she might view from that different perspective. After about fifteen minutes I concluded by saying that I hoped our acquaintanceship would become a friendship, and that differences on issues would not separate us, but give us food for thought and opportunities for listening, reevaluating and hopefully finding areas of agreement.

We were friends from that day on. She and her young son even came to visit us at Grindstugan, our country home south of Stockholm in the area known as Södermanland where she lived with her husband who was then its Governor. Consequently, it was a terrible shock when Margaretha and I heard that this bright and lovely woman had been wantonly stabbed while shopping at NK, Stockholm's leading department store. She died the next day.

Eventually a violent and mentally-disturbed young Yugoslavian immigrant, who six years earlier had been sent to a youth prison for stabbing his father, confessed when confronted with DNA evidence linking him to the Lindh murder weapon. Under Sweden's lenient criminal code he was remanded to psychiatric care. My thoughts of Anna Lindh will always be of a vibrant and bright idealist whose loss was a tragic reminder of Swedish Prime Minister Olaf Palme's slaying in 1986 because of Sweden not yet insisting on permanent bodyguards for its senior politicians.

The most likely work program item to gain consensus was the Fissile Material Cut-Off Treaty. After listening to a blistering condemnation in the Palais de Nations by the highly- respected Ambassador of Algeria, Salah Dembri, complaining bitterly of the inability to coalesce around that agenda item which would end the production of all enriched uranium and other fissile materials that could sustain a chain reaction and be used to make nuclear weapons, I decided to pursue getting it started.

I knew that I could not just come out publicly in favor of a Fissile Material Cut-off Treaty because my instructions from the State Department were not to announce America's support in favor if the Conference was divided, but only if and when all other countries were voicing support or at least none were objecting. Therefore any initiative to create a bandwagon movement toward its negotiation had to be led by others. So I discreetly inquired of those few colleagues to whom I felt closest to see if they would form a coalition to lead the initiative. That sparked them into action.

Led by the Swedish Ambassador in 2002, they formed what became known as "The Five Ambassadors Initiative." China's Ambassador immediately countered by offering a treaty for the Prevention of an Arms Race in Outer Space to be put on the agenda. So, with other activities diverting focus from the main attraction, nothing got started.

As 2002 wore on and nothing moved, I heard rumors that the US might withdraw from the wasteful and non-productive Conference on Disarmament. I received a visit from Stephen Rademaker, Assistant Secretary of State for International Security and Non-Proliferation. Rademaker flew to Geneva from Washington to deliver a message to me from his boss, John Bolton, the Under Secretary for Arms Control at State. Rademaker had only recently been confirmed in his State Department position, and I felt he was still a bit new to diplomacy. He told me that Bolton wanted me out of Geneva, and to move as soon as possible to the Organization for the Prohibition of Chemical Weapons (OPCW) in The Hague. This was a shock, but it should not have surprised me.

Bolton wanted me out of Geneva as nothing was able to get done there, but I was frankly disappointed that Bolton himself did not speak with me about his decision, and I expressed to Rademaker, not very politely, my reluctance to accede to orders from an Under Secretary when my posting in Geneva had been designated by the President. Rademaker made it clear that he had been instructed by Bolton to tell me that I had a limited time to decide if I was going to go to The Hague, and if I decided not to go I would simply be moved, body and baggage, back to Washington. He did not say the Secretary of State or the President knew of the decision, or that either had agreed with Bolton's ultimatum.

Weeks slipped by after Rademaker left Geneva to fly back to Washington. I got pulsed again by Rademaker as Bolton's deadline approached, asking if I was intending to move to The Hague. Since I had a trip scheduled to Washington for consultations in the State Department a couple of days later, I requested a meeting with the Deputy Secretary who received me on short notice despite his incredibly packed schedule. Richard Armitage was always at the department by 6 a.m. every morning where he would start his day in the gym by bench-pressing more than his body weight! I told him of Bolton's ultimatum that Rademaker had delivered, and that Bolton had not spoken to me himself about the matter. I said I had so far been non-committal, but if Secretary Powell and the President wanted me to move, of course I would. I explained that I bridled at being ordered out of a presidentially appointed post by an Under Secretary. Armitage said he would look into the matter and get back to me.

A few days later Armitage told me that Secretary Powell and he did not condone the way it had been handled but would like me to take the position as Ambassador to the Organization for the Prohibition of Chemical Weapons.

Armitage went on to explain that the U.S. had just expended a great deal of precious capital in getting the Organization for the Prohibition of Chemical Weapons to oust its Brazilian Director General, just one year after his re-election (with American backing) to a second four year term in that post. Armitage explained that the Director General, once re-elected, had depleted the Organization's funds that had been budgeted for inspections to pay salaries to favored former diplomats he had hired into staff positions. Forcing a vote in the Executive Council to oust Bustani had fractured the organization by breaking its time-honored tradition of consensus. The Director General was gone, but his friends and supporters were left in place, demoralized and furious at the US.

Armitage said that America's decision to send our first full-time *resident* ambassador was made to show support for the Organization. He added that our government was about to make a two million dollar donation to the Organization's voluntary fund to demonstrate America's commitment to that organization and to help it meet its inspection schedule. But he also warned that the U.S. could not make further voluntary donations over and above the Congressional appropriations of our annual dues as a Member State, so if more money was needed in the voluntary fund, I would have to raise it from private sources.

Although we would leave many close friends at our Mission in Geneva and at the Conference on Disarmament, I looked forward to the challenge of reinvigorating the Organization for the Prohibition of Chemical Weapons, and I began to make weekly trips to The Hague. I left my Conference on Disarmament deputy in charge in Geneva, and although I had ambassadorial rank there, I worked in The Hague simply as a member of America's delegation to the Organization for the Prohibition of Chemical Weapons while waiting for confirmation by the Senate to become our first OPCW Ambassador resident in The Hague.

For six months, from November 2002 to April 2003, I commuted from Geneva to The Hague during which time I wrote a departure memorandum for my eventual successor in Geneva. Very early each Monday morning I would catch a flight to Amsterdam's Schiphol airport where the American Embassy would have a car and driver waiting to meet me. From there I would be to taken to our delegation's office in The Hague. The office was not housed at the American embassy on Lange Voorhout, but in an office building located on Eisenhowerlaan that was only a stone's throw from the headquarters building of the Organization for the Prohibition of Chemical Weapons.

Unlike America's ambassador to the Netherlands, I had no Dutch security detail to escort and protect me, so each week our Embassy in The Hague would book me into a different hotel under an assumed name. A couple of times my wife or my daughter tried, without success, to call me in the evenings from Geneva or New York. They knew the name of the hotel at which I was staying that week, but sometimes could not remember the alias under which I was registered. I marveled at the efficiency of our embassy, as I never had to show my passport or even a credit card to the hotel staff when checking in or out.

Those months of commuting were invaluable to me in preparing for my new post in the Netherlands. It took time for me to learn the 1992 Chemical Weapons Convention, the Organization's rules and practices and to get to know the different players on the scene. Conventions and treaties are almost without exception subject to periodic review by their member states, usually at five-year intervals, and the Chemical Weapons Convention was no exception.

Preparing for the First Review Conference was one of the main activities taking place in The Hague when I arrived. The Organization's Executive Council had created an open-ended Working Group tasked to prepare for the First Review Conference, but by November 2002, it had only met several times during which it had decided to use a thematic approach in the review process rather than the traditional article-by-article approach. Five years had passed since the Treaty came into force in 1997. When it was created it was heralded as breaking new ground in arms control. It was the first comprehensive, verifiable multilateral treaty that banned completely an entire class of weapons of mass destruction, and it went beyond any previous treaty in its depth, extent and the intrusiveness of its verification provisions which included compulsory national declarations of relevant industrial and military activities, the destruction of chemical weapons within time limits (also under intrusive verification) and periodic routine inspections of declared industrial and military facilities. This first review gave the Member States a chance to fix what was not working, to discuss any needed changes and to reaffirm what was working to their satisfaction. However substantive discussions had not even begun when I came onto the scene.

Chairing the Review Conference Working Group was the Argentine ambassador who started submitting for plenary consideration notes that formed the basis of discussions at meetings of the Group. This process allowed me to hear delegations express their differing points of view, and they were many. No final draft emerged until just a couple of weeks before the Review Conference was to begin.

During that period in which I commuted to The Hague, one small pleasure was meeting and being driven by Albert Lankhamer. Albert was an experienced chauffeur who, with his big black Mercedes, ran his own small livery business. He had spent decades as a taxi driver in The Hague, and consequently knew every shortcut and back alley in that part of Holland like the palm of his hand. He could predict to the precise minute how long it would take to get to any destination regardless of the weather or traffic conditions he would encounter. He was trusted by our embassy to serve its guests when one of the embassy's cars was not available. After having been driven by a number of different limousine services and drivers, I expressed my preference for Albert, and the embassy obliged whenever he was available.

As America's first full-time resident Ambassador to the Organization, one of my initial tasks was to find a residence for Margaretha and me that would be suitable for diplomatic representation, and also well situated from the standpoint of security. The State Department had a rule that an Ambassadorial residence had to be sufficiently far from the sidewalk in case a car bomb was detonated.

Although I looked at dozens of apartments and houses offered for rent, I could find none in The Hague of sufficient size to allow for representational entertaining. I did not want to live in Wassenaar, the fashionable suburb from which it would take at least twenty minutes or much more in traffic to reach the delegation's office. I hoped to find something within five minutes of the office so that I could go home for lunch on days when I did not have meetings scheduled. Nor were any town houses set back from the street the requisite distance. In fact, but for a few, all the town houses abutted directly onto the sidewalk.

Finally, I saw one town house that seemed perfect—only five minutes from both the Organization's headquarters building and our delegation's office! It even had a beautifully carved stone Eagle atop its façade, and a front courtyard that could accommodate up to five parked cars. However, it was for sale, not for rent. I instructed the embassy's real estate broker to attempt to negotiate a long-term rental. As a result, our government leased one of The Hague's loveliest homes with a small walled private garden in the rear, only a hundred yards from police headquarters and a few hundred yards from the splendid Peace Palace that Andrew Carnegie built to house the International Court of Justice. The problem, however, was that the residence was unfurnished.

Normally it would take a minimum of six months to furnish and ready an ambassadorial residence. In our case, the State Department graciously granted an exception to their usual practice by agreeing to ship all of the government furniture from our residence in Geneva to our new residence in Holland. Margaretha, who had an amazing talent for managing the logistics of moving, shipping and tracking every item, had procured the floor plans of our new residence and had marked where each piece of furniture should be placed. When we arrived there late one Saturday afternoon, we found that the movers had indeed placed everything correctly.

The State Department, even agreed that the armored BMW I had used in Geneva could be driven to The Hague for my use there. All of this exceptional support and flexibility I attribute to Cathleen Lawrence and Peggy Nearman of the State Department's "T" Bureau. We even were able to hold our first diplomatic representational dinner one week after moving in!

The final highlight for me before I left Geneva for good was a small farewell reception with about thirty of my Conference on Disarmament ambassadorial colleagues in attendance. My brother-in-law, John H. Zeeman III, whose nickname was Hans, and my son happened to be in Geneva at the time, so I also invited them to attend.

Hans had been a Dutch naval lieutenant before marrying my sister, Joan, and immigrating to the United States. When he was growing up, his father had served as the Netherlands' ambassador to Indonesia and later to China. Hans' father had formed such a close personal friendship with Mao Tse Tung that Hans had become the Chairman's godson. Hans, therefore, was quite familiar with diplomatic gatherings. The most striking thing about my farewell reception was that even colleagues whom I never expected to show up did in fact attend.

Even Pakistan's ambassador surprised me by dropping by. We had often been at odds on policy, and he was so devious, unctuous and slippery and that I jokingly referred to him as "The Snake." Once, when he came to my office, I asked why he sided with China on every issue. That was one time when he leveled with me. It was, he replied, because China had been Pakistan's patron in helping it get nuclear capability to counter India's.

My colleagues were effusive in their comments and parting embrace. My brother-in-law told me afterwards that in all his years of attending diplomatic occasions he had never seen any diplomat hugged so warmly by each of his colleagues as I was that afternoon, and the affection certainly went both ways.

View from our residence in Geneva with Mont Blanc
in the distance.

CHAPTER XIII — THE ORGANIZATION FOR THE PROHIBITION OF CHEMICAL WEAPONS (THE "OPCW")

Staffing the new residence in The Hague was no easy job. Margaretha took charge of that requirement with one of the people at our embassy who had run the help wanted ads in the Dutch newspapers. Candidate interviews were conducted at the embassy. The result was nothing less than superb.

Margaretha selected, and succeeded in recruiting, the only British butler/house manager in Holland other than the late Freddy Heinekin's manservant. Jocelyn Hancock was intelligent, had a quick wit, a green thumb, and he kept the ambassadorial residence books of account with a CPA's skill. He had to record, for example among other minutiae, what food, wines and liquor were for official representation and what was for our personal household use. Getting this amazingly capable and charming gentleman to "hire on" was no easy feat considering the modest wage our government was willing to pay, but once again, the State Department was flexible and willing to augment his salary for his doing the gardening instead of having an outside landscaping firm render that service.

Margaretha also selected a charming and talented young Australian chef, David Cox, to whose imagination and culinary inventiveness she gave free rein, and we were not disappointed. Edith, the Phillipine maid, could never learn to serve at dinners despite valiant efforts to train her, but she laundered, ironed and cleaned very well.

A Dutch national who had been employed by the US embassy for eighteen years—first in the warehouse and then as a utility driver, pleaded for the chauffeur's position. He had the appearance of a professional rugby player. He claimed his ambition in life was to drive for an ambassador, and he seemed so sincere we decided to give him a chance. Margaretha had to be driven frequently in the beginning of our stay while she was putting the final touches on our residence for its representational function. We discovered that he was a gold-bricking liar and scoundrel who often referred to Margaretha in the embassy garage in quite derogatory terms as he found it demeaning to occasionally drive the Ambassador's wife on official business. I eventually decided to fire him, but because of his longevity with the Embassy and the liberality of the Dutch employment laws, I was told the Embassy would have to pay him close to a quarter of a million dollars in severance if he were fired.

It annoyed me that he had the habit of asking for little favors, such as permission to take a day off to be with his family, not to wear his jacket on hot days, to leave work early or to schedule a trip to suit his, not my, personal needs. I granted them all without exception. However, when he asked for leave to take his family to France to visit Disney World during one very busy political period, I told him that I needed him during those days. He became irate, probably because he was used to getting his way. As he continued to press me, I held firm. He finally lost his composure and blurted out heatedly, "In that case I will resign." I replied "Put it in writing." Thankfully, he did. I immediately wrote back accepting his resignation.

That opened the door for me to call my pal, Albert Lankhamer. I had often regretted not offering him the chauffer's position in the first place. But for Albert to take a permanent position with the U.S. embassy meant that he would have to dispose of his Mercedes and close his livery business. Nevertheless, Albert agreed without any hesitation. That was a testament to how we felt about each other.

The decision to take Albert was the right one. Albert was a street-wise regular guy, open, amiable, optimistic and smart as a whip. His connections were incredible. Together with his wife's family, Albert had not less than a hundred relatives in The Hague in every business or walk of life one could imagine. Albert was eager to improve his halting English, and we often conversed in the car. Albert never resented my offering gentle corrections. Our genuine liking for each other grew.

It astounded the embassy how many thousands Albert saved in repair bills on its armored sedans. He became a legend at US and European security courses for ambassadorial drivers where, for his speed and precision, he was referred to as the Flying Dutchman. The embassy eventually gave him an award for exceptional service that I proudly presented to him at his award ceremony.

Before I arrived in The Hague, the delegation had created an office for me by combining two adjoining rooms that visitors from Washington had used previously. I quickly positioned the furniture, art, photos and flag. Because I had been a Mac user from the very inception of Apple's computers, and because my calendar schedule and personal contact data base were on software that was not compatible with the usual government-issued PCs, I really needed to be able to access those data bases at work. I was not allowed to bring my own computer or even my cell phone into the delegation office for security reasons. I persuaded the State Department that to work effectively I needed an Apple notebook, and they accommodated by providing one for my use.

I also decided that my office would not be a "secure" area. I was determined not to bring a classified document into my office, because if the Marine guards found a classified document lying on my desk when I was not in the room, I would have a security breach on my record, and I was not willing to risk that. It was for that reason I could not have, nor did I want, anything classified on my office computer or on its backup external hard drive. Consequently, I had to go to a "secure" area to read classified or confidential documents. I was careful never to overlook those requirements, so I avoided any security violation during my years of service.

Initially, security arrangements for our residence in The Hague were woefully incomplete. The embassy had only put plastic laminate on the windows to prevent shattering in case of an explosion, and later some metal fencing was added in the rear garden to prevent intrusion. Many ambassadorial residences in The Hague were guarded by elevated police guardhouses nearby or across the street. I did not want to call attention to our townhouse as an ambassadorial residence, so I decided not to ask for police security. Instead I asked for a working alarm system, security cameras with recording capability and motion-actuated floodlights in the front and rear of the house. Unfortunately, all that took a couple of years, but I kept a low profile, stayed out of the media, allowed no photos to be published and had all our mail and deliveries go to the embassy, not the residence.

Upon confirmation by the Senate, OPCW Director General, Rogelio Pfirter, formally presented my official credentials with which I could gain access to the headquarters building.

I flew to Washington to interview some candidates for the Deputy position, and although I met a qualified army officer candidate, on the advice of Donald Mahley I chose Pete Ito, a State Department career officer.

This violated a long-standing agreement between the Defense and State Departments that the resident OPCW ambassador's Deputy would always be a military person. However, I agreed to receive a nominee of the Defense Department as the staff member next in charge after Pete Ito, and that allayed their Department's concern. As a result, Abigail Robinson, a former Army officer, became a highly valued member of my staff. Abby was charming, smart as a whip and a delight to work with.

The First Review Conference

Sometime in March, 2003, I was informed that I would not be delivering the official statement for the United States at the First Review Conference in The Hague which was to take place the following month. Since John Bolton was in charge of Arms Control at the Department of State, I fully expected that he would be coming over to The Hague for the historic First Review Conference that was to be held from April 28th to May 9th.

However, a couple of days before the RevCon was to begin I learned that Bolton was not coming, and although the Senate had unanimously confirmed me as Ambassador to the OPCW, that did not change the decision for America's keynote speech to be delivered, not by me as America's Permanent Representative to the OPCW, but by Steven Rademaker, the Assistant Secretary of State who was to read John Bolton's address to the Review Conference.

I was disappointed because I saw that as a lost opportunity to show support to an Organization in crisis by allowing me to deliver America's keynote address as our first full-time resident ambassador in The Hague, but I kept that to myself.

On April 28th, 2003, the First Review Conference of the Chemical Weapons Convention formally commenced in the large Convention Center. It began with a message from UN Secretary General Kofi Annan and a statement by Rogelio Pfirter, the OPCW's newly-appointed Director General, followed by General Debate that began with Steven Rademaker mounting the stage to deliver John Bolton's speech, the advance text of which I had not been shown.

I sat in one of our delegation's assigned seats, watching and listening as the U.S. statement was being delivered. It audaciously named both Member and non-Member States of the OPCW as possessors or future possessors of chemical weapons.

Rademaker charged in part:

> *"the United States believes that over a dozen countries currently possess or are actively pursuing chemical weapons. While some, such as Syria, Libya and North Korea are not Parties to the Chemical Weapons Convention, others have representatives here in this room. . . . We owe it to you in this room to be candid about what those concerns are. . . We are most troubled by the activities of Iran, which we believe continues to seek chemicals, production technology, training, and expertise from abroad. The United States believes Iran already has stockpiled blister, blood, and choking agents. We also believe it has made some nerve agents. We have discussed our concerns with Iran, but those concerns have not been dispelled. Those concerns need*

to be resolved rapidly and in the most transparent and cooperative manner possible."

Rademaker's statement caused a furor in the hall. Nothing could have been more damaging to an Organization already on life support that needed to be resuscitated. Ambassador Ali Asghar Soltanieh of Iran jumped up and demanded the right of reply. Soltanieh was someone I knew well from Geneva where he had served as Iran's Permanent Representative to the Conference on Disarmament. He had come from Teheran to bolster Iran's delegation at this First Review Conference. The Chairman permitted him to take the floor, whereupon he launched into an articulate defense.

Soltanieh passionately alluded to those Iranians who were killed, maimed and disfigured by poison gas at the hands of Saddam Hussein during the Iran-Iraq war, and stressed that the US, not Iran, had weakened the convention with some of its legislation. He finished by urging the US delegation not to prematurely accuse other Member States of non-compliance, but rather to pursue non-member states to join the convention. As he returned to his seat he received a loud round of applause, not a very propitious signal to me and my delegation. However, I knew this was just the opening gambit in a bigger game, so I walked over to where he was sitting and said, "Ali, that was a great rebuttal. I couldn't have done better myself." He rose with a broad smile, thanked me warmly, and said he was glad to see me again.

For the next ten days I was beseeched by ambassadors pleading with me to give the Iranians an apology for the defamatory words Rademaker had uttered. Time after time, I was warned that without an apology from the United States the Review Conference would fail to reach consensus, as Iran would block the issuance of the Review Conference's final report and it would blame the United States for the failure of the Chemical Weapons Convention's First Review Conference.

I rebuffed every plea, explaining that an apology was impossible. Even good friends tried several times to get me to relent. I finally had to chide them for continuing to press me.

As the Conference went into its second week, an Informal Summary statement was being drafted in one of the Convention Center's conference rooms in a parallel effort under the chairmanship of the well-liked and vivacious Ambassador of Malaysia, Farida Arrifin. This Informal Summary was to be the source from which the media would largely draw their reporting at the conclusion of the Conference, and for that reason it was deemed politically important. Popular with the delegates of the non-aligned Member States, Farida Arrifin was occasionally found caucusing and siding with Iran, South Africa, India, Indonesia and Cuba. I was concerned that she would not be impartial in the chair of that process, and could steer the draft away from principles that Washington wanted to see reinforced in the Review Conference report. It had been decided to undertake this summary drafting exercise as a way to allow the expression of differing points of view without poisoning the final official report of the conference, and perhaps hone some compromise language that might allow the final report to be adopted by consensus. To my surprise and gratification, Amb. Arrifin was absolutely fair and impartial. She earned the respect of all with her polite demeanor and her scrupulous impartiality.

However, on the other and main track—that of the official report—as the second week wore on there was nothing but doom and gloom. The Review Conference was due to end on Friday night of the second week, and it was already Wednesday, May 8th, with only two days left! Each morning the key players and officers of the Review Conference and the Conference of State Parties would meet in a small meeting room to plan the day. The meetings were presided by the Conference Chairman and the Director General. That Wednesday, in desperation the Director General announced that he would hold a small lunch for just the key players in his private dining room back in the Organization's office building, a three-minute walk from the Convention Center. When we assembled for that lunch with the Director General and several of his staff, seven[4] country ambassadors were also present. It became more evident to me as each course was served that the process had ground to a halt.

Ambassador of India, Shayamala Cowsik, reported that of the 117 paragraphs that had been proffered in the preliminary draft that had been in preparation for almost a year, there was disagreement on the wording of more than half! In fact, she and her delegation had been among the most obdurate in objecting to paragraph after paragraph. And with really only one full day left before the last day of the Review Conference, it seemed an almost human impossibility to find compromise language and agreement on over 60 paragraphs that for months had defied the efforts of all Member States.

However, as dessert was being served, I asked to speak. "We are all here working and hoping for a successful RevCon" I began. "Why do we have to quit on Friday? Why don't we stay for another week and finish the job?" The Iranian ambassador who was sitting at my left heatedly responded, "Because we have a big delegation here staying in hotels, and we can't possibly afford to keep them all here for another week."

A hush fell over the room. I observed Ambassador Cowsik seated across the table. She cut a lithe and petite figure swathed in her magnificent sari as she sat strong and straight as a martinet. Her chiseled features and light umber complexion conveyed her classic grace.

When I noticed her dark and piercing gaze fixed on me, our eyes locked. I thought I saw in her expression that she wanted the Review Conference to succeed, so I said to her across the table, "Ambassador Cowsik, are you willing with one or two of your delegation to meet this afternoon with me and one or two of my delegation to see if we can break loose some of the troublesome paragraphs?" She replied affirmatively.

We lost no time in repairing to one of the many meeting rooms in a side corridor of the convention hall. India's Ambassador was accompanied by several aides[5]. Also present were Bob Mikulak from the State Department in Washington; Brandon Williams, a resident member of my staff appointed by the Commerce Department; and a representative of the UK delegation observing.

We managed to find and agree on compromise language for many of the paragraphs. By about five that afternoon, word had spread around the convention hall that India and America were "making decisions that might bind the assemblage", and concern, if not anger, was building among those delegations not present in our side discussions.

The Netherlands Ambassador, Mark Vogelaar, had been elected as Chairman of the Committee of the Whole of the Review Conference. He was particularly perturbed that he had not been invited into my meeting with Ambassador Cowsik, but the result of having him there would have been to poison the atmosphere and make compromise impossible. He had persistently refused to recognize both Ambassador Cowsik and Ambassador Arrifin's requests to be heard from the floor of the Convention Hall, and they were both furious with him for what they considered was imperious behavior on the part of the

Chairman of the Committee of the Whole. When a little after 5 p.m., one of my own delegation knocked at the door of the conference room in which we were meeting to insist that we inform the Member States that our efforts would be opened up starting right after 7 p.m. that evening to anyone who wanted to participate. Both Ambassador Cowsik and I agreed. Resuming at 7 p.m. would allow people time to eat before coming to the negotiating table for a long night of work.

I hastily left to get some dinner, and by the time I returned with Ambassador Cowsik at my side to enter the long conference room at 7 p.m., every seat at the table that stretched a good sixty feet was filled. Even chairs that lined the walls were taken. Only the chair at the head of the table remained unoccupied.

"You had better take that empty seat and run this meeting," I said to Ambassador Cowsik. She shook her head and told me that I had to chair the meeting. "As America's ambassador, I cannot sit in the chair" I replied. She insisted, so I announced to all that I had been asked to sit in the chair, but would only do so if there were no objection. I added that I would not chair the meeting as the Ambassador of the United States, but would put aside my U.S. ambassadorial hat to act as an independent facilitator. I announced that Brandon Williams of my delegation would represent the United States at the table. I waited for a response. No one objected.

I suggested that we would go through the preliminary draft and discuss only the paragraphs that were in contention. Again there were no objections. As we dealt with each paragraph I allowed anyone at the table to comment, recognizing speakers in a counter clockwise direction until all comments were exhausted. Then I tried to find words to express the best option to compromise the differing views.

As the evening wore on, one after another, paragraphs that had been in dispute were agreed without further objection. By close to midnight, only about half a dozen were still in dispute, but it was clear that the group was exhausted. I suggested that we recess and think overnight about solutions to the remaining deadlocked paragraphs, with just the few principal objecting delegations meeting the following morning at the Organization's headquarters building in a private conference room to see if they could finally resolve the last remaining differences.

As I was leaving the Convention Center for the night, Ambassador Vogelaar approached me. He expressed annoyance that he had not been invited to chair the facilitation that had just taken place. I pointed out to him that any eventual success would be his as Chairman of the Committee of the Whole, and that any failure would be mine—not his—by my presiding over this last ditch effort. With that he relented, and said that as Chairman he would invite just the key players who had clung to their objections to meet the next morning.

Early the following morning when I left the Convention Center building to walk toward the nearby Organization's headquarters building I noticed the Pakistani ambassador making his way in the same direction. Pakistan was not one of the countries that Vogelaar had said he would invite to the morning meeting. I slowed my pace so as not to have to arrive at the headquarters' entrance with the Pakistani. I was concerned that if India and Pakistan were in the same room, agreement could be difficult. When I entered the Organization headquarters and passed through its security gate into the outer hall, the Pakistani ambassador and all other participants had already gone into the conference room where we were to meet. I was the only person left in the outer hall, so I took a seat and waited. Eventually, one of the Organization's protocol staff came out looking for me. He queried, "Excellency, why don't you come into the meeting?" I replied that I was waiting because the meeting to which I had been invited did not include Pakistan, so I would wait outside until that one was concluded.

After a few minutes the Pakistani ambassador emerged, and without even a glance in my direction, he strode out of the building. At that point I passed into the private office area and entered the meeting. The few paragraphs that remained in contention were discussed and resolved to everyone's satisfaction, after which those gathered walked together back to the Convention Hall.

The news of the agreed text spread like wildfire in the halls of the Convention Center. The delegates were impatient to resume the general session to adopt the Final Report and conclude the Review Conference. But the Iranian delegation was still insisting they would not join consensus unless the U.S. apologized for its accusations. I suggested that Iran and the U.S. should meet privately to try to resolve their differences face to face.

The private US-Iran confrontation was held in one of the side conference rooms. Ambassador Ali Asgar Soltanieh and I were the negotiating principals, but backed up and supported by each of our delegations. In my case I also had a group of "watchers" from the Defense Department, the Commerce Department and the State Department. Soltanieh had his own retinue of "watchers" who had come from Teheran to reinforce the Iranian delegation in The Hague.

I opened the meeting by saying publicly that Ali and I had known each other in Geneva as colleagues at the Conference on Disarmament where despite strong differences on policy and procedure we had grown to respect and trust each other for candor and conviction.

I reminded Ali that I had always been truthful and forthright with him. I said, "Ali, if I could meet your demands, they would already have been met. I cannot and will not. But I understand the predicament in which you and your delegation find yourselves and the instructions you undoubtedly have from Teheran. I can only offer you my best effort to resolve the problem by reciting Chemical Weapons Convention language. I can use no words other than those to which both our countries agreed in signing the treaty. In that document, we agreed that before accusing another Member State of violating the treaty, we would first make inquiries in an attempt to satisfy our concerns, and then if that did not dispel them, we could proceed to accuse the Member State. Right now, in the proposed text of the Final Report that obligation is reaffirmed in a paragraph far down the list of numbered paragraphs. I am willing to take that treaty language and move it up almost to the beginning of the Review Conference Final Report. You and your friends in Teheran can make of that what you will, but the fact it was moved up to such prominence and priority gives Iran the ability to trumpet that change as a major concession from the United States. That is all I can do for you. You either take it, or you will destroy the RevCon for all of us. I hope Iran can join consensus so we can hail this Review Conference as historic."

The Iranians huddled together in the back of the conference room frantically dialing Teheran on their cell phones to try to get permission to agree. After some moments, Ambassador Soltanieh announced Iran would join consensus. Greatly relieved, we all went back into the Conference Center's cavernous auditorium to conclude the first successful Review Conference of the Chemical Weapons Convention, or for that matter, of any international multilateral security organization.

Not long after the conclusion of the first Review Conference, I attended my first session of the Executive Council as the newly-confirmed ambassador to the Organization. Soon after the meeting's opening formalities were concluded, Gilberto Vergna Saboia, Brazil's ambassador, asked for the floor. He rose to make clear his and Brazil's resentment over the treatment his fellow countryman, Ambassador José Mauricio Bustani, had received at the hands of the United States. I was aware that their Ambassador was close to their President, Lula da Silva, and that Lula was angry over America's ouster of his close friend as Director General of the Organization. I guessed that Saboia was not anti-American, but that he had been instructed to make those remarks.

I immediately requested the floor to answer Saboia, but since I had not participated in Bustani's ouster, I kept it as non-adversarial as I could. When Saboia and I later met, I explained that I was glad neither of us had been serving at the Organization for the Prohibition of Chemcial Weapons when Bustani had been voted out, so I hoped he could overlook our verbal sparring and allow us to work together in the future as friends and colleagues. He said he could. We shook hands to seal a warm friendship.

A few weeks later, I got a call from the Pakistani ambassador inviting me to lunch. I was eager to accept since I had slighted him so badly during the last morning the Review Conference. The next day I entered the stately dining room of the Hotel Des Indes. Pakistan Ambassador, H.E. Mustafa Kamal Kazi, was already seated at a table as I approached. Mustafa rose to welcome me. He was thin, fit, handsome and far more polite and gracious than I had expected. There was no mention of my refusal to join him in the final Review Conference settlement talks. We spoke of international affairs, issues that would need attention at the Organization, and his offer to cooperate in ways that his instructions would allow. I began to feel a sincere respect for this aristocratic and intelligent man of the world. Finally, although I cannot remember his exact words over dessert, Mustafa said approximately the following: "I used to regard the United States as a haven for the oppressed, as a beacon of freedom and democracy, and as a friend of the oppressed and enslaved around the world. For me, the Statue of Liberty was a symbol to believe in. But lately, with President Bush's policies, its invasion of Iraq, and its threatening imperialistic superpower status, I no longer view it as I used to."

I thought for at least a minute before I replied. I said, "Mustafa, tell me, if you can, what other nation has given the lives of its young men and women as well as its treasure to bring freedom to others." He looked me in the eye and said he could not name one. I said that I hoped he would try to balance his resentments with that in mind.

From that point on we were the closest of friends. He and his wife spent many enjoyable times with us, visiting us in Sweden with their children and inviting Margaretha to Moscow when Mustafa was posted there after finishing his tour at The Hague.

It was at an Executive Session a few months later that Director General Pfirter announced that he could not manage the Organization if the Executive Council did not give him direction on the tenure policy to be applied to the staff of the Organization. He explained that at its very first Conference of States Parties, the Organization had determined that it would be a non-career organization with staff employed for only limited periods, but it had left the task of adopting a specific policy to its Executive Council.

The reason for the decision was to ensure employee turnover, and thus a broader geographic distribution of the nationalities that would be brought on staff. Pfirter bemoaned the fact that six years had passed without the Executive Council taking any decision to define the tenure policy, and he was at a loss to know whether to extend staff that had served for six years or to commence recruiting replacements.

Originally the Russians had fought for a short tenure period so that, with heightened staff turnover, they could get more Russians employed at the Organization at an earlier date. Most Member States and the Organization staff itself favored a longer period of employment. Unless the adamant opposition of the Russian delegation was overcome or softened, no sensible tenure policy would be possible.

I decided to take the bull by the horns. I placed a call to Ambassador Alexander Khodakov who, before becoming Russia's ambassador to the Netherlands, had been one of the top legal officers of the Russian Government under the Soviet system. I arranged to go over to the Russian embassy to meet with him. I knew that he would be grateful for my not asking him to come to my office, and when I arrived at his embassy I was received very cordially. I was hopeful that we might begin to cooperate constructively.

After polite introductions and the usual coffee, tea and cookies, I told Khodakov and his deputy that if the US and Russia could agree on a tenure policy we could bring everyone along with us to consensus. He asked me what I was suggesting.

I replied that I was aware Russia would want a shorter period, but I felt seven years with some discretionary flexibility that could be exercised by the Director General was what it would take to gain consensus although many delegations wanted a longer period, even as much as nine or ten years. Khodakov had spent more of his career as a lawyer than as a diplomat. He was highly intelligent and above all a pragmatist. He surprised me by immediately agreeing to collaborate without taking the precaution of first getting Moscow on board, and he courageously indicated we would work together for that solution.

That was the beginning of a strong and lasting cooperation between the U.S. and Russia in the Organization for the Prohibition of Chemical Weapons, despite very strong areas of disagreement that were not likely to be resolved. It actually shocked the Member States when they learned that Russia and the U.S. had agreed on a tenure policy, and it was adopted unanimously after extended debate and some tweaking. But it did not shock me as I had also been able to forge a close friendship in Geneva with Russia's very able Ambassador Leonid Skotnikov, who later arrived in The Hague as a Judge on the International Court of Justice.

A few months later, on the Monday night preceding the opening of the next Executive Council session that would begin on Tuesday morning, I invited the entire Russian Delegation, as well as some Russians who had come from Moscow to attend the Executive Council, over to our residence for a late afternoon reception. We served drinks and hors d'oeuvres on the terrace that fronted on our garden in the rear courtyard. Plenty of Jack Daniels was on hand for our guests who preferred Kentucky bourbon to vodka. It was a lovely evening, and for the first time our delegations were able to fraternize in a friendly atmosphere without the usual strained formality that marked most U.S.-Russian confrontations.

It was with real warmth that each member of the Russian group thanked me as they left. On arriving, their dignified and charismatic ambassador had left his overcoat with all the others at the entrance to our residence. Upon departing he had trouble finding his among all the others hanging there. Our butler, Jocelyn, said humorously "If you can't find your own, just pick the best one." Ambassador Kyrill Gevorgian eventually found his coat and was halfway out the door when he turned and retorted "Good joke, that!"

The next day instead of the usual salvos, there was no sniping between us to disturb the session. The Russians invited my delegation to their embassy on the eve of the next Executive Council, and thereafter we alternated hosting each other before every Executive Council meeting. That practice was continued after I left.

Diplomacy takes many forms. Opportunities must be seized when they arise. Many outstanding African women ambassadors were serving at that time in The Netherlands, one of which was Ghana's ambassador to The Netherlands, Dr. Grace Amponsah-Ababio. Dr. Grace, was rotund, affable, warm and huggable. She had absolutely no guile, and her heart and soul were pure as driven snow—as contrasted with sweet smiling cheeks that glistened like two ripe plums.

Ambassador Grace was scrupulously faithful in attending meetings of the Organization's Executive Council. Once I got to know her well I found out that she would buy stolen and abandoned bicycles cheaply from the municipal authorities in The Hague that had seized them, and then ship them to young school girls in Ghana who otherwise would have to walk each day as much as ten miles to and from their schools.

I asked her to get me the details so that I, too, could make a personal contribution, and when I donated only a small amount of money, it bought not just some bicycles, but bushels of appreciation as well. And when Ghana's soccer team beat the American team in the World Cup, I wrote Grace a personal note congratulating her and her country's team on their stunning progress in the games. Later, Grace was proud to tell me that she had sent my letter to the President of Ghana!

Letting the contingent of distaff African Ambassadors understand that I was interested in and appreciative of their countries and native cultures was best done by indirection. For example, it so happened that Margaretha had given me to read the wonderful stories by the Scottish author Alexander McCall Smith about the No. 1 Ladies Detective Agency in Gabarone, Botswana. I loved them and decided that I would give them to the lady Ambassadors from Africa who, without exception, had not read nor even heard of them. They must have wondered how an American Ambassador could have found and enjoyed these books before they did! But it went a long way toward informing them that I appreciated Africa, its culture and their points of view.

When the State Department was struggling to pay America's dues to international organizations that become owing each January 1st, the subject would invariably be brought up at the first Western Regional Group meeting each year. Countries that had already paid their dues that January would proudly announce that fact, and then implore those other countries around the table that had not already paid to do so while looking directly at me and our delegation.

It would have only cost a few hundred million dollars to bring current all of America's dues to the dozens of international organizations where we were more than a year behind in payment. After all, we owed it! And it would have been money well spent to reduce resentment felt by less affluent countries that had paid their dues on time.

But for the herculean efforts of a valiant few at the State Department who fought to help the Organization get its dues money sooner than most, and the wisdom of some influential members of the Senate who recognized the need to make exceptions for security reasons for the North American Treaty Organization, the International Atomic Energy Agency, and the Organization for the Prevention of Chemical Weapons, we would have been more than a year late in paying our OPCW dues for most of the years I was at post.

Aware of the need to rebuild the Organization's esprit and morale, I felt I had to somehow compensate for America's tardiness in paying its dues. I knew we might even garner some good will if I could announce that America had again contributed to the Voluntary Fund above and beyond its dues obligation. Recalling Richard Armitage's admonition that I would have to raise any extra money from private sources, I spoke to my dear friend Danny Abraham, one of America's most generous philanthropists. He graciously honored my service by donating a quarter of a million dollars to the Organization's Voluntary Fund. I was proud to announce that donation, enabling America to tangibly demonstrate financial support for the Organization despite the tardiness of our dues payments.

The role that Margaretha played in supporting me in my work as a diplomat was not a supporting role. It was a leading one and invaluable. I suppose the common impression is that an ambassador's wife has only to oversee her household staff, be kind to the other ambassadorial wives and hopefully be seen as a gracious hostess and devoted partner to her husband.

Margaretha was much more than that. She became my full diplomatic partner in many ways. One has only to ask when and how does the most informal, intimate contact take place in the world of diplomacy? It is not at the negotiating table. It is at the dinner table, and thanks to our young Australian chef we were known to have the best table in The Hague. And who sits next to the most important invited ambassadorial guest? The hostess of course!

Margaretha, with her doctorate in psychology, would unfailingly somehow get her dinner companions to open up and discuss things they never would have discussed with me. That enabled her to give me insights and information I would not have gotten otherwise. And it did not end there.

Margaretha also ran a weekly "Tuesday Salon" in our dining room where a most marvelous group of ambassadorial wives gathered regularly to converse, paint porcelain and enjoy a delicious lunch. If there was no official obligation on my schedule, I often went home during the lunch hour for a sandwich and a half-hour nap. If it happened to be a Tuesday, I would stick my head in to say hello to the raptly-engaged ladies before going upstairs.

The feeling of closeness, harmony and friendship in that dining room was truly heartwarming. Margaretha's initiative in bonding that "band of sisters" in emotional super glue proved its worth many times when I needed the support of one or more of their husbands. It did not surprise me when occasionally I was told, "If I don't agree, my wife will give me hell."

In 2005, I was asked by the Marine Detachment to be the Guest of Honor at the Marine Ball that is given annually to celebrate the founding of the Corps, and I proudly accepted. A few days before the Ball Margaretha had not yet returned from Sweden, so I went alone to a lavish dinner given by the Moroccan Ambassador at his residence. The food was succulent and I ate ravenously, even sampling all the different desserts.

When I got back to my residence late that night and retired to bed, I felt a burning in my lungs that I thought was heartburn from overeating. However, when it persisted I realized it was more than indigestion or heartburn, so I called Margaretha in Stockholm. She insisted I call the Marines to ask for medical assistance. The Marine officer on duty said he would get an ambulance to my residence in minutes. I put on my robe and grabbed my wallet and mobile phone.

When the doorbell rang, I went downstairs to open it, but only then did I realize I had left the keys to the deadlocked front door upstairs. I had to climb back up to retrieve them and then come back down, all with my lungs on fire. In the ambulance I was diagnosed as having a heart attack, and when I reached the specialized heart hospital a full medical team was ready and waiting as I was rolled right onto the operating table.

I was able to watch on an overhead monitor as the catheter was inserted, the balloon was inflated, and the stent was placed. Immediately my pain dissipated. My sense of relief was palpable. As soon as I felt better I reached under my body to find my cell phone that I had hidden there. Forgetting that it was around 3 a.m., and that cell phones were forbidden in the intensive care area, I called Margaretha to tell her the stent had been placed and that I was feeling fine.

Next I called my close friend, Mexican Ambassador Sandra Fuentes Berain, to assure her that the following morning at the Executive Council session she would have America's support for something important to her, explaining that I was in the hospital with a heart attack and could not be there in person. Sandra was someone whom I had met in New York years earlier as a client of one of my former law partners. America's reputation did not suffer when she told delegations at the Executive Council that, despite having a heart attack, I had called her at 3 a.m. to make good on a promise.

Margaretha's plane from Sweden landed the next morning, and when she came directly from the airport to see me in the hospital it was with enormous gratitude that we hugged each other. During the week I was recovering in intensive care, I was the only patient who did not have to eat the bland hospital food. Our Australian chef catered culinary delights, delivered by Albert and served by Margaretha. That became my definition of "spoiled rotten."

That same week Margaretha had to preside in my stead at The Marine Ball. When she told me all about that evening that celebrates the birthday of the Marine Corps on November 10, 1775, she described the Marines in their stunning dress uniforms, the dinner guests in black tie and their wives in long gowns, and the poignant ritual observed each year to honor those Marines who had given their lives for their country:

A lone table is set with a clean white place mat, plate, bread plate, cloth napkin and utensils. A lighted wax taper in the center of the table expresses the light of hope. A long stemmed rose in a simple bud vase represents the families who love and keep faith with those who serve. A yellow ribbon around the vase represents those waiting for their Marines to come home while the red ribbon symbolizes the search for those missing in action. An inverted champagne flute signifies that the fallen Marine will not be toasting at the Gala. A lemon wedge represents his bitter loss, the salt on the lemon represent the tears of his loved ones, and the empty chair at the table is for the fallen comrade. When the birthday cake is placed on the table the first slice is cut with a special ceremonial saber. It is given to the oldest Marine who hands it to the youngest Marine to symbolize the passing of knowledge, experience and tradition.

During my time in The Hague, I always tried to go to the Marine detachment's residence for their Friday night beer parties, or to have personal chats with those coming from or leaving for a new posting, or to shoot a game of pool with the racks, balls, and cues that I had bought for their use.

When I was about to leave The Hague in 2009, the entire Marine detachment came over to my office to present, in an unforgettable ceremony, a folded flag and memorial plaque wishing me "fair winds and following seas." At the conclusion of the ceremony, Margaretha gave a warm hug to the Gunny (the Gunnery Sergeant who was in command of the detachment). About a dozen throats noisily began to be cleared. Margaretha got the hint, and a dozen Marines each got their own warm hug from her.

All was not work at my post. The International Diplomatic Tennis Tournament of The Hague was held each year at the Canadian residence, and there was also an Annual Lemonias Tennis Club tournament. I used to play in both with relish. Even now, years later, I still play with some of those young players when we get a chance to see each other.

The Organization for the Prohibition of Chemical Weapons reached the tenth anniversary of its existence in 2007. Celebrations were held all over the world. I attended some in The Hague, Berlin, Vienna and elsewhere, but the United States had no plans for a celebration in our own country. This was a disappointment to me. I asked the State Department to arrange something, no matter how modest, but was told there was no money or staff available for that purpose. I offered to arrange it myself, and the State Department did not object.

Some friends and I made donations to Columbia University to enable an all-day event to be held in the magnificent rotunda of Low Memorial Library guarded by the statue of Alma Mater. At the Symposium entitled, "Effective Multilateralism as Exemplified by the Organization for the Prohibition of Chemical Weapons," I gave the welcoming address, and Ambassador Rogelio Pfirter delivered the opening statement.

The distinguished panel included: Columbia Professors Jose Alvarez and Laurie Damrosch; Rolf Ekeus, renowned Swedish diplomat, Chairman of the Stockholm International Peace Research Institute and former Ambassador of Sweden to the

United States; H. E. Xue Hanqin, China's ambassador to The Netherlands; Ambassador Donald Mahley of the U. S. State Department; and Congressman Christopher Shays of Connecticut.

The presentations and discussions were preserved on tape. They were provocative, insightful and substantive. The large audience that included students and invited guests garnered knowledge about a little-known Organization working to make the world safe from the threat of chemical weapons, and I had the satisfaction of seeing my country participate in a celebration from which it would otherwise have been missing thanks to the generosity of those donating[6], and of Columbia University's Law School hosting that memorable event.

The Second Review Conference

With the arrival of April 2008, another five years had passed since the First Review Conference. Once again the Organization geared up to review the Chemical Weapons Convention, this time at its Second "RevCon".

Preparations had been under way for months with meetings starting in the fall of the preceding year in an Open-Ended Working Group under the Chairmanship of UK Ambassador Lyn Parker to prepare a draft text for consideration by the Review Conference. The fact that a Brit and member of the Western and Other Regional Group was leading that effort made it vital that Ambassador Parker allowed every regional group, every delegation, and every viewpoint to receive a fair hearing in an effort to get a balanced text.

The well-liked, personable and astute Cuban ambassador, Oscar de los Reyes Ramos, seized that opportunity to lead the Non-Aligned Movement countries and China in polarizing the process, by casting the Chairman's role as far less fair than Chairman Parker had sought to be. The Non-Aligned Movement was an aglomeration of countries united by resentment of superpower domination of international decision-making that would not come together as readily to support a proposal as it would to block whatever the United States and its allies wanted.

Parker tried to counter this assault on his impartiality by offering his draft text in four instalments published every couple of months during the Open-Ended Working Group process, while inviting additional oral and written comments from all delegations.

The Working Group's efforts were further slowed by its failing even to consider an Agenda for the Second Review Conference until the final weeks of the Working Group process when differing factions tried to pack the Agenda with items they favored, while trying to strip it of those they disfavored. This obstruction was finally overcome by an agreement that anything could be raised and discussed at the Second Review Conference, even if it did not appear on the official Agenda, but by that time it was too late for the Working Group to do much further work on the draft report text.

On the eve of the Review Conference's commencement, Margaretha and I were invited to dinner at the residence of Algerian Ambassador Benchaa Dani who had been elected Chairman of the Committee of the Whole, together with some of those expected to play an important part in the forthcoming Conference. Margaretha sat next to the host on that occasion. When we drove home that night she turned to me and asked, "How can a person who obviously can speak fluent French and Arabic, but hardly a single sentence of intelligible English, expect to preside at a Conference where complicated discussions are likely to take place? Doesn't that spell problems for its success?"

April 4, 2008, finally came, and the two-week event began again at the cavernous World Forum Convention Center in The Hague. In attendance this time were 114 Member States, their Ambassadors and delegations, along with five international organizations, specialized agencies and Observor States.

Sudan's highly respected Ambassador, Abuelgasim Idris, welcomed delegations and presided over the official opening at which Saudi Arabia's popular and dashing Ambassador Waleed El Khereiji would serve as the Second Review Conference Chairperson, together with ten Vice Chairpersons of which I was one.

Ambassador Benchaa Dani had never before played a leading role at the Organization. Because Algeria and America were close alphabetically, Dani usually sat to my right at Executive Council sessions where he was invariably polite, discreet and supportive. He would do his best in slow and broken English to converse with me, but when official business was transacted in English he quickly tuned to the French translation channel. Dani was a nondescript man of slight build, medium height and pallid complexion. He wore a mask of humility under a short stubble of beard that hid his inner thirst for power, a yearning unwarranted by either his diplomatic skills or his leadership ability.

Ambassador Lynn Parker of the Kingdom of Great Britain and Northern Ireland, who had chaired the many months of stalemated effort to agree on text, for lack of an agreed draft report submitted his own provisional text in which he honestly tried to balance differing views for consideration at the conference.

The first week was taken up mainly with national statements delivered by representatives of the Member States. Each day before the general session began, the ten Vice Chairmen gathered for the early morning meeting of the Committee of the Whole, presided over by Ambassadors Dani and El Khereiji, and the OPCW's Director General, Rogelio Pfirter, in a small conference room near the main auditorium.

At these sessions it was strongly urged upon Dani that the best way to proceed was to have a single drafting group attempt to hammer out a compromise using a handful of respected facilitators appointed by Dani who would each deal with one or more troubling areas of text. Extreme courtesy and respect was accorded to Dani as protocol dictated.

Dani stubbornly rejected that advice. He insisted on convening an open assembly to harmonize the draft text over which he personally would preside! This proved to be a disaster, as English was the working language. Day after day was wasted with almost no progress toward consensus. Finally, in the middle of the second week, Dani appointed a few facilitators, but it was too little too late. The facilitators received so little delegation support that upon seeing their task was futile, they dropped their efforts almost immediately.

Eventually Director General Pfirter and Saudi Ambassador El Khereiji took matters into their own hands. They decided to appoint a Group of Eighteen, key players most likely to be able to resolve differences that remained at issue. The Group of Eighteen began to meet in the Convention Center's Europe Room. Its discussions and deliberations proceeded parallel to those presided over by Dani in another room during the last three days of the RevCon's final week. The problem was that each group had no idea what the other group was doing. There was no video monitor or other means in either room to allow proceedings to be audited by those not in the room. Not surprisingly, the eighteen ambassadors selected were resented by other delegations for their pre-eminent and privileged positions.

During the deliberations I was sitting near one end of the Europe Room's long conference table around which the Group of Eighteen had gathered. My delegation sat behind me against the wall. At the end of the table to my right sat Ambassador El Khereiji who was presiding, with Director General Pfirter beside him. The seat to my left reserved for the Ambassador of Iran was curiously empty but members of their delegation were seated against the wall behind his empty seat.

Iran had tasked one member of its delegation to stay with Dani's group and report to them periodically what was happening there. Those Member States from the Non-Aligned Movement who were part of the Group of Eighteen were spread from the table's far end halfway up the opposite side. Directly opposite me sat the ambassadors of the UK, France, Germany and others of the Western Group.

Negotiations went virtually around the clock for the last three days of the Second Review Conference that was to end on Friday. During these final days the meetings of the Group of Eighteen lasted 22 and 23 hours per day! I had platters of sandwiches, prepared at my residence, smuggled into the Convention Center and placed in a remote and unused room to which my delegation could discreetly repair.

At one point the Iranian who had been auditing the session chaired by Dani came in and whispered to me that he had been instructed by Iran's ambassador to agree to nothing, in effect blocking anything from being accomplished there. That was a signal to me that Iran was depending on the Group of Eighteen to determine the wording of the final report.

My delegation began to fade from exhaustion after the end of the first day's marathon session that ended at around 4:00 Thursday morning. There was hardly time to go home, shower, eat and get back for the 8:30 a.m. Western Group meeting, and then I had to rush out to the 9 a.m. Committee of the Whole meeting. Whenever I noticed one of my team nodding off, I would send him or her back to our delegation office to catch some sleep on my sofa.

Finally, Friday afternoon arrived. By then the Dani effort had collapsed completely. Those who participated were furious they were not in our room "where the action was." However, in our meeting where our drafting efforts were being inputted to an electronic wall monitor above El Khereiji and Pfirter's heads that displayed the competing text options, there was steadily increasing acrimony and polarization.

As the hours dragged by, the text revisions sought by the Non-Aligned countries grew progressively more extreme. It began to be apparent to everyone that reaching consensus on a final report would not be possible. Still, the Iranian ambassador continued to mysteriously distance himself from the proceedings.

I kept silent the entire afternoon and into the evening while I let the others at the table speak their peace. I knew that if I took the floor too soon I would miss hearing all the arguments. I wanted to counter only when it would be timely and more effective and perhaps allow me to get in the last word.

The Indian ambassador and others representing the Non-Aligned countries were persistent in trying to water down some of the most essential treaty obligations that had been reiterated by consensus in the First Review Conference, especially some of the intrusive measures of transparency to ensure no treaty violations had taken or would take place. Every time a Western

Group or European Union delegate made a statement a veritable chorus of rebuttal statements would ensue from the others.

At one point the exasperated UK ambassador rose from his side of the table and came around to whisper to me and Bob Mikulak (the Arms Control Office Director from the State Department who was seated against the wall behind me) that "We are getting the hell beat out of us at every turn. When are you going to say something to support our side?" I asked him to be patient, that timing was everything. He returned to his seat looking grim and dissatisfied.

I glanced at my watch and saw that it was already well into Friday evening. The Second Review Conference was scheduled to end at midnight. I turned to Kathy Crittenberger, one of the State Department's experts seated behind me. I asked her to go out into the Convention Center's auditorium and make sure that whoever was in charge stopped the official clock at 11:59 p.m.

At that point the discussion turned to a Member State's right to challenge and request an intrusive inspection of another Member State if it were suspected of violating the Treaty. Marthinus van Schalkwyk, the bright and likeable South African delegate, took the floor. No challenge inspection had ever been demanded by a Member State, so it was often referred to as a "Sword of Damocles" that hung by a thread over every Member State to serve as a deterrent to any Member State violating its treaty commitments.

Van Schalkwyk had been siding with the Non-Aligned positions all day, and he passionately accused those at the table who were seeking stronger language reaffirming treaty obligations generally, and the need for intrusive or "challenge" inspections specifically, of taking down the so-called Sword of Damocles to level it at and threaten other Member States.

Upon hearing that inflammatory statement I became uncontrollably incensed. I requested the floor and leapt to my feet. I did not speak with my usual poise. Although I cannot remember my exact words, I barked out something like "In all my five years at the OPCW I have never been furious until now. I am outraged to hear Member States accused of using the Challenge Inspection to threaten other Member States. As far as I am concerned I hope that Sword of Damocles hangs from the ceiling forever and is never taken down. I am outraged and indignant. We have always worked together with trust and respect. I see now that is no longer the case. Look up there at the monitor board and read the revisions you are demanding! You are trashing the Convention. If you want to go on trashing it, the OPCW is finished. We no longer will be the stirring example of effective multilateralism. You are burying us. This will be our funeral today."

I sat back down and waited for a reaction. The silence in the room was devastating. For five minutes no one spoke. No one moved. A kind of paralysis had stricken the Group. I could see they were waiting for me to say something more.

I took the floor again, and began in a calmer, more reasonable tone. "If you want to save our Treaty and our Organization, then let's revert to agreed text. Why, if we all agreed five years ago on language at the first Review Conference on these very points, don't we take that language once again, and go on to finish the job before the evening is over?" I then slowly read aloud the text on that disputed point that had been agreed to five years earlier.

With that, the Indian, Malaysian and Chinese representatives nodded their assent and a new mood of cooperation seemed to pervade the room. However, when discussion then turned to the issue of terrorism, the European Union and Western Group countries were demanding language mentioning the obligation of all members of the Organization to abide by UN Resolution 1540. That Resolution affirmed that the proliferation of nuclear, chemical and biological weapons and their means of delivery constituted a threat to international peace and security. It obligated States to refrain from helping non-State actors develop, acquire, manufacture, possess, transport, transfer or use nuclear, chemical or biological weapons and their delivery systems.

Iran was adamant in opposition to any mention of that resolution because of what they perceived as mistreatment of Iran by the UN, and they said they could not join consensus if that was in the report. The mood in the room immediately turned dour.

Saudi Arabia's Ambassador, Chairman El Khereiji, called out the last Iranian who had spoken and fixated him with a steel stare while he accused him and their delegation of undermining the meeting. "We Saudis know you Iranians all too well," he began. "And we know how to deal with you. So I warn you. If you persist in your obstructive behavior I will publicly place the blame for the RevCon's failure squarely on Iran. You will find out then how Teheran will treat your delegation!" This was a threat that had to be taken seriously by the Iranian delegation unless they were acting strictly in accordance with instructions from their capital.

With that the Iranians suddenly became subdued and offered no reply. I asked for the floor and said roughly the following: "The Member State that has suffered most horribly from chemical weapons is Iran. Why do you Iranians want to be the bête noir of the OPCW? Why do you want to incur the resentment of the entire international community for

346

destroying its only successful international security organization? You are isolated and alone. Why not come in from the cold and join us all in pledging to abide, not only by our Chemical Weapons Convention, but also by the UN resolutions that all UN members should respect? What are you afraid of? You could find the flexibility at least to have the text mention UN resolutions generally without mentioning 1540 specifically if that is a poison pill for Iran."

Although Iran had been chastised, villified and sanctioned in the United Nations and elsewhere, it had been treated collegially and respectfully at the Organization for the Prevention of Chemical Weapons. However, their delegation may not have been sure how much that mattered to their controllers in Teheran.

With that, and with their ambassador still absent, one of the Iranians seated against the wall blurted out "Ambassador Javits. Why don't you draft the text for us so we can accept it?" I was taken aback, but gratified that my comments had had an effect. I replied so all could hear, "The American ambassador cannot draft text for Iran. You heard my comments. Draft it yourselves."

Following that exchange, the meeting turned to the remaining outstanding points at issue that took many more hours. Finally at 6:00 Saturday morning, the Iranian delegation and its Ambassador met privately with the French delegate who had chaired the Organization's Anti-Terrorism Committee. Any mention of anti-terrorism seemed to be a red flag for Iran. However, apparently they reached agreement on language covering the terrorism issue in that private meeting because it was announced over the Center's public address system that the Review Conference assembly was ready to convene to consider and approve the final report.

As everyone drifted into the cavernous auditorium, I was told that a rumor was circulating that I had undercut the European Union by making a private deal with Iran to concede away any mention of UN resolutions. I had not even heard what had happened to resolve that issue or what the agreed text read. I wanted to scotch that slanderous falsehood immediately, as I had neither drafted language as requested by Iran, nor been party to any subsequent negotiation or drafting on that issue.

I decided to go down to the apron area just beneath the stage where I saw a group that included Director General Pfirter, Chairman El Khereiji, Iran's Ambassador Ziaran who finally decided to appear, and a few Western Group and European ambassadors. I said to them that a rumor was circulating that I had "caved" to Iran on the issue of mentioning UN resolutions. In a loud voice I asked the Iranian ambassador, "Is that true? Did I take part in negotiating or agreeing to that portion of the Report?" He audibly confirmed that I had not, and that the final text had been resolved directly between Iran and France without my participation.

Finally, the final text of the Second Review Conference was gaveled through around 7:00 on Saturday morning (with the official conference wall clock still reading 11:59 pm) by a bleary-eyed bunch of delegates. Many of the smaller countries' representatives expressed anger, and some even protested on the record that they had been excluded—not only from participation in the Group of Eighteen, but even from knowledge of what had taken place! Their protests were futile, but would fester in their collective memories until the opportunity at the next Review Conference to ensure this could not happen again.

When it was over I fell into my auditorium seat. I had gone through those last three days at the age of 76 without more than an hour's sleep each day, so focused and intent that I was able to maintain total concentration the entire time without even a yawn. Suddenly, however, I could hardly keep my eyes open. My devoted pal and driver, Albert, drove me home that morning. He boasted that he knew I would succeed again in getting a positive outcome, but I was simply too tired to thank him for his confidence. Somehow, I managed to take a hot shower after which I slept most of the day.

With the Second Review Conference successfully concluded, Margaretha and I discussed whether we should stay on in the event the Republicans won the next presidential election, or whether we had lived the diplomatic life long enough. We both agreed it was time to return home, retire and enjoy life in Florida and Sweden after eight long years away.

With the arrival of the summer of 2008, delegations to the Organization faced a reduced workload, but there were still some Executive Council meetings to be held and many issues to resolve before the Conference of States Parties would take place in early November.

Iranian Ambassador Ziaran left his post immediately following the conclusion of the Second Review Conference, and a new Iranian Permanent Representative arrived whom I met at a lunch hosted by Japan's Ambassador. Lunches at the Japanese residence were always uniquely enjoyable for the warm hospitality of the ambassador and his staff, the magnificent Asian art on display and the impeccably served exotic food and fine wines that were without equal in the diplomatic community.

As the guests mingled before lunch, I spotted the newly-arrived Iranian ambassador. I decided to introduce myself and to welcome him warmly to The Hague. I said that I looked forward to working with him as I had with Ambassador Ziaran. His expression was stiff and impersonal—his body language the same. I could see he was being deliberately cool and unfriendly. At one point in his stilted response to my remarks, he mentioned in passing that his delegation was quite angry with me. I said I had not heard that. In fact, I had always enjoyed friendly relations with Iran's delegation.

He said they were upset now because I objected to Iran chairing the Asian regional group. I responded that if that was their impression, they were quite mistaken. I only had stated that the election of a regional group chairman was a personal one, not the election of a country but of an individual to chair the group. I explained that although Ambassador Ziaran had indeed chaired the Asian Group, after his departure no election had been held. Iran simply presumed it had the right to have its Deputy Permanent Representative continue to sit in the chair, and I felt an election ought to have been held to select a new chairman.

The Iranian did not seem convinced. I told him I would prove that I meant what I said. I asked him to accompany me as I walked over to our host, the Japanese ambassador, who was the most senior member of the Asian Group. I restated my position to our host, Ambassador Minoru Shiboya, that with the departure of Amb. Ziaran there should have been an election of a new chairman by the Asian Group because the post is one held by an individual not by a country. Then I stated for the record that I had absolutely no objection to an Iranian being elected chairman of the Asian Group, since whomever the Group elected, it was solely their decision.

I then turned to the Iranian. "Please tell your delegation what I have said in order to clear up any misunderstanding. And if you ever need my help or support, please talk to me at least a week in advance of any Executive Council or other meeting. As long as it does not cross any of my red lines, I will always try to be constructive and collegial."

I strongly suspected that their animosity was attributable to one particular member, who was unfailingly obdurate and often surly in manner and debate, but as long as Amb. Ziaran had been at post he had been under control. When Ziaran left, it seemed he was free to spread his poison.

The summer passed without incident, and it was not long before the next regular Executive Council convened on October 17, 2008.

As I entered the Ieper room I had to swipe an electronic identification badge to gain entry, and then pick up a set of earphones that could be plugged in to hear any of the six official language translations of the proceedings—English, French, Russian, Chinese, Arabic and Spanish. The chamber itself contained semicircular tables that ran the width of the room with rows at which the 41 Executive Committee members were seated with placards in alphabetical order prominently displaying the names of their respective countries. In front of the room was an elevated dais on which sat the Chairperson—Slovakia's demure and outstandingly competent lady ambassador, Oksana Tomova. On either side of her sat the Director General, the Legal Advisor, the Secretary of the Policy Making Organs, and behind them in another row sat a few other Technical Secretary staff members. Covering the wall above the raised dais was an enormous electronic wall monitor. High on one side of the chamber near the ceiling were glass enclosed booths in which each official translator worked in quiet isolation to ensure the earphone system broadcast the speaker's words in each of the six official languages. Seated at the back of the room were those delegations' staff members not "in the chair" for their respective countries.

The Iranians had not given me a week's notice in advance of what they would seek at that session, but when they began trying to circumscribe the United States in an important area under the Treaty, it became clear why they had not, and even clearer that I would have to oppose them with everything at my command.

The issue involved an agenda item to "note" the United States' quarterly report of progress during the preceding 90 days required by the Verification Annex to the Convention for each Member State in the process of destroying its Chemical Weapons stockpile. Several times during that week-long 54th meeting of the Executive Council, Iran had asked to postpone that agenda item for later consideration, but without giving notice of why or what they would seek with respect to it.

Finally, on the final day of the Council, Iran said it was ready to consider the item, but refused to note the U.S. 90-day report because they contended the report was "incomplete". Iran claimed the report did not give information on the timelines for destruction of America's remaining chemical weapon stockpile to take place at two destruction facilities that were not yet built.

The United States had been granted a five-year extension of the 2007 deadline under the Treaty for destruction of its chemical weapon stockpile, and Iran was determined to make matters difficult for the U.S. Iran insisted that the US was obligated to provide "detailed plans" for its remaining destruction, and thus the report should have included the dates at which each of the two facilities would become operational, and by what dates the destruction at each would be completed—all within the extended 2012 deadline that had been granted the U.S. by the Member States.

I had no warning of this deliberate attempt to ambush, embarrass and circumscribe the United States. Not even the Defense Department or the Army could give with certainty the information that Iran was demanding because the technology that was to be used in the two new destruction facilities was novel and untested, and it was impossible to say when the plants would actually, *and safely*, be able to commence destroying chemical weapons.

When the agenda item finally was taken up for consideration, all eight Iranians in their group took turns at their microphone. I sat alone in the US chair to rebut them. The debate seemed endless with countless interventions lasting many hours.

First, I stressed the 90-day report requirement was historical, not prospective. I could not accept, nor could we provide, the prospective "crystal ball" element Iran sought. Next I insisted the Organization for the Prohibition of Chemical Weapons was a non-discriminatory organization; and since all the other Possessor States' 90-day reports had been noted without any insistence on forward-looking information, we would not accept being treated differently.

In quick succession Germany, France, Russia, Ireland, the UK, Italy and Australia intervened to support my position. Australia asked the Organization's Legal Officer to render his opinion. He confirmed that the *annual* reports might have a prospective aspect, but that the 90-day *quarterly* reports were strictly to report on destruction activity by a Possessor State during the preceding 90 days. Possessor States were those Member States that had declared they had a stockpile of chemical weapons that they were going to destroy. Some countries in that category included Russia, the United States, India, Libya and Albania, but some had finished and some were still destroying stockpiles as in the United States and Russia.

I offered Iran a chance to meet with my delegation together with the delegations of Russia and any other State possessing chemical weapons that wanted to join the meeting. When no other Possessor State showed interest in meeting, Iran put their proposed language up on the monitor board so all countries could consider the text they proposed as their price for agreeing to note the U.S.' 90-day report.

Many hours and countless interventions were needed until at last at 11pm on Friday I walked over to the eight Iranians who were all sitting together. Seeing no indication that there was any leader of their group I asked them, "Who is in charge?" They started to look at each other to see who dared take the responsibility of leadership.

One Iranian who had come from Teheran for the Executive Council session stood up. I asked him to accompany me to the side of the room where we could talk in private. We felt all eyes were on us, but we were out of anyone's earshot. I explained that we were at an impasse and would never resolve our differences, but I was not looking for either of us to be winners or losers. I wanted to do what was constructive for the Organization, and I was sure he did, too. I said that we are both being offered a compromise by Chairperson Tomova that we could both accept without either of us being seen as winners or losers. I showed him the suggested language. He made a last stab at tilting it slightly in Iran's favor, but I told him that this was our last chance to "take it or leave it" as the Chair had given us *her* wording. He and his delegation then relented and joined in the bland proposal by Chairperson Tomova that would merely "emphasize the importance" of the commencement and completion of destruction within the extended deadlines.

Much to my surprise the Executive Council session that evening did not close after the usual thanks to the meeting's chairperson, the interpreters etc. After a slight pause, despite the lateness of the hour, Ambassador Tomova pointed out that this was my last regular Executive Council meeting after six years of service in the Organization. I had worked closely together with Oksana during her term as Chair of the Council. We had become fast friends as a result. As she spoke of my years of service I could see her lips trembling and tears welling in her eyes. She had to stop briefly to compose herself. I was deeply touched by her evident display of emotion.

Then each of the five regional groups on behalf of their members took the floor to thank me for my contribution to the Organization. I was deeply gladdened and grateful. I will never forget those kind interventions, especially that of Marthinus van Skalkwyk on behalf of the African Regional Group, especially as he spoke his words so soon after I had excoriated him before the Group of Eighteen at the Second Review Conference. Marthinus said in part:

". . . It's been my personal privilege to experience his skills, his diplomacy, for two years. I see it as a privilege. We all learned a lot from him. I think he has done his country extreme justice in terms of the way he has represented his country. I have never experienced an ambassador from the US the way I have experienced him. And that says a lot in the sense that the way he is able to transcend borders and gaps between us, the way we differ. And his patience—I've admired his patience. I've sat through one or two very difficult negotiations in which he has been involved, and I have always admired the way he has handled them. He is always able to find a position. He is always able to try to see the other party's point of view. And then always coming up with a solution! So personally from me, as well as from the African Group, it has been a privilege. We are going to miss you. I do not know who is going to stand in when we do have problems and there is no Ambassador Javits to come over and talk to you in your ear and make a good suggestion. We won't forget you, and once again it was a privilege to work with you."

Touching, too, were the words on behalf of the European Union and each of the other Regional Groups.

I rose to thank each representative. I said only that I wished my wife could have heard the kind words they had said about me. Thus ended my final Executive Council meeting.

However, when the Conference of State Parties ("CSP") convened the following month in November 2008, all did not end well, nor was there an opportunity to thank anyone—not even the officials, the staff or the translators! As was my custom, I had asked the Iranian well in advance if there was anything they needed at the CSP. But again they gave me no warning that they had a trick up their sleeve and would once again try to take the United States hostage at the very last minute!

When on the last night of the two-week Conference of State Parties, they sprung their demand for a change in wording of the Final Report, it was indeed provident that when that agenda item had been considered earlier, Iran's delegation must have been out of the auditorium or asleep, because they had made no objection to the draft wording, nor did they reserve the right to request it to be amended later. Thus they had one strike against them from the outset. Nevertheless, Iran once again threatened to sabotage the entire Conference by refusing to approve the final Report if their amended language was not included.

While we waited for Iran to weaken or relent I left the auditorium for a few moments while State Party after State Party took the floor to plead with them to be reasonable. As I was walking back toward the auditorium, a newly-arrived young Iranian approached me. He seemed hesitant and respectful as he said, "Ambassador Javits. I have heard so much about you, and I am so happy to meet and speak with you. You have always been very kind, and have helped us whenever we have been in a difficult situation. Can't you help us out of this impasse now?"

I replied, "I would have tried to help your delegation had it told me what it needed a week before the start of the Conference. As I have repeatedly said I need advance warning to try to be cooperative. I did not get that courtesy, so I am truly sorry, but I am powerless to do anything now for your delegation."

The clock was approaching the midnight hour when I went back into the auditorium. My esteemed friend, yet another charming lady Ambassador of India, Noolam Sabharwal, rose from her seat and walked over to speak with me in a low voice. She asked me to find some element of compromise to end the impasse so we could get Iran on board to join consensus and approve the Conference report. I told her I was sorry, but this time I could not help Iran.

A long silence followed as she went back to her seat. All eyes were fixed on me to see if I would ask for the floor or make any motion toward the Iranians who were huddled together in the remotest, uppermost rows of the auditorium. I kept a stony and silent countenance. The Iranians finally asked for a vote to re-open the agenda to allow their amendment. The Chair asked for a tally of those supporting Iran's request. The abject silence was humiliating. Not one of their usual supporters spoke or voted in their favor. Not India, not South Africa, not Malaysia, not Indonesia. The rebuff was stunning.

After huddling on the stage with the Director General, the Secretary for the Policy Making Organs and the Legal Advisor, it was announced by Japan's ambassador that he would issue his own Report of the Conference as its Chairman, not one approved by those in attendance. He peremptorily gaveled the meeting closed with none of the usual thanks to the Conference officers, staff, translators or retiring diplomats that were leaving to go on to other posts or to end their careers.

Only a couple of days went by before the Iranians demanded an audience with the Director General to complain about their treatment at the hands of Japan's ambassador, and to question the legality of the Report that he had issued. Director General Pfirter gave them no encouragement or support.

I volunteered my opinion to many delegations that unless and until Mohsen one particularly abrasive and obstructive member of the Iranian delegation who I named left The Hague, Iran's behavior and its treatment by other Member States would not change. I learned that he was recalled to Teheran soon thereafter and that Iran acted much more collegially for some time following that incident.

Shortly before Margaretha and I were to leave The Hague, the State Department awarded me and my Delegation its Superior Honor Award for "sustained outstanding service", and in a rare tribute provided funds for a farewell reception for me at the Organization's headquarters to which over 500 people came to say good-bye. Margaretha and I greeted each person in the reception line, and then there were speeches by the Director General and others. The outpouring of affection from so many colleagues, friends, staff members and diplomats who came to shake my hand and hug me was heartening. Even one of the Cuban delegates came to bid me adieu, and that touched my heart as he might have risked his career by doing it.

When finally I arrived back in Washington, I was asked to join a staff conference in one of the Department of State meeting rooms in the Arms Control section on the second floor. Just about everyone with whom I had worked closely was seated at the long table that ran the length of the room. Business as usual was being conducted, but when I walked in that all stopped.

Arms Control Section Chief Bob Mikulak then rose to give his and the Department's words of farewell. I only wish I had a recording of that testimonial. It was far more than I deserved, but certainly what I wish my family could have heard.

Presentation of Credentials May 2003
(OPCW photo)

With my charming colleague, Indian Amb. Cowsik in her
residence in Wassenaar near The Hague

DIPLOMATIC (13)

A group of Ambassadors with the OPCW Director General. (L
to R): France's Amb. Jean Francois Blarel; Saudi Arabia's
Amb. Waleed Elkhereiji; China Amb. Zhang Jun; Japan Amb.
Minoru Shiboya; Slovak Amb. Oksana Tomova; India Amb.
Neelam Sabharwal; Ireland Amb. Richard Ryan; Amb. Javits;
UK Amb. Lynn Parker; Dir. Gen. Rogelio Pfirter; Brazil Amb.
Jose Artur Medeiros; Algeria Amb. Benchaa Dani; Russia
Amb. Kyrill Gevorgian; Mexican Amb. Jorge Lomanaco.
(OPCW photo)

Pakistan Amb. Mustafa Kamil Kazi and his family with
Rogelio and Isabel Pfirter visiting us in Stockholm

(L to R) Judge and Mrs. Thomas Buergenthal of the
International Court of Justice. US Amb. Jim Culbertson,
Margaretha Javits, Mrs. Terhi Kirsch, Mrs. Isabel Pfirter, and
Phillippe Kirsch, President of the International Criminal Court

With the OPCW Delegation at our intimate 2009 farewell lunch in The Hague (L to R) Albert Lankhamer, Kay Hairston, Sheila Romine, Scott Landsman, Abigail Robinson, Margaretha and Eric Javits, Cheryl Koevet, Deputy Permanent Representative Janet Beik, and Nicholas Granger

With Crown Prince of the Netherlands, Willem-Alexander, at
an Australian reception in The Hague circa 2007

Our delegation to the December 2004 OPCW 9th Conference
of States Parties. (Standing L to R):Brandon Williams, Deputy
Permanent Representative Pete Ito, Richard Snelsire, Amb.
Javits, Elizabeth McDaniel, Mrs. Javits, Elizabeth Sanders,
Astrid Lewis, Larry Denyer Phillip Kellogg, Jonathan Beckett.
(Seated L to R): Diane O'Neal, Jillian Walker, Luis Alvarado,
and Sue McMaster

CHAPTER XIV — MY THIRD CAREER

As the laws of physics state, "An object in motion tends to stay in motion, and an object at rest tends to stay at rest." Retirement for me did not mean ceasing to be active. I turned to writing this memoir, but I refuse to finish it here.

Margaretha's beauty, artistic talents, intellect, unfailing devotion and support inspire me to stay young at heart and active. I am grateful for each and every day we share together.

I am constantly gratified by the accomplishments of my kind and caring son, Eric Jr., a man of integrity and sound values, who has built a design business with his own talents, money and effort. He is far better known to the American public for his hats, bags and shoes than I am for my diplomatic or legal careers.

I am equally gratified by the achievements of my statuesque, athletic and forceful daughter, Jocelyn, who besides graduating Phi Beta Kappa and Cum Laude from the University of Colorado at Boulder, got her MBA at Columbia Business School, and then as a vice president of Donaldson Lufkin and Jenrette for over a decade, was acknowledged to be the best in Wall Street in Institutional Equity Sales. Now she and her attractive husband, Dr. Kamil Grajski, a brilliant executive with two PhDs, have given Margaretha and me healthy twin grandchildren, Alexander and Sienna, both bright and beautiful. There is no greater gratification than knowing the family will go on.

Just as I celebrated my 80th birthday in Sweden by skydiving from twelve thousand feet for the sheer joy of it and for bragging rights like President Bush, my life has been and I am determined will continue to be fun-filled and a "work in progress." It is for that reason my third career, investing in the fields of health and energy, will be for the benefits they offer mankind.

ENDNOTES

1. When most ballerinas would have retired much earlier, Margot still danced with her devoted friend and long-time partner, Rudolf Nureyev, despite her advanced years. I saw Margot a few times after 1975 when I was in London. She eventually retired to a farm in Panama to live out her days with Tito (who had been allowed to return) until his death in 1989, and hers soon after in 1991.

2. Star of silent films, Hope Hampton—octogenarian but still flawless in her face and always beautifully dressed and bejeweled; actress Dina Merrill and her husband Stan Rumbough; Dina's mother, Post cereal heiress and leading socialite, Marjorie Merriweather Post Davies; Ambassador Joseph P. Kennedy's family; stage actress, horsewoman and social lioness C.Z. Guest; Laddie and Mary Sanford; Wanamaker heir Rodman de Heeren and his beautiful best-dressed wife, Aimee; Randolph William Hearst; tire heir Russell Firestone; World Skeet Champion Carola Mandel; Chicago industrialist and founder of Consolidated Foods and Sara Lee, Nathan Cummings; paper and banking magnate, Samuel Gottesman; RCA's David Sarnoff, pioneer of American radio and TV, and his wife, Lisette; Jim Kimberly, the heir to the Kimberly Clark "Kleenex" fortune whose nickname was The Silver Fox, to name some.

3. The African, Asia-Pacific, Eastern European, Latin American and Carribean (GRULAC), and the Western European and Other (WEOG).

4. Japan's Hiroharu Koike, Iran's Hossein Panahi Azar, India's Shayamala Cowsik, Malaysia's Dato' Noor Farida Arrifin,

Mexico's Santiago Oñate Laborde, Algeria's Noureddine Djoudi and Netherlands' Marc Th. Vogelaar.

5. Mr. Raju Sharma, Director, Indian National Authority; Pankaj Sharma, Deputy Secretary of Ministry External Affairs; and V. B. Dhavle, Advisor and Lead Negotiator.

6. William Rudin, Bernard Marden, Fred R. Sullivan.

ACKNOWLEDGEMENTS

I am grateful to all those friends and family members who read and gave me help, comments and criticisms on this memoir in its various stages of development, especially Ed Downe, whose suggestions were right on the button; and lastly, but for the originality of Margaretha, my partner in all things, this memoir would have had no title.

CPSIA information can be obtained at www.ICGtesting.com
Printed in the USA
LVOW06s0700201013

357691LV00004B/9/P